SOARING PRAISE FOR THE NATIONAL BESTSELLER GIANT STEPS

"One need know nothing about basketball to enjoy *Giant Steps*, the odyssey from Lew Alcindor of Manhattan to a Muslim basketball star named Kareem Abdul-Jabbar who lives in a mansion in Bel Air, Calif. . . . Abdul-Jabbar's book is an autobiography, [written] with sensitive help from the co-author, Peter Knobler. . . . Abdul-Jabbar fills out his two decades in basketball with sharp insights about Harlem, parochial schools, his parents and Wilt Chamberlain. . . . The book, like the man's urban, Northern sport, is often personal and creative."   —*The New York Times*

"In a blunt autobiography Kareem Abdul-Jabbar gets open off-court for the first time . . . Indeed, *Giant Steps* is no retreat, but rather an onslaught."   —*People*

"Candid, earnest . . . memoirs of basketball great Abdul-Jabbar—offering more style and substance than most star-athlete autobiographies, with serious close-ups of his problematic, shifting political/religious allegiances. He writes vividly about life-on-the-road (drugs, etc.), about the dynamics of the game, about such colleagues as Oscar Robertson, Magic Johnson, and sometime arch-rival Chamberlain. With gentle touches of humor and just the right balance between off-court/on-court concerns: a high-scoring sports memoir all around, thoughtful rather than dramatic or flashy."   —*Kirkus Reviews*

"Kareem Abdul-Jabbar has integrity and sensitivity as a person and enormous ability as a basketball player. To those of us who played with and against him on the hardwood, the first two qualities are definitive, the last only descriptive."   —Senator Bill Bradley

"A sports autobiography by a great athlete who has some important and thoughtful things to say about himself, his profession and life at large. *Giant Steps* has its spate of 'shocking,' entertaining, now-you're-going-to-hear-what-*really*-happened, behind-the-scenes revelations ... Excellent technical descriptions of the game, and great moments relived. . . . Clearly shows once again that the great human questions transcend race, religion, politics ... and sports." —*Los Angeles Times Book Review*

"I find him to be a most sensitive, kind, and philosophical thinking man with unique talents."—Richard Pryor

"Tells it all: the tall gangly youngster who could not win a fistfight nor make a big hit with the girls; the sensitive youth who looked elsewhere when he did not receive it from his parents; his life in Harlem, dealing with racism and playing basketball, a sport that did not come naturally."   —*Newsday*

"Not since THE AUTOBIOGRAPHY OF MALCOLM X have I come across a book that touched me down to my nerve endings, but that's the impact of Kareem Abdul-Jabbar's autobiography, GIANT STEPS. . . . With the skillful, unobtrusive assistance of Peter Knobler, Kareem's story is suddenly clear."

—Pablo Guzman
The Village Voice

"A fascinating account of how a tall, awkward middle-class boy grew up to be not only one of the finest centers ever to play basketball but a sensitive mature adult who has learned to deal with his prejudices and the unique inner turmoil that few of us who are not 7'2" and black could really understand. . . . Well told, and well worth reading."   —*Detroit News*

"A procession of enlightening, frequently painful revelations that make up this fine memoir. . . . Which leads to the real point of it all: even if you're over seven feet tall, you never stop growing." —*Philadelphia Daily News*

Giant Steps

Kareem
Abdul-Jabbar
and
Peter Knobler

BANTAM BOOKS
TORONTO • NEW YORK • LONDON • SYDNEY • AUCKLAND

GIANT STEPS

Bantam Hardcover edition / December 1983
2nd printing . . . December 1983
3rd printing . . . December 1983
4th printing . . . January 1984
Bantam rack-size edition / January 1985

Foreword taken from an article entitled,
"Reaching Out to Kareem," by Peter Knobler,
November 6, 1983, Sports Section of The New York Times.
Copyright © 1983 by The New York Times Company.
Reprinted by permission.

ISBN 0-553-24511-2

Library of Congress Catalog Card No. 83-90662

Published simultaneously in the United States and Canada

Bantam Books are published by Bantam Books, Inc. Its trademark,
consisting of the words "Bantam Books" and the portrayal of a rooster,
is Registered in the United States Patent and Trademark Office and in
other countries. Marca Registrada. Bantam Books, Inc., 666 Fifth Avenue,
New York, New York 10103.

PRINTED IN THE UNITED STATES OF AMERICA

H   0 9 8 7 6 5 4 3 2 1

*In the name of Allah
the Compassionate, the Merciful.*

We would like to acknowledge gratefully the assistance of several people whose work, memories, and/or good wishes contributed to this book: John Graham, Norbert Florendo, Malek Abdul-Mansour, Kenneth Kelly (aka Wali Shabazz), Tom Collins, Stan Blum, Jay Acton, Peter Guzzardi, Mark Dissin, Barry Winik/W&W Films, Don Sperling, Catherine Moses, and Mary Lamont.

Foreword

When my friends found out that I was collaborating with Kareem Abdul-Jabbar on his autobiography, almost all of them asked basically the same question: What is a remote seven-foot-two-inch Muslim black man doing trusting his life story to a six-foot Jewish white guy?

Kareem and I had known each other when we were teen-agers, introduced in 1963 by a camp bunkmate of mine named Kenny Kelly (now Wali Shabazz), who knew Kareem (then Lew Alcindor) from New York's Dyckman Street projects. We'd hit it off because both of us trusted Kelly, because we enjoyed jazz and sports, and because we were both political skeptics. Kareem was an easy guy to like. He laughed quickly and talked frankly, and when he found that I was just as into John Coltrane and outraged by Bull Connor as he was, we became friends.

We lost contact for many years and when, during

his pro career, he developed the image of this dour, silent, hostile character, it didn't jibe at all with the sense I'd had of him. We met again in 1980, when I was writing a magazine profile of him. He gave me the serious once-over, and some of that public image turned out to be true. He was mistrustful, consistently waiting for the other shoe to fall, for me to say or do something unconsciously racist or naturally dumb. It was as if he expected me to screw up sometime and was giving me enough room to do it early.

As big as he is, Kareem uses silence to create a tension that anyone who is uncomfortable in his presence might find unbearable. It's a testing process that he has incorporated into his life. I found it unfortunate but understandable that, in order to get close to Kareem, one had to undergo this emotional frisking. I stood for it. I was determined to find out how and why he was in his own zone.

I think ultimately I passed the test because I knew Kareem as he had liked to be known, as he had known himself before the distracting pressures of stardom, money, religion, and race had pushed him inside himself. I liked him; he was smart, aware, articulate, and incredibly talented. When he was certain I was basically the same all-right guy I'd been twenty years before, he opened up.

The fact that I'm white and he's black was never a problem. He is long past rejecting anyone on general principles, and for my part race doesn't make much difference. He is a Muslim believer but hardly a fanatic, and my Semitism is cultural, not religious. We found a common bond in Hebrew National kosher frankfurters.

We spent a lot of time together, four or five hours a day for a month or more, talking into a tape recorder about the course of his life. It was quite an experience. Few people give their lives such concentrated attention, and these weren't just some let's-run-over-the-facts-again briefings; some got pretty tough. Kareem has a command of the facts; he is great at recalling specific situations—places, conversations, scenes—but not the best at analyzing what they mean. I'm reasonably good at putting together patterns, and between us we began to emerge with a sense of Kareem that he hadn't had before. We talked about his father, or a woman he'd been afraid to approach, and while he knew what had happened, we both came to a new understanding of why.

For a writer, this is also a strange piece of work. I'd never given anyone's life but my own the kind of close analysis I gave Kareem's. You don't usually spend your entire workday thinking about someone else, and, with the book written in first-person singular, it was my job to be Kareem for the year that the book took to write. Plus I had to find a voice, a consistent way for the book to sound. Kareem is a clever talker, turns a nice phrase, and I worked hard to combine his verbal style with my written one and come up with something that sounded like he was talking to you.

Normal-size men haven't been a foot shorter than anybody since they were kids, so there is a whole physical/psychological adjustment you go through when talking to Kareem. Most guys, when having a conversation amongst themselves, assume that everyone's more or less on the same level. You don't even necessarily make eye contact, just stand around shoulder to shoulder and tilt your head or nod at someone. Do that with Kareem and you're talking to his pectorals. You crane your neck and all of a sudden you're six years old again. You've got to fight that feeling, because most people defer to Kareem, and you lose his respect and your own if you refuse to be his equal.

Kareem is basically a private person. He is uncomfortable with crowds of any nature and has developed an unbreakable defense. Rather than face what's down there, Kareem escapes into his tower. Most of us, when we want to avoid people, avert our eyes downward. When Kareem looks down he sees the waiting world, so he looks resolutely forward and there is no one who can contact him.

When he starts signing autographs, it's like a feeding frenzy, with people from all over picking up the celebrity scent. Kareem is still surprised by the response. He says it's like he's giving away $50 bills.

We went to the Hearns–Leonard fight in Las Vegas and Kareem was swamped. After the bout, the car in which we had arrived was nowhere to be seen, and I was thoroughly surprised when Kareem took off on foot, walking the half-mile along the Vegas Strip back to our hotel. It was as if he was refusing to have his life stopped just because he was a celebrity. Traffic, hardly moving anyway, stopped dead as drivers waved and passengers leaned out for a view. He drew a crowd, this giant in a traveling circus, of people who had to stand next to him, shake his hand, or walk alongside and see how they matched up. Some were how's-the-weather-up-there obnoxious. Some asked questions and got very brief replies ("Good fight"), but mostly there was this strange quiet as people wanted to make contact but didn't know how to begin. And Kareem wasn't helping them.

Kareem misses a lot that way. From my vantage point—central but unnoticed, the perfect journalist's position—I could see people who clearly were impressed by Kareem for all the right reasons, people who had been profoundly moved by him and who wanted to thank him personally for many moments of pleasure. It showed on their faces. And Kareem, who for a long time thought people didn't like him—because of his race, religion, politics—was unavailable to accept their best wishes. He could not risk the disruption. Many people want a piece of him, and he feels he has to protect himself, not so much from danger as from constant intrusion. As a result he misses some of what he wants dearly: personal good feelings. Although in the past four years he has made a conscious effort to be more open to strangers, it still happens often and it's sad to watch.

But Kareem is by no means a sad person. He has a five-year-old son with whom he is growing, a high-paying contract, and an ever-developing sense of himself. And he still plays a great game of basketball.

Part of the perks of writing *Giant Steps* was that I got a chance to get on the court with Kareem. I was fifth man on my high school team, played *very* small forward. Never had a shot but got by on rebounding and scrappy defense. So when Kareem and I began to shoot around all by ourselves on this deserted outdoor court, I thought I'd died and gone to heaven.

After a couple of casual skyhooks, Kareem went up with his outside shot. From its arc I could see it was long, the rebound was going to carom over my head and land in front of him. I saw it all before me. I could short-hop the ball, slap it away from him, drive the length of the court, and tell everyone I ever knew that I'd scored on Kareem Abdul-Jabbar.

The ball landed between me and Kareem exactly where I'd thought it would. I rushed in for the steal—the whole court was open!—and ran right by like a clown.

The ball wasn't there. Kareem had reached in and, with his left hand, snatched it like a spaldeen. I hit the brakes and turned just in time to see him take one giant step and jam it leftie through the hoop. When you're playing basketball, even just fooling around, you don't mess with Kareem.

Kareem is in the process of changing. So are we all, but Kareem is actively involving himself in it. When his house burned down in 1983 and he lost a lifetime of possessions, he was forced to consider what his wealth meant to him and what he truly held valuable. In creating *Giant Steps*, he chose to dig deeply into everything he knew and believed, beginning with his childhood and running through the present.

When I switched the tape recorder off after our final session, we were both pretty beat. "You know," he said slowly, "doing this has been like psychotherapy for me." I think he was surprised, and pleased.

I was pleased but never surprised at the support and understanding given me by my wife, Jane Dissin Knobler. She was indispensable in the writing of this book, as was Cheryl Pistono, and I thank them both.

Peter Knobler

Giant Steps

1

I used to get my ass handed to me on a regular basis. On the New York streets where I was growing up, if you didn't know how to fight you were in big trouble, and I just didn't have the instinct. I was always bigger than the kids my age, so they didn't bother me, but there would be guys two and three years older who felt called upon to kick my ass at every opportunity. They were just bad, mean, streetwise nine-year-old boys ready to go for the kill.

One of the sidewalk terrors who moved into my neighborhood was a kid named Joe. Joe came from Brooklyn and didn't like anything. Say something smart, say something dumb, say nothing at all, and ultimately it would come to blows. One day he decided it was my turn. It was Sunday in the summertime, and I had just gotten back from church, standing with some of the other kids in front of my building, wearing my good clothes. You can't do much in your Sunday best; anything that's fun will get them dirty, and anything that won't get them dirty is hardly worth doing. Joe wasn't the churchgoing type. He was in jeans and a T-shirt, and like all bullies, he was using every advantage. Though I was a head taller than he was, he kept pushing me, shoving my shoulder and calling me "chicken."

I tried to avoid him. He was much tougher than I was; he liked what he was doing, and I knew he could whip me.

"Leave me alone," I said quietly. He kept on pushing me. "Leave me *alone!*" I turned to walk away. Joe took two steps and, with both hands, shoved me from behind. I stumbled, then swung around and hit him on the bicep with an awkward right hand.

"Oh," he said, this strange smile creeping across his face, "you want to fight!"

He rushed me, threw me off my feet. We were grappling on the ground, rolling on the morning concrete, and all the other kids gathered around to watch. He tried to pin me and then take some punches at my head, but with all my squirming he couldn't get the good grip, and when he tried to get back on his feet and start over, I jumped up and ran inside.

My Dad was sitting in his chair reading the paper. I ran in, crying, dirty, six years old, and told him what had happened. My father was a policeman for the New York Transit Authority. He said, "Hey, there's nothing I can do for you." I kept sobbing, trying to catch my breath. "If you can't beat him in a fight, you're going to have to stay up here."

"But I want to go outside and play!"

"Well," he said, "go."

"But this guy's gonna beat me up."

"Well, you're going to have to deal with it."

I changed into street clothes, went downstairs, and Joe was waiting for me. I tried to get by him, but he wouldn't let me, and we went at it again. He continued to kick my ass. This time he punched me all up the side of the head, in the chest, the stomach, the back. I was flailing away, and he kept popping me. So I ran back upstairs, marched past my father, grabbed my toy nightstick and headed back on outside.

When Joe saw me armed, he took off. I chased him, dodging cars and people in the street as if they were tacklers. We may have looked cute, these two little boys playing *Dragnet*, but as far as I was concerned, my life was on the line. I could hear my own breath. Joe was faster than I was and began putting some distance between us, but I kept after him. With a fifteen-yard lead he began looking for ways to turn this thing around. Off to the side he saw this big rock about the size of a brick. It looked huge. When he picked it up, I threw on the brakes and beat it real quick in the other direction. He came after me, but it seemed like I could run faster when I was being chased. I made it back into the building, ran upstairs, and cried. That was it for the day, but from then on Joe never had much interest in fighting with me. He knew I was that crazy kid who would keep on coming on.

I don't think Joe made it to twenty before going to jail.

I didn't have that many fights; I just lost all of them. One of the girls in my building, Cecilia, beat the hell out of me. She was three years older than I was, and faster than most of the guys, and extremely nasty. I can't remember why, but she wanted my behind in a bad way. I have this vivid memory of being chased all around the block. There was this big playground nearby, and I tried to keep it between us, but she ran me around the whole thing twice till I tired and she caught up. I had kept hold of my baseball bat—it was heavy and made running real difficult, but I knew if I put it down it was gone—and when she caught me, I threatened to take a swing at her knees. I was not bad enough. She took my Louisville Slugger away from me and, as I was trying to shake free, started to choke me with it. The only reason the fight ended was that she got bored.

That kind of thing happened quite a bit. I never had much taste for it, but fighting was part of learning how to deal with the neighborhood.

When I was born in 1947, my parents were living in Harlem. Housing was scarce in New York after World War II, and when my father, Ferdinand Lewis "Al" Alcindor, got out of the Army he joined my mother, Cora, in something called "rooming." One person would rent a large apartment wherever it could be found and then let out individual rooms to friends, acquaintances, anyone who had the money. My mother had talked her way into getting not one but two front rooms in an eight-room apartment they shared with six other tenants on West 111th Street, just a block north of Central Park. When I was born I had my own room, and it's been that way basically ever since.

Harlem back then was by no means Paradise, but it wasn't the war zone it is today. When I was growing up, everyone around us had a job; to be on welfare was an embarrassment. My mother would take me to play in Central Park with no fear. People would leave their front doors open. Stealing was not tolerated. Anybody who got caught snatching a purse got handled by the people in the community. Some of the worst offenders would get thrown off the roof. People didn't play around.

My parents and I moved to the Dyckman Street projects in the Inwood section of Manhattan in 1950. It was city-owned middle-income housing and, although the City Housing Authority offered us another apartment on the Lower East Side, my mother waited a year and a half while the projects were being built so we could be in there first. It was a better neighborhood, she insisted.

New York City, then as now, was divided into neighborhoods with distinct cultural identities. North of Dyckman Street was Irish, south was Jewish, and the projects were this little multinational enclave east of the elevated train tracks that ran north-south on Nagle Avenue. Only about fifteen percent of the projects were black, and the bunker mentality that now rules New York had not yet evolved. As a kid, I played with anyone who was around. We had English neighbors, and Scandinavians, Cubans, Puerto Ricans, gypsies. The people who lived right above us were Russian, had emigrated to America right after World War II, the Diviatkins. The old man had me up there an hour one day trying to teach me to pronounce his name.

My parents had strong ideas about discipline and manners. It was important to them to be respectable; they were definitely not going to have a thug for a son. Their primary focus, as far as I was concerned, was my education. In fact, it was almost all we talked about.

There wasn't a lot of emotion on display in the Alcindor household. My father was stern and powerful. I knew he loved me, but he didn't often go out of his way to let me hear about it. A large man—six feet three inches tall, 200 pounds—he carried himself as if his mere bulk and the silence he maintained were a life statement. "Big Al" could be intimidating, and some of the people in the neighborhood were deathly afraid of him. He could walk down the street, and if he didn't want to hear you, you weren't there. He was never brutal or violent, but he maintained an aura of menace that it took a very persistent, or extremely foolish soul to penetrate. It was his natural state; he had to concentrate when called upon to be even sociable.

But there was clearly a muse on the loose inside him as well. He enrolled in the Juilliard School of Music right after I was born and graduated five years later with a degree in musicology. A trombone player, he jammed with Art Blakey and Yusef Lateef, and played in as many groups as would have him. Trombone was perfect for Big Al; it's not really a soloist's instrument, and subtlety out of such a large piece of equipment always seems a surprise. A trombone player is literally shouldering the burden of

5

his music, so when he steps out of the ensemble to take his shot, you've got to respect him.

My father put his intimidating size to use. He was in Juilliard on the GI Bill, but he had rent to pay and a family to support, so he got a full-time job as a bill collector and claims investigator for a retail furniture store, and played whenever he got the chance. I got all dressed up and went to his graduation and was very proud. But the life of a serious musician was no easier then than it is now. With his classical training my father went looking for employment, but he found that blacks were simply not being hired by symphony orchestras. Finally, after several years of trying to make music his livelihood, my father found a career that made his bearing his work. He worked for the city, first as a corrections officer at the prison on Riker's Island, then as a police officer for the New York Transit Authority.

My father had found his niche. In 1955 there was little room for argument with a policeman; conversation was not required, only obedience. A classic strong, silent type could let his authority speak for him, and my father's silence spoke like thunder. Al had a great deal of respect for order, and with the laws already written, all he had to deal with was their not being violated. Which is not to say he was heartless. One time while I was in high school, Ronald Spry, who lived in the next building over, got caught jumping a turnstile and was brought into the district office where my father was working. Big Al didn't let Ronald get booked, which would have shamed him and his family. Instead, he took Ronald downtown to where his father was working and let Mr. Spry wear out Ronald's behind.

But most of the time my father would put a cool distance between himself and his emotions. That's the way a lot of policemen cope with the daily potential for disruption—and my father was particularly well-suited for this line of work. Unfortunately, he found it difficult to warm back up when he came home. I could come to him

6

with problems, and he could cope with them—that's what he did all day—but it was a rare moment when I felt I was more than a professional case, when he made me feel he knew and cared that these were *my* feelings that were battered or my personal aches that needed soothing.

When he went to work for the Transit Authority, I would only see him one shift out of three. If he started work at eight A.M., I'd see him in the evenings, but if he had the four P.M. shift, I'd be asleep by the time he got home, and if he went on at midnight, he'd be asleep when I arrived from school. He was there—there was always the man in the house—but I could go days without talking to him, and then when we would get some time together he wouldn't have much to say.

My father is a great reader. My friends thought of him as an intellectual, or at least a man of learning, because there were always books in the house. Al would go downtown to the used bookstores on Fourth Avenue and buy paperbacks, read them, sell them back by weight and buy more. There were magazines lying around at all times—*Gun Digest, Life, Argosy, True*—and all through my years in that house, I would be browsing and reading. My taste in women, for better or worse, was formed by the cartoons in the magazines my father read: narrow waist, great curves, big breasts—caricatures, but hard to deny. I could have picked Jayne Mansfield, or Anita Ekberg, but the woman I wanted had a little more class. The Sophia Loren Syndrome.

Big Al's literary leanings were a mixed blessing. It was made clear to me early on that books were important, but often my father would rather read them than talk to me. I would ask him a question or start a conversation, and he wouldn't even acknowledge that I was there. If I was asking something factual, he'd tell me to look it up; if I kept after him, he'd get annoyed and chase me away. There was no feeling in the world like asking your father "Where does electricity come from?" and not getting his eye off the printed page. I wanted to know about politics, machines, history—"Why is that like that?"—but pretty soon I stopped asking. I learned the facts of life, and almost everything else, out on the street.

Though my father's presence dominated the house, I spent most of my home time with my mother. She was as outspoken as he was taciturn, and she had plans for me. Her Lewis was going to be educated; I was always going to do my best, and if there was good to be gotten, I was going to get it. She had been born in North Carolina and knew Jim Crow personally. She never liked him. Not active politically, she fought national battles on the family level. She didn't have economic power—while bringing me up, she worked part time as a price-checker at a large department store—but she found ways of making her feelings known. Through all of the drubbings I absorbed in the street, she would drill into me, "Don't let anybody intimidate you." That was her cause.

We used to buy our groceries at the Associated Food Store down on Dyckman Street. Urban tensions being what they were, this was the stage for the occasional street scene. A guy named Ozzie won immediate and undying fame when, after three Irish troublemakers started messing with him as he came out of the market, he put down his packages and whipped them all right there on the sidewalk. Ozzie was a hero, and his life was considerably simpler from then on.

One afternoon my mother and I, on our way back home after buying some material and dry goods downtown at Macy's, stopped into the Associated to pick up some groceries. I couldn't have been more than six and was trying to keep up as my mother bustled down the aisle to the refrigerator section. The store manager decided we were dangerous customers, or maybe he just felt like wielding a little power that day. He intercepted my mother and told her to check her bag up front. The store was full of people with all sorts of baggage, but he was going to make us the examples. My mother took this for what it was, another in a lifetime of petty harassments, and told the man that if he had to satisfy himself that she was no thief, he could inspect the package when she left. "There's nothing in this bag that you sell," she said loudly. "You sell dry goods here? No. I'm going to get my milk and a loaf of bread and be on my way." She never stopped moving.

Wasn't good enough for the manager. He made a pass at her package; she resisted and stormed to the register to pay and go. This man didn't make this kind of scene with his Irish and Italian customers. He started shouting. She was in a rage, yelled sharply back and swung her shopping cart blindly into a display case, bringing a pyramid of hard rolls crumbling to the floor. I was up to my thighs in baked goods, kicking at them, following my Mom, who called everybody a whole bunch of unmentionables and made her exit. She never went back.

I listened to my mother. She would tell me where I was and was not to go. I could fool around in front of the house or in the big playground nearby, but if I was going anyplace else, she better know about it. If there were certain kids she didn't want me to play with, she'd tell me, and I wouldn't play with them. I was her only child, and I was a very good little boy.

Being an only child had its advantages. While I missed out on an older brother to show me the ropes, or a younger sister to torment, I did get my own room, a fact that went a long way toward shaping my personality. With such privacy I was unique among my friends. My room was my sanctuary, where I would lick my wounds after another sidewalk disaster or retreat to read or daydream when no one else would talk to me. It looked right out on the Cloisters, a medieval-period stone monastery that the city had made into a park and museum, and in my many monkish moments I could manufacture the calm I needed. I grew up in that room, from three years old through high school, and though I outgrew the bed and bumped my head on the doorway, it held all my secrets, and I had plenty.

My parents enjoyed their new house and used to throw some hot parties. My mother is a cosmopolitan lady and a talker, and she loved to have a good time. My father's most intimate connection was to music. His warmth and generosity, his desire and ability to make people smile, almost all his humanity seemed to show up there. When it really got to rocking, a whole new man would emerge. He could be the main attraction, dance up a total storm—he was an excellent dancer—and then, at song's end, sit back down and have nothing to say.

During a big wintertime bash, I would wake up, burning, with thirty coats piled on my bed, but that would be okay because I knew the next morning I'd have my own celebration. On Saturday mornings the day after a party I'd be up at six on the dot; the living room would be full of quarter- and half-filled soda bottles—the little kind that are now art deco classics—and I'd have a Coca-Cola party before my folks woke up and caught me.

I was a pretty obedient kid. My mother told me what to do and . . . she was my mother; I had to obey her. I paid attention to my father, too, because if I didn't give it up, Al was going to have my butt for sure. I got spanked a couple of times, but I learned quickly. I have always been a quick learner.

My mother was insistent that I was going to get a good education. While she could have waited until the following May for St. Jude's Elementary School to open for its six-week spring session, she enrolled me in first grade at P.S. 52 that September, 1953. For me, at first, school was fun.

In first grade I was a man. My mother walked me the first day—the new school was three blocks from home—and kissed me good-bye at the school door. The second day I wasn't being walked and wasn't being kissed. Too old for that kind of stuff. I shook my mother's hand and set off on my own. (It was only many years later that she told me she gave me a half-block's headstart and followed me to school for weeks until she was sure I'd be safe.) I shook hands with the policeman who took me across the street and made it to school just fine.

When May came around my mother transferred me to St. Jude's because she felt the Catholic school offered a better learning program and more discipline, her strong suit. She had converted from Baptist to Catholic in order to marry my father, and she was about to raise me with the zeal of the newly converted. Plus, the school was only a block away.

My first day at St. Jude's all the kids were scared, but I had been going for seven months and was an old school-hand. Kids were crying, didn't want to leave their mothers, and I said, "No, come on, we're gonna have fun!" Parochial schools had a policy of putting public school kids back a year, so I was in kindergarten—no work. I was already advanced; I could write my name, so I had nothing to do but go crazy, which I did with pleasure. The first day there I pulled the chair out five times in a row just as Lawrence Trainor was about to sit down on it, and got a laugh each time. Lawrence took a few times to get wise, and I loved to have people laugh at me. The classroom was on the ground floor, and when the bell rang at three o'clock I would climb out the window and go home. I was happy and bouncy, and though I was never a discipline problem, I think they were worried about what they were going to do with me. But it was only six weeks, a parochial school boot camp.

Out of the house everyone was more lively. My father had been brought up in Brooklyn, and on the weekends when we would visit my grandmother in the Brownsville section, I caught glimpses of a relaxed man I did not know. His father, my grandfather, died when Al was nine, and as the oldest son, Al raised his younger brother and two sisters and was forced to become the money-earner as well as trailblazer. Like lots of others during the Depression, he got his childhood taken away from him. Through junior high and high school my father was an iceman, carting fifty-pound blocks of ice from the wagons up as many flights as he had to, to help support the family. It developed his physique and honed his anger and independence. It also taught him Yiddish, which he learned to understand and speak from delivering ice to the Hasidim in Canarsie.

So this was the old neighborhood, and we'd drop in at the barbershop or hang for a while at the candy store, and the people who knew him as a boy would treat him kindly, and he would be loose with them.

I was loose with everybody, but sometimes it didn't work out too well. Always good for a practical joke, I was really bored one hot summer night and went looking for fun. I was tired of listening to the radio, had run through all my toys and my relatives. I wanted to go outside, but it was hot and dark, and my grandmother wouldn't let me. There was crime out there, she said, no place for a little boy. I wasn't buying it, but all I could do was hang out the window and look up and down the street for entertainment. Nothing. "Okay," I told myself, "I'm going to play helicopter." I got a piece of string and tied a knot in it and proceeded to swing it and whoosh it and helicopter loudly all over the apartment. Got no rise out of anybody.

My father's good friend, I'll call him John, used drugs on and off for years. That evening he was in the bathroom shooting up. I liked John a lot. He was everything my father wasn't: outgoing, personable, and always good for some playtime. So when he opened the door and weaved into the living room, I wanted him to fly in formation; we were going to be the Brownsville Blue Angels. I bothered him and bothered him, but he shooed me away, lit a cigarette, and lowered himself onto the couch for a nod.

I was disappointed. I was also a practical joker, and the best part of my extensive repertoire was the old tie-your-shoelaces-together gambit. Not that it had ever worked on anybody, but it was always worth at least a chuckle and a couple of moments in the spotlight. I crept up to John with the squeaky silence of a seven-year-old and undid his laces. He didn't move. I picked up one strand and tied it to the other, being careful not to put my face too close so I wouldn't get kicked when he brushed me away. But John was out cold, and even when I knocked at his ankle he didn't move at all. Geez, this was no fun. I went back to my fantasies and my flying machine and forgot, for the moment, all about old boring John.

But things were real dull at Grandma's that night, and I needed some air time. So, "Hey," I decided, "I'm gonna buzz friend John!" I was swinging my propeller and sounding like a soprano kazoo choir, and I got real close when my twine hit his cigarette and knocked hot ash all up John's chest and neck. He woke up, burning, stoned, confused. I knew I was in trouble and jumped back quickly. He swatted the ash off him and started to get up to see what the hell was happening when, wham, his feet just stopped and he fell like a bozo between the couch and the coffee table.

"I'll kill you!" he yelled, hobbling after me. I shrieked and scooted into my grandmother's room, where I was expressly forbidden to go, and hid under her bed. My grandmother laughed and protected me, but I was scared out of my mind. Still, it's the only time that trick worked.

John, by the way, totally cleaned himself up and is now back on his feet.

School was very important in my home. My father was interested in my report cards, and my mother was vitally concerned. She wanted the best of everything—for her, for me, for our family—and saw schooling as the key to my future. There was no desperation; it wasn't like I had to lead my family out of the darkness—we were neither poor nor ignorant. What my mother carried in herself and instilled in me was ambition. With my father's respect for order, and my mother's vision of success, I was primed to do well in Catholic school, and I did. I learned to read early and quickly. My homework got done because my mother made me do it, and after she'd drilled it into me how important it was, I did it for myself. Plus, the nuns would not permit me to be lazy. I was always near the top of my class, and once they recognized some glimmer of intelligence in a kid, the sisters would not let up. You would apply yourself, or you would stay after school. They had the word of God, and you were going to learn how to spell it.

Still, I did a lot of looking around. Once in the springtime when I was in the second grade, there was a lot of noise going on outside. My desk was right next to the window, and when the teacher, Miss Doyle, turned her back to the class and began to write something on the blackboard, I leaned out and tried to find out what was happening. There was a big crowd, and I hissed to a kid standing nearby, "What's going on?"

"It's Willie Mays!" he told me. Willie Mays was playing stickball with the kids right outside of St. Jude's! I craned my neck and, for one fleeting second, caught a glimpse of the top of his head. Boy, I wanted to be out there.

When I ducked back inside Miss Doyle had me in her sights.

"But Miss Doyle," I explained, "it's Willie Mays!" Much more important than St. Thomas Aquinas.

"Yes, well," said Miss Doyle, "you better sit down."

By the time I made it outside for lunch Willie was gone.

One very important piece of information came my way accidentally. In third grade one of my classmates, Michael Farrell, brought a Polaroid camera to school. It was a new-fangled invention back then, and we all gathered around looking at it and poking it and wondering how it worked. Some of us may have had Brownie Starflashes, but we'd never seen anything like this. What do you do with a camera in third grade? You take a class picture. So the whole class—the boys in their white shirts, blue ties, and navy blue slacks; the girls in their jumpers and knee socks—lined up in front of the blackboard while the sister focused, and remembered to keep her finger out from in front of the lens, and squeezed. The flash flashed and she read the instructions and flicked the switch and waited a full minute, then she opened the back of the camera and peeled the photograph clear. "Back to your seats now, class, and we will pass this around."

When it finally got around to me I was shocked. I knew I was the tallest boy in the class; I had always been taller than everyone my age, but there I was dead center in the back row, towering over everybody as usual, and as I looked at the grainy black and white photo in my hand, I thought, "Damn, I'm dark and everybody else is light!"

I hadn't noticed, and nobody had told me! In the projects nobody had said anything, and the subject hadn't come up in school, but, hey, I was darker than the rest of these kids. I didn't tell anybody, didn't mention it to my parents when I got home that afternoon. I just had this special bit of info, and I tucked it away.

I was always a good reader, generally faster than most of my class, and in the time we were supposed to be plowing through one story I could absorb three. At school I would read the assignment and then flip through the book until I came to a story that never failed to please me. In my reader this ugly, gawky, black duckling was tormented by the other guys his age, had to go off by himself and lick his wounds. But when he began to grow he blossomed into a beautiful black swan that glided majestically into maturity. At least that's the way I remember it. Other, lighter, children may have seen only the duckling as black, not the swan. I saw otherwise.

I never felt like I was black until I was made to. For fourth grade, whether to save money or work out some personal problems or just to live their lives without a nine-year-old boy underfoot—I've never been sure why—my parents sent me to an all-black boarding school in Pennsylvania, and I learned about being black in a

15

hurry. Up until that point, color had not been a major issue. It wasn't ignored, we weren't living in any dream world, but race had not been the sole determining factor in what my life had been like. I'd been more apt to play with someone who was friendly than with someone who was black.

The Holy Providence School in Cornwall Heights, right outside of Philadelphia, housed forty boys and perhaps three hundred girls from the fourth through eighth grades, as if they were detainees. The place looked like a Mediterranean abbey, with its long, massive buildings and their red tile roofs, many arches and arcades. It was run by nuns and by those boys who had proved they were willing, in fact eager, to establish domain the hard way.

I got there and immediately found I could read better than anyone in the school. My father's example and my mother's training had made that come easy; I could pick up a book, read it out loud, pronounce the words with the proper inflections and actually know what they meant. When the nuns found this out they paid me a lot of attention, once even asking me, a fourth grader, to read to the seventh grade. When the kids found this out I became a target.

Nineteen fifty-six was a hard year for me. At five feet eight inches, I was bigger than all but one boy in the school, but at nine years old, I was as tough as almost none of them. It was my first time away from home, my first experience in an all-black situation, and I found myself being punished for doing everything I'd ever been taught was right. I got all A's and was hated for it; I spoke correctly and was called a punk. I had to learn a new language simply to be able to deal with the threats. I had good manners and was a good little boy and paid for it with my hide.

My mother had told me never to be intimidated, but she hadn't told me how to prevent it. The school bully was a seventh grader named Sylvester Curtis, and I managed for the first few months just by good fortune to

16

stay out of his way. Sylvester was the kid who muscled to the head of the lunch line every day, bullied the lower classmen, chose the sides for touch football so he'd always win. He needed to be dealt with, but I was not the one to do it.

The currency at Holy Providence was marbles, and one afternoon Sylvester was demonstrating his supreme control over his subjects by throwing his rolling cash flow out the dorm window and laughing as the other boys ran to pick it up. The scene had a loud soundtrack, and when one of the sisters strode up and demanded to know just what exactly was going on, old Bright Eyes here piped up, "Sylvester Curtis is cockin' marbles!" She set out after him and, when she was through, he came after me.

I took a terrible beating, and there was nothing I could do about it. When he finally let me drag myself away, I knew I had to find some way of making it through the year. The nuns liked me because I did well in class and was polite, but they couldn't protect me. I had no allies, and I was surrounded by predators. As many fights as I'd had in my life, I had twice that many before Christmas. Something had to change or I was not going to survive. I had to get mean.

The impulse to clown around, which had won me friends before, had to be stifled; this wasn't family friend John chasing me now, this was someone serious about wanting to do me harm. There was nothing I could do about schoolwork; it never occurred to me to give up learning, but one thing I did learn was not to be too smart out loud. Any contact could get me a whipping, so I was looking to have no contact at all. As big as I was, I simply tried not to be there.

About the only place I was even semisafe was on the basketball court. In New York my father had shown me how to get the ball up to the basket ("This is how you protect the ball," he'd say, and elbow me in the face), and I had fooled around in the playground by myself, but at Holy Providence basketball was the only thing you could do, and since I was the second tallest guy in the school, I was automatically on the team. One of the local Catholic men would pile us in his car and take us to a seminary nearby where we would play against other Catholic elementary schools. It was organized ball but just barely, crazy games with kids running wild up and down the court. I was playing with boys older but smaller than myself, and where they were comfortable with their bodies, I didn't know what to do with mine. I hadn't grown into what I was walking around in, as if I were wearing somebody else's suit and kept tripping over the cuffs. I was gangling and awkward, and on top of being uncertain about what exactly I should be doing, I was right in the middle of trying to be invisible. I would run up to one end of the court and watch as the play got made, then run down to the other end and be out of it there too. If one of the guys on my team actually threw me the ball, I generally made a mess of it. That was if I played at all. I was no child prodigy.

But one day I stumbled upon a strange and delightful experience, kind of like that exciting yet amazingly unexpected feeling you get when you know, quite definitely, that you've entered puberty. In the first half, I was in the game, which was already unusual, and a rebound fell my way near the right of the basket. I fumbled with it, trying to conquer the dribble, and it almost got away. Finally, with a guy from the other team at my back, I looked over my shoulder, saw the basket, turned into the lane, and with one hand put up my first hook shot. It missed. Hit the back rim and bounced out. But it felt right, and the next time I got the ball I tried it again. Neither of them went in, but I had found my shot. At halftime my teammates, surprised that I had showed some coordination, encouraged me to practice it, and from then on, whenever I got into play I would shoot it. Nobody showed me how, it came naturally.

Shooting touch is developed mostly through comfort and orientation. Most people are comfortable when they're facing the basket, the balanced, squared-shoulder approach of the classic jump-shooter Oscar Robertson, for example. But turn them ninety degrees, and their focus goes off, their perception changes, and their touch. Maybe it was because I wasn't facing anything head-on— more likely, it was a matter of a nine-year-old's limited strength and coordination—but I found I was totally at ease and inexplicably confident when I turned my back on my opponent and shot the ball unmolested. I practiced that shot all winter long and, if I never got very good, at least I had a trademark.

But that was it for high points at Holy Providence. I couldn't snarl and get away with it because everybody knew I couldn't back it up, so I had to disappear. I found ways to ignore kids who I just knew meant me no good. And if that meant missing the one or two people who might have turned into friends (though as far as I could tell there weren't any of those), that was okay. I didn't need friends, I needed to be out of there.

My parents came for me in the spring, but not soon enough. Two weeks before school let out I got jumped. There was a long, narrow corridor leading out of the dining room, and two tough morons who didn't like this teacher's pet pressed their backs to one wall, feet to the other, climbed above the doorway, and fell on me as I was going back to my room. If you punched somebody in the face you got a pummeler's prestige, and they were busy working on their reputation. I rolled around and covered up as best I could, but they had a great time before they ran away. I couldn't see who did it, but I *know* to this day who it was. I was humiliated, and I wouldn't mind meeting those guys now.

My parents noticed the change in me as soon as they picked me up. They said I didn't smile anymore. They had put me in a numbing environment, and now they were telling me how disappointed they were that I had gotten chilled. I had never really been gut angry at my parents before, but I was angry at them now for having sentenced me to that year. And I was colder.

As soon as we got home I took off to see all my friends from the projects. It was June, and St. Jude's still had a few days of school left, so the next morning I walked over there and saw all the kids in my class. They were happy to see me and I was overjoyed to see them. The nuns let me stay the whole week, and I was never so glad to go to school. But I wasn't as giggly as before, and I swore I was never leaving New York again.

2

I loved summer in the city. St. Jude's ran a day camp, and each year I would swim and play softball and romp around with my friends. The summer after third grade I had won the award as Best Athlete, but after I got back from boarding school, they wouldn't give it to me anymore. I could run faster than anyone my age, and swim as well, and hit a softball farther, but I had gotten too nasty, had too much "street" in me. Which was funny because I had picked all this up in suburban Pennsylvania. As unaggressive as I'd been up there, what little rubbed off on me had put me far ahead of the project kids. The Philly boys had bruised me, and I wasn't going to give anyone the opening to hurt me again.

But I still had a good time. I had my friends, and we had our games. We played sandlot football, six on a side, crazy games with equipment. The summer after fifth grade I had my bike, and I'd ride all over. I was playing Little League, and to get up to Inwood Hill Park where the fields were, I had to go through Good Shepherd Parish. Good Shepherd had been one of only two Catholic churches north of 181st Street, but when the projects were built they couldn't—or wouldn't, I've never been sure which—accommodate the new arrivals, and so St. Jude's was built. St. Jude's territory was the projects at Good Shepherd's back end, so St. Jude's had the new development's blend of ethnic and racial backgrounds. Good Shepherd was almost one hundred percent Irish. I would be riding up there to play baseball, and these Irish kids would be chasing me yelling, "Nigger! Nigger!" Once I had to swing my bike chain and plow through a whole crowd of them. There weren't any gang fights, but you had to be ready for these people.

My best friend at the time was a boy named Johnny Harrison. He had been in my class since second grade. He ate over at my house all the time, and we were always together in the street. We never missed each other's birthdays; he liked to build model ships and airplanes, and I'd always give him one. We played and talked and were real lockstep buddies. At St. Jude's day camp, we had all gone swimming one day in the George Washington High School pool when his sister had gotten in trouble and was very quietly drowning in water just over her head. I couldn't swim either, but I was tall enough to grab her under the arm and take her to the side of the pool. If I had a "first fan," it was her. Johnny's mother and mine were close; the families liked each other. This went on for years.

But in the sixth grade we started to drift apart. It was 1958, the Civil Rights Movement had begun in the south, and segregation became a topic of conversation. Though there was no cataclysmic break-up, Johnny was white and I was black, and we just didn't see each other as often as we had. We were there in school each day, but he would go off with his white friends without inviting me.

There were now two more black kids in the class so, want to or not, I would play almost exclusively with them. I felt bad about it, but Johnny and his friends didn't seem to want to have much to do with me. I was no longer simply one of the crowd; I was black and alone.

By seventh grade Johnny and I were hardly talking. Though nothing had ever been said, we both had that adolescent instinct that tells you when you've been slighted, and if John had let his resentment gnaw at him, I had tried to avoid thinking about it at all.

One day we were sitting in the lunchroom—me, to my right a guy named Brian Gallagher, and to his right John. It was lunchtime and we all had our trays in front of us and were pulling the usual lunchtime nonsense, pushing and shoving. We had this chain reaction going— the kind of scene where your mom always says, "Someone is going to get hurt!"—and Brian lurched into Johnny, and Johnny took offense. He figured it was my fault, got out of his seat, walked over and tried to smack me in my face. Seeing him coming, I ducked, and his slap caught the top of my head. He jumped back, ready to fight. Maybe he was thinking of how easy I had been the last time we'd been friends, but I was well over six feet by this time and had stopped losing fights. I stood up and Johnny took a run at me. He led with his right—John was left-handed, and never too good at boxing—and ran directly into my own straight right, which caught him flat on the nose and knocked him backwards. The floors were hard institutional linoleum and had just been polished that morning, so when he hit on his behind he slid for a couple of feet. I didn't break his nose, but I must have busted up something in there because he was really bleeding.

They picked him up, took me to the principal's office, and immediately called my father. I was worried; my Dad was not in favor of breaking school rules or disrupting his schedule. Al got there, asked me what happened, and, when I told him, said, "This is bullshit.

23

He shouldn't have been hitting you," and left. Lots of people had seen what had happened, but the principal still kept me in the office until three o'clock and then let me go.

Harrison was waiting for me outside, he and his friends. He was yelling at me, but I had learned to ignore people, and I turned the ice on him, stared over him, then laughed at him, which got him even madder. "Hey, nigger!" he screamed at me. "Hey, Jungle Bunny, you big jungle nigger."

I just laughed at him. "Fuck you, you . . . milk bottle." It was the only white thing I could think of. It really pissed him off, but he didn't come anywhere near me. We never spoke again.

John and his family moved to Florida the next year.

Basketball played a larger and larger part in my life as I grew taller and taller. I was on the St. Jude's team in fifth and sixth grades, but ended up mostly as comic relief. I'd be the tallest guy there, and before warm-ups you could hear the other team buzzing, "Shit, man, what if he can play?" And then the game would start, and I would sit.

The man in charge of all athletic activities at St. Jude's was Mr. Hopkins. I was at an age when my awkwardness could have become a trademark, and he gave me a confidence well beyond my abilities just by letting me know that, no matter if I could dribble a ball or read one word, he was going to care about me. He was in a position to have a positive influence on a lot of kids, and he did.

In seventh grade I began to have some effect on the game. That was a big year because we got new uniforms. I was always a big sports fan, and my favorite New York football Giant was the fullback, Mel Triplett, number 33. I got his number. Plus, according to my mother's cosmic numerology, 33 was right up there. So that was that, I've had number 33 ever since.

By eighth grade we were a team to contend with. I had spent the summer playing with the guys who would travel up to the projects for a game. Actually they would come up to see the girls and end up in a game to play or show off. But my entire social activity consisted of basketball. I could almost feel myself growing. I amazed people. They'd say, "You're in seventh grade, you can't palm the ball." One day I couldn't, next day I could.

I spent the whole summer practicing how to dunk, and when my eighth grade season started I finally had my chance in a game. One of my teammates, Patrick Dorish, had the ball on a fast break; there was one man back, and I was at the top of the key. Patrick drove, the man stayed with him, and as Patrick went by he just flipped me a pass and kept on going. The ball came up in my hands, I took one dribble and jammed it. The whole place went crazy. Might have been all of sixty people there, but they went insane. I was bouncing up and down, ready to go for some more. Give me the ball! We scored the next six baskets in a row, and the place was filled with a machine-shop din.

In the fall we won a gold medal by beating Good Shepherd in a three-man tournament held in Central Park. We lost in the finals of a Christmas tourney at All Hallows, another Catholic school in the Bronx, because they had Christian Brothers officiating the game, and they let me get beat up underneath the boards without calling any fouls. I complained—it frustrated the hell out of me and got me mad—but the Brothers just told me, "Well, we have to make it interesting."

We tied Good Shepherd for the district championship. Early in the season they had come down to our gym and beaten us, and for our game up there we were looking for vengeance. The day before, I had practiced my jump shot the entire afternoon. I was ready. A whole lot of students and even some nuns came and cheered us on. Good Shepherd was the traditional powerhouse, and St. Jude's, in our eight-year history, had won nothing. We beat them by ten points—I scored thirty-three. And all of a sudden the school began to rally around the basketball team. Some of the boys in the class were jealous because the girls were out there cheering for Lew, but I was loving it.

We won the rest of our schedule, and Good Shepherd did the same, so when we met in a final playoff it was for all the marbles. We lost, in overtime, and I hated to lose to those guys, but we won a trophy, and we put it in the school lobby where you could see it every day as you walked inside. That had been a consuming drive for me, that display-case distinction. It's easy, once you have it, to take money or fame for granted, but the prestige of that trophy to a thirteen-year-old boy is hard to match in a lifetime. It was a victory of pure emotion, a totally new experience, a triumph of gladness and surprise I would never again be allowed to feel. At my quietest, if I concentrate very hard, I can only recapture a faint glow of that consuming pleasure.

I started being recruited when I was in seventh grade. I wasn't very good, to say the least, but my size was startling, and the coaches must have seen something I didn't. By the next year, when I was six feet five inches, I could have attended any Catholic school in New York City on full scholarship. The Hill School, a private prep school in Pottstown, Pennsylvania, made me an offer. My mother was doing some sewing at the time for Alexandra Potts, whose family was, you might say, very influential in Pottstown. Mrs. Potts wanted my family to know that the Hill School administration would allow me to integrate their institution. No, no, no, no. I passed on that one.

My friends Johnny Graham and Arthur Kenney, both a year ahead of me at St. Jude's, had gone to Power Memorial Academy, a Catholic high school downtown at 61st Street and Amsterdam Avenue. Power had contacted me in seventh grade, and while Arthur was being recruited, I went along and checked the place out. The school had a good academic reputation and a great gym: full court with six other baskets, open on Saturdays during the winter so you could go down and play all afternoon. It was Catholic school, so I'd have to toe the line, but I was used to that; at home or at St. Jude's that's all I ever did.

In eighth grade Arthur took me down there to shoot some hoops and meet Jack Donohue, Power's basketball coach. I had a good feeling about Coach Donohue almost immediately. He knew how to talk to kids like they were really there. There's a thin line adults walk between teaching kids through emotional closeness and offending them by encroachment—some adults just line up offside—but Coach Donohue was both personable and authoritative. He told good jokes and seemed like an easy guy to be around. The only other coach I met and liked was Jack Curran at Archbishop Malloy, but Malloy was way the hell out in Queens, and it would have taken me two hours each day to get there and back. Plus, Coach Donohue would get us pro basketball tickets and take us to Madison Square Garden to watch the Knicks. That's when I saw my first pro games. It was wonderful. I saw Kenny Sears and Carl Braun play. I saw Cousy. That's old history to the guys in the league now, as if I'd met Abe Lincoln or run with Kunta Kinte, but then it was an education and a thrill. Coach Donohue knew what he was doing. No way was I going to go anywhere but to Power.

I graduated from St. Jude's after eighth grade and hit the streets. That was a big summer for me, 1961. I played a lot of basketball and hung with the guys I met on the court. I literally grew away from my old friends. The girls my age didn't have the right curves, and the older ones didn't want any part of me. My white friends from school made it extremely clear through their indifference that I wasn't at home in their crowd, and I didn't have a lot of other people to turn to. And my basketball compadres were all right. We used to hang out at Roy's, a little coffee shop down on 156th Street and St. Nicholas Avenue on Sugar Hill in Harlem with a hip jukebox—Art Blakey & the Jazz Messengers and Horace Silver stacked up next to Martha & the Vandellas and the Shirelles—and thirty-five-cent hamburgers. We'd play some ball, then drop in on Roy's and eyeball some of the girls. I was learning from moment to moment.

I hadn't done much wandering outside of the neighborhood before, but with these guys I got mobile. They were all two or three years older than I was, a crucial difference at that age, and since having style was a way of life, I had to develop some quick cools. Running with the fast crowd was new to me. Because I seemed by size to belong but was still so young, I learned to watch and take it all in. I was never the one who started the action; I had no experience, no background to tell me what was acceptable foolishness and what was plain dumb. And I didn't want to look foolish; I wanted to be one of the guys. I was in over my head, but I felt like I was growing up by the second.

I took to my role as observer as if I were born to it. My size offered me a consistently unique perspective, and the years at Holy Providence and St. Jude's had convinced me that I did indeed view my surroundings differently than other people, but mostly I found that in any given situation I was being allowed or even expected to be simultaneously in a crowd but not of it. It seemed like I had always been the youngest, the biggest, the fastest, the smartest; now I became the quietest.

There was only one kid from the projects who remained close. Norbert Florendo's family was Filipino, and Norbert was the guy with whom I shared those heart-to-heart discussions about the important things, like was Brigitte Bardot beautiful or just sexy. After college he was going to be a draftsman, he told me. I said I was going to be an architect. We'd sit up in my room, play chess and talk about what we'd read lately or seen on the latest episode of *Route 66*. On those days my view of the Cloisters was a real bonanza.

Apart from Norbert I had seen my best friends, the entire crowd from school, turn their backs on me for no reason I could fathom. If I could simply have blamed it on their being white kids and said to hell with them, I would have been more relieved, but I had thought of these people all along as friends, not whites, and that made my abandonment both political and personal, and, above all, painful. So when my new crowd came open to me, I joined in but was careful to keep my guard up.

Plus, there were some things I couldn't do. My father was a cop, so when the guys started jumping turn-stiles or palming Clark bars in the candy store I couldn't go along for long. Once in a while I would shimmy up the drain pipe to the elevated subway platform and sneak on the train when I was short on cash—that was an important fifteen cents, and it gave me a certain thrill knowing that I was beating my father. I gave that up pretty quickly, though, because I didn't want to chance getting caught. On the streets, but still essentially inside my mother's house, I continued to be a very good boy. I knew how to have fun, but some of it I knew I couldn't have.

The guys I hung out with near home were Johnny Graham, Munti, Kenny Kelly, and a fellow named Vino. Johnny I knew from St. Jude's, Kelly was new to the neighborhood, and I met Vino because he used to play the saxophone out his apartment window facing the park where we played ball. Vino was two years older than I was and came down one time wanting to play me one-on-one. I beat him, and he couldn't believe he'd lost to this fourteen-year-old kid; he's been in and out of my life ever since with his crazy self.

They called him Vino because he liked wine. He also liked company. Vino would go out and get all the guys around him to drink a little bit, and he would drink a little bit, and he'd get high and happy, and they'd get

29

high and happy. Then he'd get them to drink some more, and he'd drink some more, and he'd get drunk and uncomfortable, and they'd get drunk and uncomfortable. Then Vino would keep going beyond that and just be totally sick and get everybody sick, and then he'd pass out, and we'd have to take him home. This went on regularly. So one summer night he went out and started into his routine, but nobody drank with him, and when he passed out on the IRT local we left him there.

It was hot, and Vino must have slept from the projects down to South Ferry at the southern tip of Manhattan and back several times, did the whole circuit half the night, because when he woke up he was at 242nd Street, at the city line in the Bronx, in the *trainyard*. They'd taken the train off the line and jammed it with the rest of the out-of-use cars into what looks like a junk heap but is actually the guts of the transit system. Vino woke up, and it was dark. He was drunk, and he didn't know where he was, and he started to run. He ran the length of the silent cars, through three or four full trains, picking up speed like a runaway. Panting, oozing sticky wino sweat, careening through open doors, he took two more steps and then, like Wile E. Coyote, realized he was in midair and fell four feet to the ground on his face.

It took him hours to stagger home, bruised and dirty. After that Vino didn't stop drinking, he just stopped getting so drunk that he had to depend on us.

At the same time, Vino was the guy who intimately introduced me to the music of John Coltrane, and for that alone I am forever in his debt. I had listened to Trane on "My Favorite Things," but hadn't appreciated all that he was doing. In the confines of my room Coltrane taught me about freedom and release and holding everything under wraps and wailing anyway. I responded to Coltrane, and to the whole world of jazz that was just beginning to open up to me, with real passion. My father's music had made its impression. Even if I had been kept at arm's length from it by his silence, I knew the effect music had on his life; he had spent one entire two-week vacation sitting at the kitchen table with a soldering iron custom-crafting a stereo amplifier for his hi-fi. If he never told me in so many words, he made it extremely clear that music was as important as any one thing in this world; music and books seemed to be his only consistent pleasures. My mother was always listening to Sarah Vaughan, Nat "King" Cole, and Count Basie. I tuned into Art Blakey and Cannonball Adderley and Charles Mingus, and the hours I might have spent alone no longer had to be solitary. Though this was what my father played, I made it my own, my discovery. We rarely discussed it.

When I graduated from St. Jude's in June I was fourteen years old, six feet eight inches tall, and my glands were on the rampage. All I wanted to do was play ball and get laid. I was not notably successful at the former and a total failure at the latter. I had a tremendous crush on Barbara Nielson, a Puerto Rican girl from the projects. Her father was a stage technician at the Apollo Theater, which was cool, and she was very pretty and had the right curves. But it was never a go; she couldn't stand me. She had an aunt, though, eighteen or nineteen, who thought I was cute and probably wanted to give me some, but I was too stupid to understand the signals. I had no experience whatsoever, only this raging need, which I had no idea how to fulfill. I was very withdrawn. At that point in a boy's life, when forces are moving and juices flowing that you never knew you had, the main objective is to be exactly like everyone else. Don't want anybody laughing at you; don't want anybody looking at you; don't want any attention at all because at any moment things down there could shift, and you had no idea what might happen. Uniformity is security, accident is outrage, pray for peace.

I was definitely not like everyone else. Aside from my size, I couldn't dress well, had no social graces. Prime product of a Catholic education; every sin I conceived was original. And the Lord knows I was horny. But with no prospects and a built-in self-destruct mechanism, the best I could do was masturbation. Best time for that, right before confession. I was totally psyched out. If Jews have their stereotyped guilt, Catholics have to deal with repression. They teach you to suck it up all week long, and then, when you come clean at confession, they lay it on you some more: "What! You want some pussy?! That's the worst thing you could ever want!" It's like the devil is running your life through your balls.

I went to confession because that was what you were supposed to do. I had been an altar boy and had sung in the choir just like my mother had wanted. I wasn't making any of my own choices, and here they were trying to take something else out of my hands. The chaplain from my parish, and also at Power Memorial, was Father Burns. Where other priests had oil-and-vinegar-sized cruets for the communion wine, his had some volume to them. I would be pouring the blood of Christ into his chalice, and he would give me some very strange looks until it was good and full.

Father Burns used to meddle ferociously. He wanted to know all about his boys. He'd get me into the confessional, and from behind the screen I'd hear, "So, who's been out there violating the temples of their bodies?" Father Martin, at a parish near home, went a little further. I'd go up to confession on Saturday and say, "Father, I touched myself in an impure way." Father Martin would jump in: "Been jacking off, huh? Stop that stuff!"

Power Memorial Academy was an all-boys school run by the Brothers. A stolid brick building, it had once been a hospital but now looked more like a B-movie prison or a munitions factory. Wards that had once housed the diseased and recuperating were now classrooms, and the cafeteria used to be a morgue. The stairway walls were solid concrete; they retained no warmth, and they didn't give. And in the center of the stairwell was a caged elevator that stopped at even floors only. In September, 1961, nothing odd was being acknowledged at Power.

The first day I got there, sharp as I could get in my three-piece suit, I was given a demonstration of how the place worked. I walked up the six flights of stairs to where they tucked the ninth graders and did my best to fit into the chair-and-armrest desk that already had several generations of initials carved in it. (I had grown two more inches over the summer and was now six feet ten.) Some of my St. Jude's classmates were there, but having spent a summer on my own I didn't have much to say to any of them. I was ready to pay attention in class and get on with it.

My homeroom teacher was Mr. Kuhnert, a genuinely caring adult who, if you were polite and respectful toward him, could be the nicest man in the world. He taught algebra, and during the first class a freshman named John Walsh started cutting up. Walsh was a wiseguy, clearly looking to make a name for himself and establish his territory early, and for a full half hour he kept on cracking. Finally, toward the end of the period, Mr. Kuhnert told him to stand up. Walsh stood six feet five inches, about 230 pounds, figured he could take care of himself, and was looking around and trying not to grin as he rose. Mr. Kuhnert was about six feet six, and he walked over, picked Walsh up by his lapels until the kid's back was against the wall and nothing but his tiptoes touched the floor, whispered a few quiet admonitions dead into the boy's face and put him back down. That ended John Walsh's reign as class clown and did wonders for our comportment.

At Power they took their Catholicism seriously. The Pope, I was told time and again, was infallible. And since the Brothers were a lot closer to the Pope than I was, their infallibility was not to be questioned either. I learned by edict, and though there was some encouragement to compare and contrast, what this schooling ulti-

33

mately came down to was either acceptance or rejection, authority or anarchy, sanctity or sin.

I bought it. Made the Honor Roll first semester, did my homework, asked no questions, told no lies.

Tryouts for the basketball team were held in late October. I had come to Power with no great reputation, notable for being enormous, not particularly good. Whatever potential the coaches saw in me, I hadn't begun to deliver on. My coordination was beginning to catch up to my size—I was starting to have some idea when I jumped up where I was going to come down—but I had no strength, zero muscles, and I wasn't very aggressive.

When I showed up at Power's first practices I was scared. I had seen the pro game; I had played in the Harlem streets, and I didn't think I had it. The game was too rough, and I didn't know how to be bad. I was not an aggressive boy, let alone an aggressive rebounder, and I think it must have showed on my face. I had size but no stature, and I was easily intimidated by guys who moved with authority, who got in the pivot and held it through force of will. People dunked over me and I couldn't do anything about it. I didn't move well to go get the ball, reaching with my arms instead of attacking with my whole body, and I had no idea how to make my presence felt.

It was a struggle. Once practice started I was tired all the time. I had to wake up early to get to school, didn't get out of practice till almost five o'clock, came home, did my homework, watched TV, went to bed.

I practiced with the junior varsity, and I wasn't that good. We were handled by Mr. Percudani, the freshman and JV coach, not Coach Donohue, and we would scrimmage with the varsity, but I didn't think I was varsity material. So I was shocked when, on the morning we were scheduled to play our first game against Erasmus Hall High School in Brooklyn, Mr. Donohue called me down to his office and gave me a varsity uniform. He had even thought enough to give me number 33. I was very proud, and more than a little scared, but I tried not to show either when I went back to class. Mr. Kuhnert, who had become as much of a friend as a high school teacher was going to be, saw my uniform and was amazed.

The Power team rode the subway to Brooklyn, and I tried to be cool, but this was my first real shot, and I wanted to be brilliant.

It was a disaster. Erasmus killed us. They had an All-City guard named Charlie Donovan who would go the length of the court and score, take half-court shots and make them. One time he drove to the basket, and when I went in to make the block he put the ball under my arm, off the backboard and in, with English. We were destroyed, and I looked awful. After the game I sat in the locker room and cried, like a gigantic baby sitting there weeping. I hated to lose, and I absolutely hated to look bad doing it. All that day I had allowed myself visions of glory, and now they'd been thrown back in my face. What was worse, there didn't seem anything I could do to prevent it from happening again.

We scrimmaged Lincoln High School that same month, in preparation for our league opener. They had Dave "Shorty" Newmark, a seven-footer who went on to Columbia University and then the pros, and they were knowledgeable, cunning basketball players who played rough. They boxed me out well, and bounced me around while they were doing it. I tried to get tough but just ended up fouling and being ineffective. After the game, as I fumed in my frustration, Mr. Donohue came over to me. "I hope you're learning what it's all about to really want to win," he said brusquely.

Mr. Donohue coached through benign humiliation. He challenged your pride, knowing that the worst thing that can happen to an adolescent is to look bad in front of the guys. The coach was a master psychologist; he could size a player up in a moment, pinpoint his personal vulnerability, and then lean on it so the guy would do anything to get the coach off his back. He took the game personally and insisted that we do the same, that we make ourselves proud by winning and playing well. We had to play our absolute hardest, nothing else was acceptable. Pride was his life force; for us it was a live nerve that he could teach us to brush. One stroke, a good practice, and we could tingle for days. Deny it, or stamp on it—he found unique and inspired ways to abuse you—and life was hardly worth living. First, he found the pride in each of us, then he taught us how good it could feel. What he was ultimately after was for every one of us to learn to light our own fires and glow our brightest.

But this is cosmology. He was a basketball coach, and he knew what he was doing. He revered the Boston Celtics for their passing, discipline, and consistent winning, and he impressed on us the value of these attributes. We were not particularly flashy, the coach would not stand for a lot of hot-dogging, but we passed and took good shots and played with high enthusiasm and an element of fear. You did not want to look bad in front of Mr. Donohue for you would carry his insults with you for a lifetime.

Coach Donohue sized me up immediately. "What are you, a stiff?" he'd shout at me after another rebound would roll off my hands and out of bounds. The big gym would echo, practice would stop, and the guys would titter. "What are you, a farmer? Are you alive?" He'd grab my wrist and make a big show of checking his watch. "Let me feel your pulse." Mr. Donohue was great. He could make everybody laugh, and humiliate you to death, but through it all there was an unstated yet undeniable quality of affection. And he got me to the point where the next time anybody came near me I was going to knock them down and get that ball.

I needed every bit of that because basketball, I was beginning to learn, is a rough game. We scrimmaged Boys High and some guy bit me on the arm. There were serious teeth marks in my arm! We came over to the huddle and I said, "Mr. Donohue, this guy bit me!"

"Yeah, right, okay," he said, busy cooking up our

next series. "You got any more jokes, you can go down in the locker room and tell them."

I wasn't going to argue with him, so I went back out on the court. We were running up and down, and the mark was getting red, and he saw it and said, "He did bite you!" No kidding, coach. Mr. Donohue stopped the game in midplay and threatened Micky Fisher, who was coaching Boys High. "You better get whoever did that out of here!" he yelled, and they threw the player out of the building.

It was a whole lot of hard days in the gym, but as the season progressed, the game became familiar and I started to relax. I was still anxious on the court, but I learned about dishing it out as well as taking it. Power played a Saturday morning Catholic High School television Game of the Week against Fordham Prep, and I picked up twenty-one rebounds, and after that the coach was all over me. "You know what you can do now!" he would shout. "Maybe we should get cameras out here every game and just tell you they're gonna be on!"

Once in a while, as he had done the year before, Mr. Donohue would take me to Madison Square Garden. They used to play doubleheaders back then, a Celtics game and then the Knicks, and I would watch and learn. I wasn't even thinking about playing pro ball, I just wanted to pick up some pointers and win at Power. Mr. Donohue loved the Celtics and made me pay close attention to Bill Russell, who, along with Wilt Chamberlain, was in the process of redefining the role of the center. Russell would grab a rebound and quickly get it out to Bob Cousy, who would get it to Bill Sharman, Tommy Heinsohn, or the Jones boys. They'd score, and Russell wouldn't get past the free throw line. I'd say, "But Coach, he's way behind." And Mr. Donohue would explain, "But you know what he did, he's letting his team run." And you couldn't argue with the Celtics' success. I learned how to use the outlet pass from watching Bill Russell. I also learned how to guard people and intimidate shots from watching him in those games. I don't block shots in the same way he did, but the concept was made clear to me then: Help your teammates when they get beat.

As my game got stronger I got cockier. Having seen some pro ball, one day I shot a turn-around jump shot in practice, your basic Wilt Chamberlain fadeaway. And I banked it in. Mr. Donohue stopped practice. This was a low-percentage shot that left me nowhere near any potential rebound, and he wanted to nip this little experiment in the bud. He said, "Shoot that one again." So I shot it, and it went in. He had me shoot seven. I made six, and after I made the last one, I was laughing because here I was proving him wrong, but I knew he was going to come down on me anyway. He said, "Yeah, you can make it in practice when there's nobody guarding you, but don't try it in a game."

We had a pretty good team. By the Catholic High School Athletic Association league opener I was starting at center, a fourteen-year-old playing with the big guys. One of the first things I learned, to minimize intimidation and mask my freshman fear, was a game face. We had just won a thriller over All-Hallows in my first game at Power's home gym when Mr. Kuhnert came over to me and said, "You drink ice water out there or something? You're real calm." I shrugged, didn't crack him a smile either. It had been too close a game for me to be happy, I was just relieved that we hadn't lost. I was a freshman playing on the varsity, and it was a strain.

We lost six games that year, the last one in the Catholic high school playoffs to Holy Cross, eventual finalists, but from the first tryouts to that day I had grown another inch, and my play was beginning to be refined. Colleges wrote, asking me to visit their campuses. I was fourteen and college was assured! My parents were joyous in their understated way, and my confidence was on the rise. We won the postseason Iona tournament with five straight victories; word was starting to spread, and it wasn't too long until school let out.

Summer, 1962, was a problem. I had a reputation now, and some moves, and I wanted to spread one by working on the others. I was meeting the city players and wanted to be one of them. My mother, on the other hand, wanted to keep me off the streets. Coach Donohue was building a basketball camp in Saugerties, New York, so he and my mother formed a strong alliance. I tried to fight them, but what could I do? Appeal to my father? Run away? I was sentenced to three weeks in the country.

But before I got sent away, the guys and I took a few chances. I had a year of high school in me now, and what I knew, I knew perfectly. Couldn't tell me a thing. I was looking for action.

We had a good time playing chicken on the subway. The AA local tunnel between 155th and 163rd Streets in Harlem was pitch black and absolutely filthy. The tracks were cleaned once in a while so the trains could run with whatever efficiency they could muster, but the grime of the entire city collected down there like dog shit on a crepe-sole shoe, and you never knew what was going to go for your ankle. The catwalks that connected station to station stood at door level no more than a foot from the path of the train, with only a guardrail sunk in the cement for safety. In the eighteen years I spent riding those lines before I left New York, I never saw anyone on those catwalks.

Except us. All that summer a bunch of the guys would go down to 163rd Street. While most of us waited for the local, some of our lunatic fringe would take off down the catwalk and try and beat the double-A. When the train came the rest of us would pile on, lean out the windows, and try and smack the runners in the heads as we thundered by. I had the good reach, but I was always worried that I'd catch my hand on some girder and leave my arm behind. The rest of the people on the train probably thought we were crazy, but we were having a real good time.

There were no subways in Saugerties; there were

no streets to run wild in. In fact, where I stayed, there were no streets at all. Mr. Donohue was still in the process of renovating this farm property upstate. The place was named Friendship Farm, and while the main house where we all slept was built in the 1780s, the rest of the "camp" didn't actually exist. A half-dozen guys from Power's basketball team were put to work building cabins, chopping logs, installing screening. Saugerties was only an hour and a half out of the city, but it could have been Wisconsin as far as we were concerned. There was a dirt court where we played ball every day, and we all swam in the Hudson River, but aside from that there was nothing to do. I was dying for music, and all you could get on the radio were cattle-report stations, Ferrante and Teicher, or WABC. Any kind of jazz was out of the question. I had no real friends up there, certainly nobody like the guys I was running with in Harlem.

The way Coach Donohue had set it up, basketball was the only fun thing to do, so I played a lot of basketball. I was out there on the court all day, every day, trying to immerse myself in the game and forget where I was. My body was coming around, my coordination clicked in naturally, and out of sheer frustration and intensity, I finally started developing some significant aggression. I stopped thinking of myself as the kid on the court and found even the older guys giving me my due. I didn't have much to say to anybody, made no conversational strides that summer, but my game took the great leap forward. I found out exactly how much I had improved when I got back to Harlem and saw right away that nobody on the court could stop me. It dawned on me then that I might have something here.

By tenth grade, high school meant basketball. I had made scholastic Honor Roll as a freshman and established to anyone interested that I was a true student, but the Catholic concept of education was a bit brutal for my tastes, so I concentrated on what I found most important at Power: my game. I played all the time, afternoons and weekends in the fall, team practices, pickup games in Harlem. I started hanging out with Eric Brown, a black kid who was a year behind me. He was from the Patterson projects in the South Bronx, and we'd go up there to play. There were girls in the South Bronx, and now I was one of those guys who would show up at the projects to play ball and watch the ladies. But I was still watching from a distance.

At the preseason scrimmages, where I'd gotten bitten and beaten a year before, Power was now wearing the other teams down. The games were played in quarters— you'd go maybe eight quarters in an afternoon against various schools—and we started to dominate. We went up against Erasmus Hall and Bishop Loughlin and rarely lost a period, never a game. My shot was falling; I was going after rebounds with a vengeance; I was looking to pass, and with Coach Donohue on my back I was so afraid of embarrassing myself that losing was out of the question. I was picked as a preseason All-American by some of the basketball magazines, but my friends and I didn't pay much attention to that; it was more important to be All-City.

The first game of the season was in Madison Square Garden against the defending Catholic High School Athletic Association champs, LaSalle. Their best player was Val Reid, All-City, and they'd beaten us twice the year before. We didn't have any legacy of victory—Power Memorial hadn't won the city championship since 1939—so there was no historical score to settle here, just teenagers' pride in the big payback. We thought we were pretty good and went gunning for the city champs. We beat them by twelve points and lost all awe for anyone, turned our season around in one game. From then on we were the team to beat. Nobody beat us.

The team was made up of me; six-foot-eight-inch Art Kenney, who couldn't jump at all but was aggressive as hell and bulled for every rebound; Oscar Sanchez;

George Barbazat, who coached at Long Island University; and Bobby "Radar" Erickson. Danny Nee, who went on to coach at Ohio University, was on the bench. Nobody at Power had seen anything like this. The whole school began to rally around us. Where maybe fifty people used to come to the games, now the big gym was packed, and there were lines snaking down the stairwell, through the lobby, and outside onto Amsterdam and 60th Street. Nobody ever used to show up for away games, but now hundreds of kids and even some of the Brothers would travel to root for us. We were the school's main attraction, moving in one season from a winning team to a dominating team to an undefeated team to a team of national note.

At first it felt really good to be so increasingly well-known and popular. They were our victories, the coach's and the team's, and we were glad to share them with the student body and even the teachers. Who would've thought we could cause such a stir? But as the season progressed, and the wins piled up like bricks in the whole school's foundation of pride, the games began to lose their thrill. I was no longer playing simply for myself and my teammates, guys I knew and wanted to win with. Somehow I now had a thousand people's self-esteem to shoulder, people I didn't know or particularly care to know, and I was being told—not asked—to be responsible for it. Victory was no longer confined to any one given high school basketball contest but was invested with a lot of other people's currency that I couldn't afford to lose. Coach Donohue made a big point of basketball being a team sport, but I knew whose fault it would be if Power lost; I knew who people would come to first. There was pride and prestige at stake, and in practice Coach Donohue never quit riding us; so there was his stinging criticism to face if anyone came anywhere close to beating us. Losing became unthinkable, and basketball stopped being fun.

The games were work. I learned how to play well and not get chewed out, how to win, how not to lose. It was hard work for a fifteen-year-old, but it had its rewards; they were just not what I'd thought they would be. I got acclaim and a lot of attention, my name in the papers and on the street, but there came with it the increasing knowledge that none of this was personal. They were screaming my name but few of them knew me, and those who did didn't know me as well as they thought. I was well aware that what goes up must come down. Still, we kept winning and I kept climbing.

I was a big story—*High School Goliath Powers To The Top*—but I couldn't talk to the press. I'd been reading the sports section since I'd learned how to read (I was, and continue to be, a serious Dodger fan), so I knew some of the writers' names and some of what was being said about me. Of course, it felt great. When the first article on me appeared in the *Journal-American*, my father got all excited and bought fifteen copies and sent them to friends and relatives all over the place. But back then there were seven major daily newspapers in New York, and Mr. Donohue decided that rather than let me be overrun by reporters or overwhelmed by requests, he would permit no contact at all between me and the media. I could read all the hoopla, but not add to it. Once in a great while he would let some reporter whom he knew to be reputable have a few moments with me, but mostly he kept them away. I think he felt my head might get turned around, and he didn't want to take the chance that I'd start disregarding my studies or his discipline. His team concept was very strong, rightly so, and he must have felt it was in my best interest not to have to deal with any potential disruptions. I didn't mind, I was getting good write-ups without having to go out of my way. There were always strangers hanging around the gym, but Coach Donohue kept me out of their way and them out of mine. You never could tell who those guys were.

The few times I did speak with a reporter were generally at Madison Square Garden. I'd be sitting there at a Knicks game with Coach Donohue, or we'd be standing in the promenade at halftime, and one or another of them would come over and start up a conversation. The coach was always right at my side, and after a few sentences he'd usually shut things down.

There were plenty of people who wanted to talk to me, and I knew some of them were sharks. Coach Donohue knew a few of the basketball figures who had been involved in the fixing scandals in the early 1950s and warned me away from them. He was in on the grapevine, wary and well-informed, and sometimes he would tap me on the knee and point out one or another sleazy dude and say, "This is a guy who will ruin your career, ruin your whole future. They're only interested in one thing, making money. If he ever comes around, don't even say a word to him." A lot of these guys, the coach explained, would pose as college scouts in order to get next to high school ballplayers. They'd give them money or whatever a kid might be looking for and then turn around and use their access to get money from the colleges trying to recruit them. Point shaving, recruitment violations—there were plenty of quick-buck possibilities that could wreck my life, and I was never tempted to look at these guys twice.

Coach Donohue and I spent a lot of time together. On his way down from Yonkers, he would pick me up in his black Falcon sedan and drive me to school a couple of times a week. We talked about upcoming opponents, schoolwork, how terrible the Knicks still were. He didn't want me cutting up in class and getting sent to post-three o'clock detention and missing practice; he made major points in that area. He was friendly, and though we never really had the kind of man-to-man talks that elevate friendship to intimacy, he was at least outspoken and clear in his good feelings for me.

I had a lot to talk about and very few adults to discuss it with. My mother, though interested, was too involved in protecting me from real and imagined disasters to be much help in encouraging my independence. If I could have ridden in a tunnel from her door to school and back every day without pain or interruption, broken only by the weekly communion detour, she would have been more than pleased. Rather than let me make mistakes and learn from them, she preferred me never to stumble upon a situation I didn't know. Perhaps because she herself was so thin-skinned, she thought I'd be torn up in a scrape. If she'd thought I was racing the A train, she would have gone crazy, so I told her nothing. My father, on the other hand, I could tell almost anything— and be certain it wouldn't register. He wouldn't tell me not to do anything; I just couldn't get his attention.

Though I might have been ready, I didn't spill out a whole lot to Coach Donohue either. I never told him about my parents; I never told anybody. I thought this was the way parents were supposed to be. We never talked about the ladies, though I could have used some guidance, but what fifteen-year-old ever talked to a grown-up about girls? There were things going on in the world that I was vitally interested in, however, and sometimes despite myself I would strike up a real conversation with my coach.

The year 1962 was a time of turmoil in America. Black people were thinking of themselves as . . . black . . . people. My pride in myself was growing, and I took every slight to every black man or woman personally. The Freedom Rides were riling up the South, and just as I was beginning to take my life in my own hands, black people were starting to lay theirs on the line. The headlines were full of southern disruptions, and one day the coach and I got to discussing it.

Coach Donohue had been stationed at Fort Knox in Kentucky and told me about the South. A New York boy, he had had his own troubles adjusting to the way life ran down there. He hated what they did to blacks, and he didn't see it changing any. He had known enough crackers in his unit and in town, he told me, to convince him that their ideology wouldn't die until they did. He saw it taking generations, the racial trickle-down effect, until finally through advanced assimilation racism might be eliminated. He was sympathetic, knew that the time had come for a change, but he told me it was going to be a big job.

Tell me about it. I'd been introduced to the dark side of southern hospitality only a few months earlier.

The daughter of one of my mother's friends had been going out with some guy who didn't exactly meet with the family's approval. Because the girl, Alice Silva, refused to stop seeing him, her parents sent her to school down in Goldsboro, North Carolina, about fifty miles outside of Raleigh. Out of state, out of mind. It put a damper on the relationship, but it didn't help things much between mother and daughter. The school in Goldsboro held graduation in April, and since my parents couldn't get away, I was sent down there on my Easter vacation.

This was Easter, 1962. They were having all these Freedom Rides and sit-ins, people were getting shot and mauled with fire hoses, police dogs and cattle prods, and they put me on a bus down to Goldsboro, N.C. And of course, good boy that I was, I didn't say anything. "You'll have a nice time," my mother told me, "there'll be parties. . . ."

I boarded the Greyhound, and as soon as we got past Washington, D.C., I started to see these signs, Johnson's White Grocery Store, Corley's White Luncheonette. I had to see all this shit. I was crammed into one of these tiny seats, my legs were all over the aisle, and I was going crazy.

When I arrived in Goldsboro—this was the first time I'd ever been alone outside of New York or Philadelphia—I didn't know what to do, how to handle myself. I had to ask people, "Are you allowed to walk on the same side of the street as white people?" The facts of black life in the South were explained to me, and I got to see Goldsboro. Had to be down there for six days. That's what I did on my Easter vacation, compliments of my parents.

I received another little bonus from that excursion. I was standing there, out of my element in North Carolina, when my head began feeling like it was about to explode. The lights were all of a sudden too bright; there was a pounding like a wrecking crew on a submarine at four hundred fathoms, and there was nowhere to escape the pain. It was my first migraine. I found a dark room and sat down for a half hour until the ringing went away, but I've had that kind of piercing migraine disorder, sometimes for weeks on end, almost every spring from that time on.

So I knew a little of what Mr. Donohue was talking about. He was certain that racism wouldn't die until the racists did, and so was I. What I didn't tell him was that I hoped it would be soon and that if I could help them along, I would be delighted. I wasn't quite ready to pick up the gun, but I was intimate with the impulse.

3

Power was a normal all-boys Catholic high school; the corridors bustled; the classrooms were thick with terror and decorum, and there was this tension that you couldn't quite place until you'd gotten far enough away. Brother McLaughlin, Power's Dean of Discipline, haunted the hallways, busting kids for lateness or loitering. His whole deal was the inevitability of your apprehension. If you lost your books, or left your locker open, if your hair was too long, your pants too short or too tight, he'd hand you a slip, like a summons, and keep you for an hour after school. Cutting class was unthinkable, but if you didn't hurry in the halls you stood a good chance of being late, and Brother McLaughlin was always there to put the arm on you. He nailed me a couple of times. You had to be in the building by ten to nine each morning, and I'd get there at five to nine, or nine, and he'd catch me, write me a slip and say, "Come see me this afternoon." The jive turkey. Some dudes who he caught would just not go, hoping that he might forget. And sometimes he would. But then he'd see you, and remember, and then you got five days, a whole week when you never saw the sun shine.

Colmenares almost got put away for life. Any time I went to detention he was there, sleeping or reading in the back. If you got caught sleeping, you had to stay another hour. If you got caught reading, you got five whole days. Parochial school justice. Colmenares would sit in the back and throw chalk at people; he'd imitate Brother McLaughlin or call people out and try and make them laugh. Kids would want to kick his ass in detention, but if you got caught so much as turning around, you'd get five days. So Colmenares was up to his tricks one afternoon—"Walter!" he'd hiss. "Go clean the erasers!"—when the dean walked in right in the middle of it. "Mr. Colmenares," the dean said evenly, like St. Peter checking the guest list, "that will be one month."

The quiet room hushed even more. "Yes, Brother," said Colmenares.

"And you will stay until the end," the dean added. That meant he had to do two sessions every day all month long.

I believe Colmenares dropped out of Power because he had two high school careers for all the time he owed.

One time Brother McLaughlin stopped me in the hall and looked at the pin I was wearing on my lapel. "What's this?" he wondered. It showed a black hand in a powerful fist holding a torch with the words "Freedom Now" written boldly across it. "It's from SNCC," I told him. "Snick?" he said. "Student Non-violent Coordinating Committee. It means that my people want freedom ... now." "Oh," he chuckled uneasily and started to move away; "I thought it was your Honor Roll button." Better, I wanted to say, but I didn't have the nerve.

There was only one black teacher at Power: Brother

Watson. (If there were any more, they were passing for white.) Brother Watson was useless. I had him for French, and he was supposed to be a drummer, which sounded pretty hip, but I showed up in class one day with an Art Blakey record, and he'd never heard of Art Blakey. Hopeless. Whatever kind of drumming he was into I didn't want to hear. A white religion teacher, Brother D'Adamo, told me in class one afternoon that "black people want too much too soon." His concept of race relations was that blacks had to "work for their equality." I knew my way around Harlem by that time, had seen enough hard-working people come up against stone-wall prejudice and worse not to take Brother D'Adamo's unbending work-ethic philosophy at face value, particularly from his face, and I told him so. We had a definite difference of opinion, but he could never convince me, and I was too young for him to take seriously. The power balance was all wrong; here I was forced to be a Spokesman for My People while at the same time crammed into a desk, taking down everything he said and giving it back to him the way he wanted to hear it if I was going to get a good grade in his class. I could earn my equality by accepting his definitions. In that class I decided to be separate, not equal.

Power seemed to attract more than its share of questionable characters. One of my teachers would periodically disappear during class and then come back and forget everything he'd just told us. This was a mystery, and a source of much malicious gossip, until one of my classmates came out of the boys' bathroom and saw the man slip around some lockers, take a nip from a silver flask, and check the corridor for shadows before returning to his duties. The teacher in charge of the school yearbook left under clouded circumstances, and despite the fact that the next year's yearbook went all to crap, he was never invited to return. One of the other teachers would have made a good hoodlum. He was big, maybe six feet three inches, and spoke the kind of English you'd expect from a longshoreman, and he'd beat the hell out of you if you fooled around in his class. High school kids will always wise off, and without the moderating influence of girls to shine or be shy for, the guys at Power pushed it to the limit. So to stem the tide, this Brother played by his own rules. If a student mouthed off once too often, the Brother would swoop down behind him and pound him with his sizeable fist. He'd hit him a shot halfway down the back, and it would reverberate in the boy's chest like personal thunder. Sounded like he was hitting a drum.

Mr. Coleman was another odd freak. Break up his class and he'd get you in a one-handed pincer hold by that muscle connecting your shoulder and neck, right above the collarbone. You couldn't pull away because of his authority, and his grip. He'd grab that muscle and sure seemed to get off on watching you squirm. No lasting damage, and no love lost, but Mr. Coleman established who was boss.

But the best of the lot was Mr. Hugh P. McGlade, moderator of the St. Thomas More Political Science Club. The guys had a field day with him because he was so out of it. He'd come into class and say, "Do you have any questions you would like to ask me, gentlemen? I will be glad to answer them. Just write them on a card." The dudes in my class would write, "Are you a faggot?" He'd read it out loud and say, "Gentlemen, what is this word, 'faggot'? What does it mean?" Meanwhile we were all dying and rolling all over the floor.

Collecting money for the Catholic charities was a yearly preoccupation at Power, and each teacher found his own way of encouraging his students to contribute to the missions. Mr. McGlade's was thoroughly unique: He would let you throw money at him. On Collection Day, McGlade would sit at his desk, cover his head, and the guys would fire on him. This was back when there was still silver in the dimes and quarters, they had good heft. You could whip it sitting down or taking a running start and wing half-dollars at him from across the room. All the good Catholic boys' fear and resentment loaded into their right arms. It was the righteous combination of Christian charity and a good scourge. And the Church kept the coin.

But Power didn't corrupt everything. I had the occasional good teacher and made several friends. I've always been a reasonably articulate guy, answered what I had to in class with the most considered language I could muster, and I must have impressed the teacher in charge of the debate team, Brother Harrington, because he invited me to sit in and practice with the squad. I liked the idea, domination with the mind, so about once a week, between the end of class and the beginning of basketball practice, I would work out with the debaters. We'd be assigned pro or con, read the facts for about five minutes and go at it. I wasn't a flamboyant stylist, made no grand gestures, controlled my teen irony. Brother Harrington liked my restraint. I was simply looking to outtalk everybody, leave them speechless. I just stood there, tried to move as little as possible, and spoke from the height of reason.

Some of the guys at school were cool. Neil Chusid's folks had been Jewish, but for some reason they had converted to Catholicism and sent him to Power. Neil hipped me to Bob Dylan, and I returned the favor by turning him on to Thelonius Monk. My man Jose Marmelejo came from the Dominican Republic and played on Power's basketball team. He was six feet two and a great leaper, got all kinds of tip-ins. Also played some hot Latin Eddie Palmieri licks on the piano. He was a nice guy, and we used to hang out a bit, but every three months they used to bomb his neighborhood in the Dominican Republic, and he'd have to go back down there. Ignasio Gonzales was from Havana. There was this Cuban fighter named Sugar Ramos, and Ignasio and I used to call each other *Azucar* and laugh. Ignasio had to carry an alien's card with him at all times. He showed it to me, and I was fascinated by it but couldn't figure why. Every once in a while I'd say, "Let me see that thing again," and turn it over in my hand. He couldn't have been or felt more alien than I did, and I wasn't carrying any I.D.

Joseph Traum used to call me "Schwartz." "Hey, Schwartz, what time is it? What do you say, Schwartz?" He was born in Germany, spoke German, and I thought he was just being friendly, giving me a German name, making me a brother. He always grinned when he said it, as if my induction into the Teutonic family fold was giving him some untold pleasure. This had been going on for two years when I finally learned that *schwartze* in German means black and that for two years he'd been calling me a nigger to my face and having a good time doing it. On the day that I pieced this little scam together, Traum came sauntering down the hallway like always, popped me five (it was the new greeting and all the rage), and gave me his usual morning greeting: "How you doin', Schwartz?" I cupped my hand to return the favor, leaned over to him and said gravely . . .

"What do you want, Weiss?"

Traum took one more step, then froze. Got him in the classic double take. He looked up at me, no words coming out, waiting for the one-armed bandit behind his eyes to jackpot him out of this one. I gave him the serious sidelong glance, then broke up and laughed very loudly. Maybe he thought I was going to hit him. But we were friends, and we remained friends. You had to admire the guy for pulling off such a daring winner over such a long stretch of time.

My best friends during high school were Norbert and Johnny. We used to call John "John Bull," because he was so strong. A good football player, he broke his foot scrimmaging in eighth grade down by the Harlem River Drive. Lost an athletic scholarship because of that, but he was a good sax player and went to Power on a band scholarship. He was a year ahead of me in school, but we were always together, like brothers.

Norbert was the only guy I could talk to about sensitive issues; I knew he wouldn't make fun of me, and we never lied to each other. He was Filipino and I was black, and we were both just starting to get seriously interested in our origins. We didn't just hang around the street corners; we started to explore the city, and one afternoon we visited the Metropolitan Museum of Art down on Fifth Avenue. We were both fascinated by ancient cultures, so we headed straight for the Egyptian Room, walked in, and found a large white stone sarcophagus with sides about six feet high. Norbert couldn't see inside, but I could. I peered in. It wasn't empty! I looked around—no guards watching—and stretched one arm all the way to the coffin's bottom.

"What'd you find?!" Norbert whispered.

I opened my palm and showed him a stone the size of a walnut.

"Wow, that must be two thousand years old!"

I slipped it into my pocket as if it were glowing. We toured the entire museum and didn't pull the treasure out until we were on the subway headed safely uptown.

Norbert and I passed the stone back and forth, holding it gingerly. This was serious antiquity; I had never touched something that old.

"Yeah, but . . ." I turned to him, "what if there's a curse on it?"

"You mean, like a mummy's curse?" Norbert said shakily.

"Yeah, the Curse of the Mummy's Tomb!" I pushed the stone into his palm. He pushed it back at me. It flew between us. By the time we got uptown we had ourselves totally psyched.

"You took it out!" he yelled at me.

"Yeah, but you're holding it!" It came back quickly.

"Let's throw it away."

"We *can't* throw it away! I saw in the movies that you've got to pass the curse on, you've got to *give* it away. Otherwise it's got you in its power!"

54

Norbert had a brother, Dave, who was three years younger than he was. "Let's give it to him!" Norbert chimed. Which we did. Dave lived to tell.

The basketball team went undefeated through the entire '62-'63 season. By midwinter I had all the confidence I could handle on the court. Some wins were routine, some hard-fought, and as our reputation developed, other teams came gunning for us. Coach Donohue was emphatic about our not hog-dogging, and as the center of attention, I had to be very careful when to allow my emotion to show in my play. It would have been simple to stuff over everybody, growl at and intimidate our opponents. But, because I was so clearly better than most of the people I was playing against, it seemed unpleasant to shove it in their faces. I had absorbed too much abuse from aggressive strangers to feel comfortable embarrassing anyone else.

But, boy, embarrass me and you were in a world of trouble. There was a lot of fancy maneuvering in those games, and if anyone went out of his way to show me up, then he was going to get his shots thrown off the court or take three straight dunks through his face. I'd dribble the length of the floor and jam it. All Coach Donohue had to do to motivate me was to get me to remember some time I'd been made to look bad in the past. Nasty tongue that he had, he could pick the exact moment we needed some fire and light one under me with a few choice recollections from freshman year. He could make me go nuts. I never quite realized what he was doing; all I knew was that I didn't want to look bad in front of Coach Donohue.

I was an innocent, the kind of idealistic teenager who wants to live in a world where things run the way they should. I was offended by bad calls, or by no calls at all, which is how the officials decided to even things out. I had developed into not only a giant—there were huge guys playing basketball even then, Swede Holbrook types—but an agile and fluid ballplayer. I knew it, they knew it.

But they must have felt I had an **unfair advantage** because they let me get beat to shit. But I was cool; I didn't complain. I tried to transcend them, to play over their heads.

We clinched the CHSAA Manhattan division by beating defending champions LaSalle at home and met them again in the city championship semifinals. Val Reid gave me the official elbow in the mouth, cut me up until I was tasting my own blood, but we went on and whipped them and then won it all. I got very excited when we finally took the title, but the exhilaration faded within a day. The best awards are the ones you don't expect, and we had peaked too soon. It was good to be city champs, but the feeling after the final was more relief than triumph.

Coach Donohue let me make the rounds when I was chosen to each of the newspapers' All-City teams, and each writer asked the same obvious questions and gawked and made the same cute jokes, the journalistic equivalent of "How's the weather up there?" Was this all there was?

Mr. Donohue was also Power's baseball coach and encouraged me to come out for the team. I had been a pretty good Little League outfielder and pitcher, but by high school I just wasn't interested. My studies had fallen off during basketball season because of the time demands and the pressure. While I would have loved to have played baseball just for fun, winning was running in my blood like a drug, and I didn't want to need that fix all springtime too.

When school finally let out I hit the streets with authority. I had an eight-week Friendship Farm sentence to look forward to, so I made every New York day an event. I went everywhere looking for a game—the Bronx, Long Island, down to Greenwich Village—and hung out with the guys in the street. We were a fine crew. Each of us had his own specialty. Mine was basketball and ogling women. Harold's was robbery. He was the greatest sneak thief in the world. No mere second-story man or liquor-store gunslinger, Harold had developed the gas station burglary to a fine art. Never one for a confrontation when a good move would do, he would case the place, wait until everyone working the lifts and pumps was occupied, go in, ring up the cash register without making any sound, take out all the money and leave. Did that a number of times. He never taught me the cash register trick, and I wasn't about to go on a field trip with him, but he was never hurting for disposable income. Harold's dead now.

Julio was another of my ballplaying compatriots. Julio was very intelligent, very aware, and Julio wanted to be a gangster. That was his ambition, to join the mob. He and I used to go down and play at this fenced-in asphalt court at the corner of West Third Street and Sixth Avenue in the Village. There'd be traffic piling by, and the subway grumbling underneath us, and always a good crowd and a ready argument. Seemed like half the time you'd be playing ball and half the time you'd be running your mouth. You called your own game, and the honor system was severely put to the test. Winner stays on, so all the jawing was essentially about not wasting a day on the sidelines, but you'd hear the most outrageous lies, threats, bellying up and bravado, often for the sake of the casual fans leaning three-deep on the chain link fence like inmates watching freedom. The games were mostly black, with the occasional local Italian sharpshooter making an appearance but rarely getting the ball, and it must have been a curiosity to some, a trauma or treat to others, having this Harlem cultural exchange down on their playground.

The ladies in the Village were terrific. Postbeatnik, prehippie young women, they dressed with a breezy informality and smiled to their admirers or themselves when someone on the sidelines would loudly extol their virtues. "Lord, mama!" and all along both sides of the fence heads would turn as a dancer in tight jeans and a leotard, or two short-skirt high school foxes, would strut on by. If one of these wonders ever stopped to watch, the game took a twenty percent jump in intensity. I never knew what to say. My time had not yet come.

While I was doing all this looking, Julio was searching out other opportunities. "Hey, man," he whispered after a run-and-gun affair one Saturday afternoon, "there's the Good Humor man." The ice cream vendors stood with their carts on all the Village's strategic tourist corners. Old men, most of whom had probably walked their beats for my entire lifetime, they were a New York springtime staple. "Yeah, so?" "He must have three, four hundred dollars on him," Julio calculated excitedly. At a dime for a Chocolate Malt that didn't seem likely, but I didn't stop Julio's roll. "Tell you what," he said, "we're gonna follow him to where he puts his thing up, old guy like that, and then we're gonna rob him!" He was ready. I said, "Julio, you're gonna do that by your*self*," went and got on the A train, and went home. Julio kept that up until he finally got busted. He went to jail that summer, and I didn't see him for ten years.

But Julio was Robin Hood compared to some of the hard guys. One kid got murdered for twenty-five cents delivering Christmas trees on Christmas Day. That made the front page of the *Daily News*.

I saw a gunfight one night on 140th Street. I was walking up St. Nicholas Avenue to Sugar Hill, and I heard an unmistakable flat "pop." There was no ring to it, no echoing ricochet off any canyon wall like in a Hopalong Cassidy movie. This shit wasn't intended to bounce off anything, it was supposed to put you down. I looked around, and there's this sedan weaving down the one-way street, with a cop car maybe twenty yards back—and there are these flashes jumping out of both of them! I was three-quarters of a long block away, but I could hear that flat report. *Pop pop pop pop.* Didn't sound like *Dragnet*. The front car slowed down; the cop car stopped. I ducked behind a lamppost and stood there watching. Nothing and nobody moved. It was like that for three minutes. I was standing in the only light on the block, as if this lamppost was going to protect me. What am I, a fool? I said, Hey, I'm getting the fuck out of here. Never found out what happened. Glad not to know.

Johnny Graham got jumped on Dyckman Street by a bunch of Irish guys. He and some friends had just come from the store, and when these guys started to get physical Johnny tried to defend himself by hitting someone in the head with a bottle of orange soda. He missed, hit the wall, and the glass busted in his hand, but the jagged handle was serious and everybody beat it back to the projects.

One of the guys who'd been hanging with Johnny lived in the Bronx. He was going with one of the project girls and was new to the neighborhood, didn't know where to run. Later that night I was over at my friend Joe Grice's house when I got the details. The Irish boys had circled the stranger and had been getting ready to kick his ass when he'd pulled a knife, cut a few guys and run. He made it home, back to the Bronx. The cops weren't collaring the Irish; they were out there looking for some phantom black killer. Of course, we didn't know anything about it.

This one guy, Butch, was pretty tough. He wasn't a bully or anything, just a street-wise, slick type of dude. Butch was semiliterate, called everybody "Gentlemens." He'd have on some Italian-style shoes, clean gabardine pants, a T-shirt with suspenders, and a snap-brimmed fedora or a pork-pie hat. Sometimes he'd dispense with the suspenders and have on the knit shirt. Butch was famous in our neighborhood. He'd been coming home from work one day and some white boys had leaned out of Barry's Bar up there a couple of doors off Dyckman Street and called him a whole bunch of "niggers" and the like. Butch had hustled into the projects walking kind of fast and headed straight for Joe the Boxer—that's all the name we had for him. Butch got Joe and Butch's brother Sherman, and they went back to the bar. These guys were seventeen, eighteen, nineteen—nobody older than twenty—and they went in and kicked ass. Turned Barry's Bar out! That's the way you got the good reputation.

I never ran with those guys, the toughest guys I knew were only on the fringes, nothing big-time, but my mother and my coach again decided for me that what I really needed was two months in the country. Friendship Farm had expanded up to twenty-five kids, but it was still family and still not Harlem. The court had been black-topped, but the backboards were like the side of a barn, battered and beaten. They had literally been hammered. You learned to adapt. After seeing that a ball could hit the boards and stay there as if it were sandbagged, I found that if I just put the ball high enough over the rim, it would drop down and in by itself. Made for a light shooting touch, if nothing else. I played ball and swam and wished I were back in the real world.

The real world closed in on me real fast when I returned for eleventh grade. On September 15, 1963, while I was attending mass with my mother, the Sixteenth Street Baptist Church in Birmingham, Alabama, was bombed by white folks. Four little black girls were killed. As I watched the ineffectual moral outrage of the black southern preachers, the cold coverage of the white media, and the posturings of the John F. Kennedy White House, my whole view of the world fell into place. My faith was exploded like church rubble, my anger was shrapnel. I would gladly have killed whoever killed those girls by myself. Those red-necked cracker bastards should all die, but I knew in my gut that they would get away with it, that nobody cared about black people except black people, that we needed vigilance and protection. We were alone in a world more hostile than I had been led to believe. Forget about equality by assimilation, harmony through brotherhood, freedom through justice. If they had their way, we'd all be dead. Johnny Harrison, my abandonment at St. Jude's, the trip to North Carolina—these weren't isolated incidents; this was the way the world worked, and I had better get used to it. We had no allies. The government couldn't care less; behind the pious pronouncements from Washington and the local law-enforcement communiqués, it was obvious that the identity of the killers was common knowledge, and no white folks were talking. Until thirty years before that, they'd been lynching black people in Alabama; did anyone really expect the state troopers to set the dogs on a few rambunctious good ol' boys who just blew a couple of blacks up? Who's to say they weren't involved already? The liberals had money but no power, and it wasn't their ass on the line, so how far could you trust them. God certainly wasn't stepping in; they'd just bombed His house!

All spring, 1964, I kept to myself and hung out in Harlem. At least there I never felt people were falsefacing me. I looked around school, and these were all white people pulling this weirdness. At least if blacks were going to juice it up they'd be doing it in style, with proclamations about the goodness of the grape, not hiding in some stall sucking on a monogrammed flask like a candy-assed hummer. These gray motherfuckers were supposed to teach me how to live? Who was I supposed to grow up to be? Brother Watson?

I walked around Harlem; the place was a mess. Who owned these tenements, these roach-infested, coldwater rat traps? White people. Who owned the stores? I'd been downtown; I could compare prices. Who was gouging the neighborhood on groceries, clothing, rent? White people. Who controlled the jobs that these guys playing craps on the stoop couldn't get? And who was making money selling them wine? Landlords, store owners, pawnbrokers—white people.

I walked into a pawnshop one afternoon looking for a saxophone. I'd heard Coltrane and Vino and thought maybe I could fall somewhere in between. The small store was cluttered with other people's valuables—watches, radios, jewelry. Musical instruments hung from the ceiling like cocoons. I was browsing intently when I picked

61

up the conversation at the counter. A black man, not well dressed but by no means a bum, was trying to pawn something, I couldn't see what. He needed money, but the white proprietor in the teller's cage wasn't going to give him his price.

"Hey, man," the guy at the window said, "this is valuable stuff!"

"I'm sorry, sir," said the proprietor, "this is the best I can do."

"Aw, man, I know you can do better. I been in here, I know what this is about."

"I'm sorry, sir, that is all I can do."

"Aw, man." And then he started to beg. He had to have this money. First a tear, and then, as if he'd startled himself, he moaned the way no person should moan in front of a stranger. He begged beyond the piece he was pawning, begged the man to help him, to acknowledge his humiliation and *give me this money! Please!*

The man in the cage was embarrassed but unbending. "I'm sorry," he said. His customer tried to pull himself together, fumbled pocketing the unsold valuable, and returned to the street. I was staring into dark corners, trying not to be there. The man spoke to me slowly. "May I help you?"

I couldn't talk, couldn't focus. If I looked him in the eye, I might have hit him. There was exhaustion in his voice, but I hated this man.

"You got saxophones?" I finally managed. They hung all around me.

"Yes, sir." He had started to come around the counter when I snapped, "Forget it," and walked out.

St. Vincent's School on the East Side held weekly dances, a downtown party, so to speak. Eric Brown and I got respectfully dressed and headed on down to see the ladies. Power was good that way. Though it was all boys and you were denied the daily revelations coeducation might bring, it did introduce you, every once in a while, to a species of young woman you didn't run across much uptown. So Eric and I were duded up and ready.

I was always getting looked at when I entered any room. I'd learned to live with that by then, but when we arrived, there was an air of anticipation that I hadn't expected. A song had started when Eric approached one white girl. He could dance, and she looked like she could be moved in that direction, but when he asked her she said no. Gave no reason, just "No." Eric turned around and headed for me and then the door.

We thought about throwing bricks through the school's windows. Hey, we didn't crash this party, girl, we were invited! Eric hadn't asked her, but we knew. She wasn't tired; her dance card wasn't filled. It was very clear what the matter with her was.

Eric wanted to go get drunk and crazy, but we just prowled the streets, loud and lonely. Probably scared a few passersby. We found the Plaza Hotel, which was all lit up as usual and looked like a European equivalent of the plantation Big House. As we stomped by, Zsa Zsa Gabor was standing outside holding court to a blister of photographers and her entourage. "Hey," we called at her from across the way, "fuck you, Zsa Zsa!" and encouraged her to do likewise to the entire white race.

But I still had white friends—Traum, Chusid, Kenney—and even made some more. I'd meet white guys playing ball, mostly Italians, who I'd like. I knew I liked white people individually—I never lost sight of that—but the people in power, and the power they wielded over black people's lives, were definitely no good. Because Harlem had been a Jewish neighborhood before it became a black one, Jews owned much of Harlem's property, and it was Jewish businessmen who were gouging black customers, so there were these faceless people called Jews who were easy to hate. But there were plenty of Jewish guys I met who, contrary to what I might have heard in parochial school, were real nice.

Power was overflowing with white kids and, while they were mostly just acceptable, they weren't bastards. The teachers weren't venal, only unenlightened. There was some discussion of current events, but it was academic and carefully distant. While I was connecting directly with Birmingham and Bull Connor and billy clubs, no one else seemed to be taking anything personally, as if nothing were really in one's own control. Power was an institution run on misplaced faith—in God, the government, the administration, the faculty—and, though I couldn't articulate it at the time, the school encouraged a terrible sense of futility. As a student, if you were looking for inspiration, advice, or action, you had to trust in a tight Chain of Command with you at the bottom. Your life was taken out of your hands. You were the last one approached, and you were never consulted, you were told.

They weren't telling me what I wanted to hear. At Power it was more important to march in the Columbus Day parade than to demonstrate for equal rights. At first I spoke up in class, created opportunities to discuss what was important to me. But nobody really wanted to get into it, and soon I simply kept my ideas to myself and started the long walk through high school.

Junior year is dead center, all the way in and halfway out, and the scramble for college was on. My grades were good and my education was important to me, so I started talking to Coach Donohue about where I might go from here. Letters from colleges and universities had begun arriving in ninth grade and by junior year there was a deluge, all correspondence handled by Mr. Donohue. He received everything that came for me at school, and all mail on academic letterhead that showed up at my house was forwarded to him unopened. High school was getting old, and I was always after the coach about my future.

"Lew, don't worry," he'd tell me, "you can go to any school you want to."

"Did Harvard write me a letter?" I'd ask. I never

saw any of the mail; it was like getting love letters and not being able to read them.

"Don't bother about who's written the letters," Mr. Donohue would say. "Any school you want to go to, you can go to."

For a while I was excited and proud—I can go to college anywhere!—but soon even that faded. I still had two years of high school to sit through.

The basketball team continued undefeated. Thirty straight, thirty-five, forty. The team was solid, good shooting, tight defense. I enjoyed rebounding even more than scoring, demonstrating with every snatch, with every rejection, that I was not one of these Negroes who was going to be pushed around. We went out to win each game, and we had some scares. Mr. Donohue was teaching us and cajoling us, but mostly he kept on our backs, and practices were, if anything, more intense because he had to maintain our motivation. He didn't want us taking anything for granted.

But one winter afternoon we were ragged. We were at home against St. Helena's, a Catholic high school from the Bronx, and though we were definitely out of their league and should have been whipping them by twenty, minimum, we were sluggish and only up by six at the half. I was playing badly, one of those lousy games when for no good reason nothing goes right and there doesn't seem to be much you can do about it. I may have been keyed up for our next game, against DeMatha, one of the best high school teams in the country, two days ahead down in Maryland. They were excellent, and we'd have to be tough to beat them. So maybe St. Helena's was an annoyance, and I was trying to ignore them as one might walk through a cloud of flies.

We trooped out the east end of the gym, down the drafty stairwell to the next landing. There was a big crowd, as usual, and you could hear the subdued buzzing as students stretched and wondered at the boring game. I ducked my head to get inside the locker room and again as the team was ushered into Mr. Donohue's office. Outside it was getting dark, and our heat started to fog over the grilled windows as the team stood around, some of us sitting on the beat-up wooden chairs and filing cabinets in the close little room. I sat, weary and distracted, as the coach closed the door with his left hand and the latch snapped.

Mr. Donohue was in a rage, storming from wall to wall. We're terrible, we don't deserve to win this or any other game, we're asleep, we're a disgrace. And then he pointed at me.

"And you! You go out there and you don't hustle. You don't move. You don't do any of the things you're supposed to do. You're acting just like a nigger!"

No! I looked up at him, my eyes burning. The word jumped at me like lasers. He couldn't have. I knew this man; he didn't say that. Donohue kept berating me, then moved on to the rest of the squad.

I don't remember the rest of the game. We won, and I'm told I played well. When I got back to the locker room, before I could strip off my uniform and be scorched or soothed by a shower, Donohue called me into his office alone.

"See," he said happily, "it worked! My strategy worked. I knew that if I used that word, it'd shock you into a good second half. And it did." He kept talking, about DeMatha and determination and playing up to my potential, but I just sat there watching my sweat drip onto the dust balls. I knew what he'd been trying to get at. He meant I'd been playing lazy and slow, like something and someone I didn't want to be. But was that what he thought of blacks? Was I shiftless, too, couldn't be trusted with the game? Didn't I smile enough fo' de fans? Should I be twirling the basketball like an ol' watermelon? Mr. Donohue! I sat in his office wondering, Am I here all alone?

We had to leave for Maryland right after the game, but when I hurried home to pack I told my parents. My father was upset; my mother was livid. I wanted to

leave Power that day. Talked about transferring to the
Hill School over the weekend, or tossing it all in and
going to George Washington High School in the neighborhood and just partying until college. But I couldn't
transfer without my parents' permission and without losing a year of eligibility, and though my mother was
outraged, she didn't want me being left back a year, or
spending two more semesters playing basketball when I
could be on my way to college. I was trapped. No apology
was acceptable, no moment at Power tolerable, yet I was
faced with another year and a half before I could get out.

Word traveled fast. In the Power hallways everyone
was talking about what Mr. Donohue called Lew. It was
1964, and black people weren't above using the term,
but usually as a fraternal symbol and never in front
of white folks. It had never intruded here where I
spent so many hours, so many days. How could I live with
it every day? Usually we'd joke about the names the coach
called us. Not this time. I never said anything more about
it to the coach. What could I say?

We went down and beat DeMatha and everybody
else they threw at us. We won the city championship for
the second straight year and were voted the number one
Catholic high school team in the country. I made All-City
and All-American again. Only a year to go.

No way I was spending two months up on Friendship Farm. I didn't want to see that man at all. It was
going to be a vital summer in New York, you could tell.
The streets were steaming, people were steaming in them,
and I was going to be on the scene. I applied to
HARYOUACT (the Harlem Youth Action Project) and
got a job in their journalism workshop as a reporter on the
editorial board. I'd be working in Harlem (making thirty-
five dollars a week, which was serious money at the time),
playing in Harlem, getting comfortable in an environment I respected and wanted to learn more about.

When Mr. Donohue found out I wasn't showing
up for his camp, he was shocked. He had reorganized the

summer, he told me. There would be three one-week sessions now; he had advertised it as a basketball camp and for the first time he had paying campers, not just the Power family. The place was refurbished. And besides, he said, "You're a draw to new campers."

I wanted to tell him to go to hell. But my mother still wanted me off the streets and made it very clear she was prepared to give me a hard time in order to get her way. And, in spite of my anger, I somehow felt I owed Mr. Donohue one last favor, to clean the slate. He had truly cared about me, though I doubted he still did (How could he have? I asked myself), and I wanted to be out of his or anyone's debt. Eight weeks was impossible, but I agreed to a three-week appearance, and everyone went away satisfied. I didn't have to be up there until August, so I had a hot summer to look forward to.

4

Harlem! It was 1964, I had just turned seventeen, and my color was being made clearer to me with each nightfall. I was twice an All-American, going to be a senior, bigger than anyone I knew. And I was looking to grow into my culture, I only had to find it.

I'd never had the time or the confidence to truly explore Harlem. I'd visited the community as a ballplayer, almost like an out-of-towner come in for the games, but we'd had our own beaten paths—from the courts to Roy's to the subway—and the group I'd played with had never been real interested in giving me the Harlem Historical Guided Tour. I had to tramp those streets by myself.

The Harlem Youth Action Project was a city-funded attempt to keep some of the smarter kids off the street. Our office was a jumble of desks and machines in a forty by forty-foot basement of the 135th Street YMCA Annex. You walked through the lobby and down the stairs and came upon what must have been a Ping-Pong room or some sort of recreation hall. Flourescent lights, institutional linoleum floors, lots of clatter as the ancient black manual typewriters were being pounded, and a cold-press typesetting machine that must have been donated, certainly not bought. It would be warm and summery bright on the street, but in our news grotto there was always a subterranean crispness that kept you on your toes. There being no windows, we were encouraged to bring our own light with us, and we did.

The journalism workshop's weekly paper covered the news and advances of HARYOU's other summer workshops: dance, drama, music, community action. We would get to work at ten o'clock, decide on our assignments, and then scatter through the streets for research. I had a lot to learn, and a revelation warehouse was right down the block, the Schomburg Center for Research in Black Culture, which stood like a beacon down on Lenox Avenue. It was part of the public library system but all black, the only place of its kind in New York City. I first walked in there to find information for an article concerning Striver's Row, which I had seen once or twice—elegant, light straw-colored brick row houses on 138th and 139th Streets between Seventh and Eighth Avenues—but knew next to nothing about. At the Schomburg I learned that the entire area was architecturally noteworthy and had been central when Harlem first became a refuge for blacks. In the early 1900s W. T. Handy had lived there, and Eubie Blake, and when the rest of Harlem deteriorated into a ghetto, the people in these houses resisted the fall and maintained the beauty of their blocks against the hard times. In turn-of-the-century innocence these people were known as "strivers" and the houses came to be called Striver's Row. Later the buildings were designated as historical landmarks and protected against Harlem's further fall.

I hadn't known any of this. They were just nice-looking buildings stuck in the middle of the ghetto, and

I'd thought very little about them the few times I'd passed by. Now they fueled my pride. The Schomburg Collection was full of exactly the information I wanted and needed but never knew where to find. I became a fixture at the place, learned how to use the microfilm machine and read up on the Harlem of the twenties and thirties. One of the teachers in the drama workshop, a fellow named Roger, was another Schomburg regular and pointed me toward Marcus Garvey, the black nationalist, and W. E. B. DuBois, the black revolutionary. I was enthralled. I read the poetry of Countee Cullen, Paul Lawrence Dunbar, and Langston Hughes. Novels by Richard Wright. Kelly had hipped me to Ralph Ellison's *Invisible Man*, so I wasn't totally in the dark about black literature, but I found there was so much I didn't know, had never been taught or even told existed. The Harlem Renaissance— what a vital time, and no one had ever mentioned it to me. The Schomburg was an entire building filled with facts each one of which I wanted to put under my skin.

I would step out of the Schomburg and into Harlem, 1964. Black nationalists were hawking newspapers on the avenue; jobs were scarce, and the sidewalk crap games were going strong. Street-corner speakers were declaiming about white devils and low pay and high time we did something about it. Malcolm X was on the soapbox, James Brown on the radio, and a serious sense of action was in the air. In June three civil rights workers disappeared on the backroads of Mississippi, and anyone with half a brain kissed Schwerner, Goodman, and Chaney good-bye.

Our newspaper shilled for our accomplishments, but after a few weeks we got down to issues. It occurred to all of us on the editorial board that we had access to more than just the ears of our friends here; if we wanted to have some effect—and we could!—we had to speak for the community, not just to it. We fanned out. I covered Martin Luther King, Jr.'s press conference when he arrived in New York. In fact, the next time I saw *Jet* magazine there I was, all the way in the top left-hand corner of a news photo, leaning over Dr. King with my trusty tape recorder in my hand, looking for the last word. I was anything but a Power Memorial junior; I was starting to feel like what I thought of as a man.

On July 18, 1964, a Sunday, I was heading home from the beach. It was sticky, and the heat that I had picked up on the sand combined with the subway musk to bake me like a traveling calzone. The evening was planned; me and the guys were gathering for another streetlight prowl, but I had some time to kill and thought I'd check out the action on 125th Street, maybe buy some records or look at some shoes. There was supposed to be a CORE protest rally that afternoon, maybe there was a news angle I could cover on my way home.

I poked my head out of the subway entrance and was faced with a firefight. The sun was glinting low in the sky, and in the bruising half-light before the city's power turned on the streetlamps shots were fired and glass was being broken as hordes of people were smashing windows, rampaging in packs through the six-lane street. There was smoke in the sky, fire around the corner. Footsteps, as men and women ran the avenue, that gritty sound of old leather on worn pavement, were oddly clear, as if a thousand paths were being shown to me. Harlem was rioting.

Two nights before, on the Upper East Side, a white off-duty policeman had shot a black fifteen-year-old high school student dead. The cop said he'd thought the kid was armed, but there was no knife, no gun, nothing but a black boy killed by a white man. Once too often. A day had passed, and the police department had issued excuses, denials, explanations without that gunshot ring of sincerity. Nobody believed the cop would do a moment's time; and if anyone was believing his penitence, it still wasn't good enough. The cop was on the force, and the boy was dead. White people had been murdering blacks for too long. That night the streets belonged to the people.

Scared the shit out of me. Torn between my

newfound journalist's news sense and the unsettling scent of blood, I watched from the subway steps. I had ducked bullets behind a lamppost, but this went beyond a skirmish; this was out of control. I found myself running, grunting—I didn't stop till I was at 137th Street and Broadway. Anger wasn't new to me, nor was power, but I was burning without release. No amount of running would give those people control of that street—I knew that—and *that* made me angry. The fact that I understood, *felt* the impulse to put a brick through Woolworth's front window, didn't make me any less aware that it would do no good. I knew cops shot kids, I knew the cops were white and more often than not the kids weren't. This was one not-very-unusual confrontation when the white guy was stupid enough to get caught, when publicity took over and demanded morality where little could be expected to exist. The killing spotlighted not the uniqueness but the absolute commonness of the crime. The fact that no one was admitting to it caused the riot. It was not the death—that happened all the time, everybody had a friend who'd died—but the lie that was intolerable. It made all of Harlem face the fact that they didn't even have the strength to exact an acceptable apology. What else was there to do but go wild?

The next morning I reported for work, and the entire editorial board hit the streets. Morning showed devastation but no results, just a lot of unfinished business. The police had been called in, ostensibly to keep the peace but actually in an angry attempt to protect property. Black heads had been smashed by the mostly white phalanx of law enforcement officials trying to assert and maintain its authority, but stores still got run through, and the store owners, also mostly white, had to choose between losing their stock or risking their lives. As early as safety could be assured, men were out boarding up storefront windows, surveying damage, planning for the coming night's security. This thing was definitely not over. It was ironic to watch black handymen nailing huge plywood sections over broken doorframes and window shells, directed by the white men whose property was at stake. Under siege, even old friendships between employer and employee were strained in the sunlight.

We interviewed people all over the Harlem streets and got exactly the angry, ghetto-dialect, eyewitness reports that white journalists and newscasters have such a hard time accepting at face value. We were all eyewitnesses and didn't need convincing; the conclusions at street level were inescapable: Starting with the cop's victim, a whole lot of innocent people had been beaten up and shot at by the police because they were black. It was that clear, but the message never got through. Newspapers and TV broadcasts focused on property damage and police injuries, not Harlem's powerlessness. By nightfall nothing had changed, and once again the streets were full.

It got bloodier. If the first night steamed with outrage, the next exploded at Harlem's endless futility. The police were better prepared, given twenty-four hours warning, and injected with an element of pride—these niggers were trying to run their city, to abuse their regulations, to usurp their turf. The fight was for more than simple order now, it became a personal challenge to each individual cop. If they could not by force of will, or force alone, control Harlem, then what authority did they really have? Here was a police force struggling for the survival of its self-esteem against the community it was supposed to protect.

The riots continued for five days. CORE issued statements, and the black nationalists were on the podiums. Kids were running in the streets shouting, "We want Malcolm! We want Malcolm!" but I never saw Malcolm X, who had already made his split with Elijah Poole's Black Muslims. The collective leadership of our newspaper published a special riot issue, including an editorial condemning the police for punishing black people while protecting white interests, and we were proud, but not pleased, that what seemed so obvious and persuasive an argument

74

could be heard nowhere else in the press. I was, once again, righteous, angry, and alone.

A week later I was up at Friendship Farm again for my enforced retreat. In other years I had known only that I was out of my element, but now I knew what I was missing. I plotted and schemed ways to beat it back to the city, but they kept campers coming up there in waves, and being the main attraction, there was no way I was slipping away. No one was coming near me, on the court or off it. As a celebrity with no responsibilities except to play ball, I didn't have to exchange the first word if I didn't want to, and not feeling particularly beholden to Mr. Donohue, I found no need to be anything but simply there. I'd been dead-center inside an urban uprising, and now a combination of former friends and fawning strangers wanted me to come play in the woods. Forget about it. If I didn't want to catch someone's eye, I just looked over them, and I was sullen and suspicious enough to question the motives and reject the advances of any and everybody who approached me. My silence, I found, intimidated people, and in their nervousness they made jokes (no laughter), asked questions (no answer), and came up with observations (no response) that needed a warm, receptive audience to save them from seeming stupid. Maybe they were trying to be friendly, I didn't care. I certainly wasn't about to help them out, so most contact with strangers was forced and uncomfortable. Tough luck. These turkeys wouldn't last a day uptown.

When I got back, the anger was still in the streets, but the nights were less fiery. The riots had released enough tension that municipal promises, when finally made by City Hall, were to be given time to prove unworkable rather than assumed to be jive. It was hard to stare a dead end in the face; most people wanted to step back. It was as if the whole of Harlem was heaving after a fight.

I wasn't ready for Armageddon either. Mostly, I needed the comfort of friends; so I hung out, played ball, and went and watched the Rucker, which was a basketball tournament and black cultural extravaganza all in one.

Nowadays white people know about the Rucker Tournament. It has been discovered and duly noted by the press as a summerlong meeting ground between professional basketball players and the uptown playground types. But back then you either had to be a ballplayer or have a serious tan to be hip to it. Holcombe L. Rucker, a black social worker, had created the tourney in 1946 as a means of getting attention for the Harlem brand of ball and getting the attention of the guys who played it. Just as white college basketball was patterned and regimented like the lives awaiting its players, the black schoolyard game demanded all the flash, guile, and individual reckless brilliance each man would need in the world facing him. This was on-the-job training when no jobs were available. No wonder these games were so intense, so consuming and passionate. For a lot of the men on that court this was as good as it was ever going to get, and it was winner-stay-on. Who says the work ethic didn't live in the ghetto, that Calvinism and social Darwinism were outmoded credos? These were philosophers out there, every one-on-one a debate, each new move a breakthrough concept, every weekend another treatise. I took the seminar every chance I could.

Some of the best were Fred Crawford, who played for the Knicks and Lakers, Miles Aikens, Helicopter (because he could sky and hover). These guys had some names. There was Foothead—"Hey, Foothead, what's happenin'?"—who had a long, narrow skull, a head like a foot, and must have picked the handle up early; it's not the type of name you'd accept late in life. These cats were deep!

I met Wilt Chamberlain at the Rucker Tournament. I'd first heard of him when I was in fourth grade at Holy Providence and he was an All-American at the University of Kansas. Coming from Philadelphia, Wilt was a big hero to the locals. I'd never heard of him, had a hard time remembering his name—"Chamber-what?" I'd always ask—but when they told me he was seven feet tall I thought that was amazing. Our coach sent away and got us some autographed pictures. There was Wilt, in full leap, grabbing the ball with both hands about eight inches over the rim. His face was lit up in a grin, like "This is nothing!" I'd never even considered, let alone seen, anything like it. I studied that photo for months.

My parents ran into him on the beach at Atlantic City. He was holding court, standing and attracting a lot of attention, trying to run into some ladies. My parents had a picture of me, six feet one inch in the sixth grade, my confirmation picture, they told him about me, and he signed it for them. After that—real contact with a giant star—I was always interested in him.

My father took me to the old Madison Square Garden when Wilt was with the Harlem Globetrotters, and I saw him dunk a few, but the play was nothing special. Coach Donohue took me to the Garden when Wilt was playing for Philadelphia, and I watched him grab every rebound, dominate the game, and get beaten by Bill Russell and the Celtics. But I never really felt Wilt's power until I saw him up close.

The first time was when I was fifteen, a freshman in high school, six feet ten inches tall. I'd gone up to the St. Nicholas project on 129th Street between Seventh and Eighth Avenues where the Rucker Tournament was held, to watch. I was too timid, skinny, and nowhere near good enough to get in a game—and besides, CHSAA rules prohibited high school athletes from participating—but I needed to know how this thing was really played. I was up there with my friend Wesley Carpenter who lived all the way uptown, and we spotted Wilt, all of twenty-five years old and a Rucker celebrity, at midcourt taking off his street clothes to reveal his tank-top and uniform shorts underneath. There were only two men for me to be like in the NBA, Wilt and Russell (clearly I couldn't be Oscar Robertson, Elgin Baylor, or Jerry West), and here was one of them, not so very much larger than I was, standing on the same blacktop. I didn't move, couldn't find anything to say that wasn't dumb. But Wesley was an outgoing guy, had a lot of nerve. He said, "Come on, let's just go meet him." I would never have done it alone.

It was summer, and dressed in the ballplayer's universal haberdashery of shorts and a T-shirt (always ready for a game), we sauntered over trying to be as cool as we could be, our sneakers slapping the asphalt like flippers. Wilt saw us coming. He had just completed his third year in the NBA and was no newcomer to Harlem, so he'd developed his own style of dealing with strangers. In this crowd, in this setting, he knew he was being approached by connoisseurs. My anxiousness no doubt showed in my eyes, and he could have pulled the gruff withdrawal that one too many uninvited well-wishers can bring on, but though I was too young to offer him any real challenge, I was one of the few people in the world who didn't have to look up to him.

Wes decided he would make the introductions since it was obviously beyond me. I told Wilt my name, and he said, "Oh yeah, I heard of you. You're that young boy that plays for the Catholic school, supposed to be getting good." Wilt had heard about me! When I thought about it later I got all charged up, but right then I was cool.

"I really admire the way you play the game," I told him, shaking his hand. He looked me up and down like a trainer examining a racehorse. "You've got good legs," he said. I looked down, trying to see what Wilt saw in me. He folded his shirt and pants, then turned back to me. "I wish I had legs like that," he said. I was thrilled—Wilt had taken notice of me!—and when the conversation died I just said, "Nice to meet you," and turned off into the crowd. From then on when I saw him at the Rucker I'd go up and have a few words.

In 1964 Wilt had his own Rucker team. He owned

Small's Paradise, a bar and jazz club right across from the HARYOU office on 135th Street, and he was taking on challengers. Twice an All-American, I still wasn't playing up there, but I saw some amazing basketball. There were legendary players working on their immortality, and at some of the games they seemed like warring gods. Crowds gathered early, lining the court ten-deep, climbing trees for the classic bird's-eye view. The windows overlooking the court were all filled with faces, and there was as much loud and fanciful lying among the aficionados as there was gliding and swooping among the players.

But there was no need for exaggeration; it was hard enough to keep track of what you actually saw. Wilt's team from Small's was playing one afternoon against an all-star lineup from Brooklyn that Zeus himself would have had a tough time cracking, if b-ball had been his game. Connie Hawkins led it, perhaps the greatest ballplayer of all time, totally in his element on the asphalt.

The first time I saw Connie was by accident. A man who lived next door to me, Mr. Brooks, was a paraplegic and played on the Bulova Watchmakers wheelchair basketball team. One day when I was in eighth grade, he took me and my father out to the Brownsville Boys Club to watch him play, and afterwards we hung around to see what the next game on the court was about. It turned out we had happened upon the legends: Connie, Billy Burwell, Roger Brown. These dudes were dunking, going up and doing a 360 and dunking behind their neck! Their warmups was like the parting of the Red Sea.

Connie played a lot of street ball, and I'd go watch him and not only learn new moves, I'd get taught a whole new concept of the game. These were my Sunday revelations. The Hawk would snare a rebound and swoop downcourt as each of his teammates circled in their own improvised patterns. He would fake his man a couple of times, as if testing his engines, and then gun it. Palming the ball, waving it around in one of his huge hands, he'd take off some twenty feet out and glide to the basket like a Black Phantom, then hang, hesitate while two or three defenders each took their separate shots at him, somehow circle underneath the basket, let go the ball, and put it in off the backboard—with English. All he needed to top it off would've been a victory roll. No one had ever done that before. No one had even thought of doing it.

Connie was only about twenty when I was in high school, and already he was an endangered species. He had gotten involved in a betting scandal (from which he was ultimately exonerated), so his pro career was stunted and his ambition damaged, but he was an amazing athlete. His physical gifts were unique, and he had such a natural grasp of basketball's mental demands that he never had to work very hard on his game. He practiced his ball handling and his shot, but if he had worked on his wind and lifted some weights, and had been given the opportunity to play when it was his time to play, he would easily have been recognized as the greatest ever.

On his team this day were Pablo Robertson and Jackie Jackson. Pablo was a magician with the ball; he would dribble through people's legs and back again, slice into impenetrable defenses, and make passes that were not simply true, they were truth. Jackie was six-five, maybe six-six, but he could leap so that his arm reached a foot-and-a-half, two feet above the rim. Their team and Wilt's went at it.

Wilt posted himself low, backed in, used his massive shoulders and trunk to batter whoever was in his way, then turned and shot his trademark fall-away jumper. This tended to work pretty well for Wilt; he was averaging better than forty points per game in his NBA career at the time.

But Jackson was serious. This wasn't just a game; this was all that was real. With his Genghis Khan mustache and a shaved head, he knew that the meaning of life hung on the rim. As Wilt started his fade, Jackson came running on a sharp diagonal from all the way the other side of the court. He leaped, looked like he was climbing stairs, and at the top of his arc, his arm above the white box over the rim at the eleven-foot mark, he mashed the ball right as it reached the backboard. Pinned! Might have been goal-tending in the NBA, but they didn't play that shit here. The crowd stomped a soulful celebration as Jackson pulled the ball down and shot it out to Hawk, who was in midflight to the hoop. It was the most amazing play I've ever seen on the court, and the whole place went crazy.

It was like that all afternoon. Pablo would dribble through everybody. The Hawk would come down and shoot in Wilt's face, right over his hands, or get him up in the air and make the sweet pass around him. They put it to him for three quarters, really made Wilt mad. Finally, of course, Wilt had to get every rebound, which he did. He refused to be beaten, and every time he got the ball inside, which was often since it was his team, it was a dunk. Ten times in a row. Pass to Wilt, dunk. Pass, dunk. Shot, rebound, dunk. Total domination. He'd take people up with him. One time I can remember like a photograph: His head was almost above the rim; there were players draped all around his neck, and it looked for all the world like the end of *Moby Dick* with Gregory Peck lashed to his prey, beckoning his crew to the quest. Wilt Chamberlain as the White Whale.

I got close to Wilt that summer. He lifted weights at the 135th Street Y where our journalism headquarters were, and I made a point of dropping in whenever I heard he was around. Once when I was shooting the ball in the gym, Wilt came by and we started playing some HORSE, matching shots, him trying to hit some hooks and me taking the fadeaways. We didn't go one-on-one, I wasn't even tempted, but at least now I had a speaking relationship with him.

You could tell when Wilt was at Small's because his black limo or his fuchsia Bentley would be sitting like a high-gloss sentinel out on the street, and it gave us a nice boost the first month just knowing he was in the territory.

Small's was heaven for me, a black focal point for two of my favorite pursuits: jazz and basketball. And the pin-point focus was Wilt.

Wilt was the only star I knew, and I stood in awe of him. He lived the life of public success, and I'd hang around Small's and watch how that worked. I had the good reputation—All-American, national champion—and it turned out that Wilt and the guys had been following my career, partly because I was a New Yorker and perhaps because sooner or later I would run up against Wilt, and his underlings were secretly tickled to think some young kid might give their boss a hard time. But when they met me and found out I wasn't one of those cocky loudmouths but a silent observer type, they took a liking to me, and I found myself a Small's regular.

Wilt's close friend Curtis Lawton, and Charlie Polk—who functioned as Wilt's valet, making sure Wilt's way was paved, bringing Wilt's car wherever he wanted it—made a point of making me comfortable. I even had my own drink that the bartender knew to fix for me when-ever I showed up; it was an Orange Sling, which is really orange juice with an egg beaten up in it. I wasn't a big drinker; Vino's example had cured me of any impulses I might have had in that direction, but I was extremely flattered that so prestigious a hang-out as Small's Para-dise would grace me with such recognition. I'd had tastes of the celebrity world, mainly being treated like a big deal in the newsroom of New York's daily newspapers on the All-City go-rounds, but this was the first time anyone whom I respected had treated me with a celebrity's respect.

Wilt must have liked having me around, a man at the top of his game enjoying the presence of this kid who was only starting to be aware what he might grow into. One afternoon as we were standing at the bar he said, "Come on, we've gotta play some hearts." We got in his limo and drove over to Wilt's house.

Wilt lived in Park West Village in the high nineties on Central Park West in an apartment that had to be termed Oriental Modern. It was one of the early slick cooperatives, a two-bedroom place done up in antique gold finish, with a big couch in the living room, paintings on the walls, good stereo, great record collection. Wilt was known for his expensive tastes, and the place showed it. I walked in, and if I had been hard to draw out before, I clammed right up tight—I didn't know what cool was, but I knew very strongly that I didn't want to be uncool.

There were five of us—me, Wilt, his business partner and former Harlem Globetrotter teammate Carlos Green, Tom Hoover who played for the Knicks, and NYU and pro ballplayer Calvin Ramsey—sitting around Wilt's big dining room table. The four of them were hearts junkies, they used to close Small's at four A.M., go back to Wilt's place, and play till dawn. And now I was being included in.

Twenty bucks bought a lot of cold cuts in those days, and since Wilt was the man with the wealth he sprung for the spread. We were sitting around, me and these men, eating sandwiches, telling stories. I was used to hanging out with older guys; it was all I'd ever done, but the level of sophistication here was higher, the circle faster, the names dropped hipper. What did Russell say when Wilt took it over him? What was Elgin always bitching about? When don't you mess with Oscar?

I didn't know how to play hearts; I'd never played it in my life. Some kind of card game combination of bridge and Go Fish, it looked like. They explained it to me and dealt the first hand open so I could get the hang of it. Oh yeah, they told me, house rules. Normally this is a betting game, but we're not playing for money today, you not knowing the ins and outs. If you lose a game you've got to chug a quart of water, drink it straight down.

So the cards were dealt, thrown, taken. I was playing it close to the vest and not doing too badly. Hoover lost a game; he hoisted the quart bottle. Another hand. Cal Ramsey lost and downed his quart. I lost and downed mine. Wilt wasn't losing. I lost and downed another. That's not easy, taking a second quart of water straight, with no breath, on top of the first and a couple of sandwiches. Plus, I had no idea how to play this game, and whatever ideas I had about finessing my way through this thing were disappearing fast. I lost my third straight hand in a hurry.

"Hey, man, I can't do this," I told them. "I can't get this last quart to go." I was a rookie, I didn't know how to play the game, I figured I could ruff my way out of it.

"Oh, there's one more rule we forgot to tell you," Wilt said, his voice somehow deeper now when I needed him. "You drink it or you wear it."

"Oh, come on, man . . ." I started, but Tom Hoover, who was six feet nine, and Carlos grabbed my shoulders; Cal got both my legs with his arms, and with me struggling and at first trying to reason with them and then starting to shout, they dropped me to the floor while Wilt—it was his show—went for the water.

They poured it all over me, starting at my head and working their way down. I squirmed and sputtered, but they had me pinned solid and all I could do was get real wet.

After that I kind of lost my appetite for hearts.

Throughout the next year Wilt went out of his way to show me what he saw as a good time. He took me to the Latin Quarter, one of New York's last remaining Las Vegas-style nightclubs, and I watched him play the room. It was Wilt, Carlos Green, me, and my date, Sandy. (I had met Sandy during my summer at HARYOU. Her people were black Portuguese, and she was definitely the finest looking girl I knew. I figured if I was hanging with Wilt, I had to be up to the task.) I still have the picture, a grainy old black and white of the four of us around a table, Wilt smiling and in his element, me poker-faced in a thin tie taking it all in. I would have found it much easier to go one-on-one with him athletically than socially. I was still learning how to read a menu, that in a joint like the Quarter the roast beef came naked, that it was two bucks for a baked potato and another two bucks for spinach. The maitre d', captain, and waiters fawned over us, from the stage they announced "a celebrity in our audience" and shone a spotlight on our table, and while the attention made me even quieter, Wilt thrived on it, his barrel voice booming each time he laughed. Wilt didn't care that all of these guys just basically had their hand out; he was capable of having a good time with the whole place watching him, *because* the whole place was watching him. He was boisterous and funny and he liked me, and this was his way of both showing off and teaching me what he probably felt was a lesson in how to have money. What I learned from it was that this supposedly high-class floor show was boring, the place was totally jive, and I would rather have been down at the Five Spot listening to some good jazz.

I'd never known anybody with real money, piss-away money. All my friends were working- or lower-middle-class guys who had developed the ability to have high times at low cost. It had occurred to me not long before that, hey, I stood a decent chance of making some dollars playing basketball, but I hadn't pursued it past the concept of a good suit and a fine car. Wilt liked to be number one and go number one.

Anything you could think of that a seventeen-year-old wants, Wilt had. We drove up in his Bentley to see his horse run. Wilt owned a trotter, and we spent the day and night up at the track in Saratoga, New York, touring the barns, talking with the trainer. We had some dinner, put some money down, and sat in the clubhouse and yelled for Wilt's silks in the stretch. The horse was going up against Brett Hanover, who was to trotting horses what Henry Aaron was to baseball players, but Wilt's horse was good; Brett Hanover, who won something like his last seventy-seven races in a row, only beat him by half a length.

Wilt had a nice jazz collection, hundreds of records, and I took to stopping by and borrowing a few. Then, of course, I had to return them and, as long as I was there, talk for a while and borrow some more. Sometimes I'd just call. The first time I tried it I was extremely nervous, but Wilt was so friendly he made conversation very easy and me very comfortable. I was in a social no man's land; none of my friends were hanging out with celebrities, but I was not truly capable of keeping up with Wilt and his crowd. That summer we'd walk into some of the downtown jazz clubs like a Harlem delegation in size order; first Carlos and Cal, two six-foot-four-inch black guys in T-shirts and shorts, enough to draw some eyes; then six-foot-nine-inch Tom Hoover, then me, then Wilt. Shut those places down! I'd have a good time, but when things started getting late and serious, it was time for me to go home.

I was careful not to get underfoot. My mother made that point to me clearly. "Lewis," she said, "Wilt is a grown man with plenty of things to do and people he will want to be seeing alone. He might not want you over at his house all the time, you have to remember that. I know you like being there, but he's a man, and he might not want to spend all his time with a boy still in high school." It was hard to tell me, at seven feet tall, that I was still a kid, but she did it. So I tried not to make a pest of myself. I even mentioned it to Wilt. He said, "You know, your mother's all right. Make sure you always listen to her, she's got a lot of sense. . . . But, no, don't worry about it."

Wilt was very generous to me in bizarre ways. One day he picked up two pure silk suits from where they'd fallen in his bedroom and said, "Here, take this, this is for you." Wilt, who dressed with flash and taste and money, was giving me some threads! The suits needed cleaning, he said, but I was big enough to wear them, so he put them in a large shopping bag, and I took them home. When I showed them to my mom she was horrified. They were nice suits all right, one chocolate the other like cocoa butter, and raw silk with the little slugs to them, but they looked like he'd worn them in a sauna. He had probably been out dancing in them for days. They were all pitted out, with huge stains underneath the arms and halfway down the back. And they smelled! God, they were awful.

But I had to try them on. They were Wilt's suits, after all. It was astonishing. We were supposed to be the same height, but the shapes of our bodies had almost nothing in common. The suits didn't begin to fit. He was so massive in the chest that the shoulders were too big; the behind was enormous; the legs were too long. No wonder Wilt always looked like he'd hitched his pants up around his chest, he had no waist! I thought about keeping the clothes anyway, just as a souvenir, but my Mom said positively no, they'd just stink up the closet. She threw them out.

One thing Wilt had in abundance that I had no part in was the ladies. Maybe it was the aphrodisia of power or the allure of wealth; maybe Wilt was just a great conversationalist; I don't know, but every time I came by there was another absolutely beautiful woman who looked like she could change my life. I wasn't having a lot of success on my own, in fact I wasn't having any, so when faced with these incredible foxes I just dissolved. I was in the throes of puberty, with zero experience. All I knew was what I wanted, I could spell that right out. How to get it was beyond me.

I walked into Wilt's apartment one time, and there was a heart-stopping, stunningly beautiful woman with a sweet, sweet face and bright eyes, soft skin and fresh hair, and thighs that made me want to cry on the spot. She was small and tight, with large breasts that were almost caricatures; all of this packed into a form-fitting Danskin.

"Come on in," Wilt invited me, and I headed for his records before I could do myself damage.

"I'm returning these six, can I borrow some more?" I managed.

"Sure, take what you want," he told me and returned to whatever he had been doing in the other room. I knelt before the stacks and thumbed through them with a passionate intensity. She was in the dining room, then the kitchen. If I looked at her, I'd turn to stone. If I didn't look at her, I'd turn to stone. I sneaked a peek and she caught me, approaching as if about to pet a poodle.

"Do you want something to eat?" she asked, filling the doorway. I couldn't see if Wilt was watching me. "I can fix you a sandwich if you like."

I started to answer, and the sound that came out was like I was speaking in tongues.

"Daabraaaglphyaa . . ."

She looked down at me and laughed. Wind chimes, jasmine, the A Train Express.

"Will tuna do?"

I looked up at her, cleared my throat, and nodded.

The next time I came around Wilt's place she was gone.

I never had real heart-to-hearts with Wilt, and certainly not about the ladies. (Much as I knew, they would have been extremely one-way conversations; I had nothing to discuss.) If I had, I would have had to tell him about me and Kristal, and then there would have been trouble.

Kristal was Danish. Blonde hair, blue eyes, and a warm and attentive smile. She wasn't just another hunk of meat you'd find at Wilt's; I knew the first time I met her that she was very special. She didn't recede behind Wilt like all his other women, or get loud and pushy to compete for center stage. There was a calm about her that drew not only eyes (she was beautiful) but somehow attracted a quieter and more significant attention. There was an intelligence and a sense that her world was larger than the confines of Wilt's shadow, that she was no concubine, and her time at his side was determined by her choosing.

And she liked me, maybe found in my quietness

something of her own. All she had to do was look at me while other people were talking, and I would melt. She and I would sit and talk when Wilt was in the other room, and I felt an illicit tingle, as if we were hiding intimacy in plain sight, that at any moment Wilt would roar in and catch us entwined. She taught me Danish—we had our own language!—and I couldn't imagine how someone so gentle could have gotten caught up in Wilt's whirlwind.

We had a silent bond; I was the only one who saw through to the true Kristal, and I knew she knew I was the boy with her secret. I had to work hard at not letting the room fall away when we were in a crowd. I think I was in love.

Seventeen-year-old boys are not known for their cools, and I was less cool than most, so when I started rhapsodizing about Kristal to Curtis Lawton one afternoon, he pinned me immediately. Curtis was a schoolteacher with a compassionate understanding for young people, and we used to talk about everything: grades, girls, where I was going to go to college, basketball. He was a sympathetic compadre who straddled both my worlds. As Wilt's friend but without the star's means, Curtis may have been a little jealous of Wilt, so, presented with this opportunity to watch a kid live out his fantasy, he told me that perhaps Kristal might enjoy hearing this from me directly.

Gee, how could I ever?

Maybe I'd like to go over there one night.

But . . .

Wilt was in Europe. Wouldn't be back for two weeks.

Well . . .

Curtis brought two splits of champagne from Small's to Wilt's apartment where Kristal was staying. Lew would like to see you very much, he told her; he'll be coming by, and it would mean a lot if you would be nice to him.

It was dark out, nighttime, when I rang Wilt's bell and she opened the door. I was wearing my good slacks and a nice shirt (a tie would have been too formal, but my hair was carefully brushed, and I was maybe a little *too* clean). She looked beautiful as usual, and she asked me in, closed the door behind me, and the place got real quiet. I didn't know where to begin, but she brought me into the living room and sat down. No master of small talk, any conversation in this upper realm being a struggle, here I was trying to say what had been very specifically left unsaid. I got right to it.

"Gee, Kristal," I said in my best soft-sincere tone, "it's so nice to be here with you." She smiled. "Geez, you know, I really like you a lot."

Her blue eyes held me, and I just knew she was going to say something to make me stop shaking.

"Aw, that's nice," she purred. I wanted to touch her hand, but I hesitated. "But you know I'm Wilt's girlfriend." She kept me looking at her face. "You know that, don't you?"

"Yeah, I know it, but I like you anyway!"

"And I like you."

But that was as far as I could get. And it was plenty. We drank our champagne and sat next to each other. I couldn't find a way to put my arm around her and believe she would want me—that magical question that, in adolescence, can't be asked until it's answered—so I sat and chatted bravely, talking high school and thinking out an emotional blueprint from which I simply could not lay a foundation. After forty-five minutes I ran out of conversation and was left with only my sweet awkward intentions. Kristal was as nice as ever. She gave me a peck on the cheek as I stood at the door, and I glowed for hours.

I never had much success with the ladies. I was always the most retiring guy in the crowd, last to be noticed by the girls looking for the ringleader or Romeo. I was always hoping for some young lady to read my silence as sensitivity and have enough of her own to let me know she was open to romance. I was a dreamer.

Going to an all-boys Catholic high school where they as much as checked your palms for hair also didn't help. Plus, generally hanging around with older guys, I was always the least experienced, the most impressionable.

And those guys would lie something fierce. The dudes that were doing all the talking—Vino, Victor and Kelly—they'd lie about all kinds of shit. Vino, that was his specialty. He'd come back and tell stories about orgies he had been to over here and wild parties he'd gone to over there. Like, "Oh, yeah, and there were these babes from Brooklyn, and they took us to this place like you've never *seen*, man, and there was us and these six chicks and. . . ." Or, "So we left this pad in the projects, man? And we was grabbin' at each other and it got to where we just couldn't wait so . . . I got some in the stairwell." That's how it would always end up: He got laid. But when we were at parties with Vino nothing ever seemed to happen, except for him getting drunk and acting crazy.

But I believed these guys; I believed most of what people told me. They were running all over town sampling the vineyards, and I was woefully alone. Made me feel like I was in the Dark Ages, and a lot of times I just crawled on back into my cave. They had the old gift of gab and were nailing the mamas with no great difficulty—every challenge answered, every objection overruled—and I felt, gee, I can't be like that, so I must not be what the girls want.

Maybe, I thought, I'm too nice to them. None of the other guys would do it—"What are you, crazy, girl? Don't be asking this man to do that!"—but I wasn't above helping girls with their packages, walking out of my way for them, even opening doors. All the nice girls liked me; I was too stupid to try to do anything with them; that's why they liked me.

Things never quite went my way. There was a girl who lived on Riverside Drive and 156th Street, Cheri Benoit, who I really liked and who was starting to return the favor. She was a year younger than I was, and she'd come up, and we'd sit around and kiss on the couch when my parents weren't home. When they were, I'd get antsy and say, "We gotta get out of here"; so we'd go downstairs, and it would be thirty degrees outside, and I'd sit out there on the bench with her all bundled up.

One day we were walking together, and Cheri said, "Come on, let's run down the hill." She took off, and I was trailing after her in my best athlete's lope when, one sneaker over another, I tripped and sprawled forward like an oaf. I took two steps while pitching out of control, trying desperately to maintain my balance, but the hill only got steeper and I finally just went down. My knees skinned against the pavement, tearing huge holes in my pants as I tried to break my fall. I lay there, stunned. After enduring and then outgrowing all my on-court humiliations, I had to be a hopeless clod in front of the first nice girl who lets me touch her. Cheri ran back, saying, "Gee, can I help you?" I pulled myself up, palms scraped, these great big holes at least six inches across in my pants, blood coming out of my knees. Why me? We ended up going to her house; she stung me with a whole lot of iodine, and I hobbled home.

Not long afterwards, Kelly and I were discussing the various assets of the neighborhood ladies. Kelly was into music; we'd go down to the Village Vanguard and hear some jazz together, and he was reasonably well-read with an agile mind. He was a good friend if you got him alone, but he did go on about getting the job done. He didn't know I liked Cheri; I was always very careful not to let anyone in on who I was seeing. Didn't want a lot of loose talk.

"Man, I had Cheri up there the other day," he told me confidentially, "and I almost got something."

I thought, Oh, no. But I didn't let on as Kelly gave me the details.

I didn't talk to Cheri for six months. I figured Kelly was telling the truth and, since he was good-looking and a proven charmer, she was locked up. Besides, the whole thing was now somehow tainted. I kind of missed Cheri, but I figured there was nothing I could do.

Finally I ran into her. She had been confused, then angry, then sad, wondering what ever happened to me. Though she was a year younger than I was, I had never thought of her as vulnerable, only either uncaring or taken.

"But you and Kelly . . ."

"You know, I talked to Kelly," she said with a sixteen-year-old's dignity, "but that's it." Still, at that age hurts run real deep, and things were not really right between us for a long time.

Vino was also a talker, but Vino had ample opportunity to get some. Older and out of school, he lived with his parents, both of whom worked and weren't around the house too often anyway. During the summer I'd get up at around 10:30 A.M., put on my shorts and sneakers, grab my basketball and head over to Vino's. He'd be hung over and immoveable, but even in this weakened state he'd be looking for an angle. One time he conned me into walking all the way down to the Chinese restaurant on Dyckman Street and buying him some brunch. I was a nice guy, went, and brought back the food while he lazed around in bed some more, but when the word got around, it was like Vino had suckered me into playing the slave. There was no such thing, I learned once more, as a kind act in the street.

But I paid him back. One Saturday morning later that summer I came over and found Vino asleep but his girlfriend wide awake in the living room. Now, it was known to everybody that Vino's girlfriend was giving it up, and I don't know how I did it—I was never aggressive, except this once—but I got us seriously into it. She was vitally interested, and I was working some lower division digital revelation, and, as I had been told so often, *I was gonna get some* when . . . she got nervous. Vino was sleeping not twenty feet away and, though that was a large part of the morning's attraction, she ultimately could not risk blood warfare. She didn't say "No," she said "Not now."

It never came to anything, but it was highly insulting to Vino when he found out. How he found out was, I told him.

"I was up in the Bronx," he was bragging months later, "and me and this chick were getting loaded and she really wanted it . . ."

"No she didn't, Vino," I said sharply. "But I'll tell you what did happen. I had *your* old lady up in *your* apartment, and I was *gonna* get some . . ."

"No, man, that shit didn't happen!" he shouted.

"Yes, it did," I insisted. "Let me tell you about it. . . ." Vino figured I was lying, but he never sent me on any errands again.

I wasn't without my opportunities, being All-City had some benefits, but often I was too naive to know what the signals were, and on top of that I was particular. If they didn't look like Sophia Loren, I wasn't interested. So what happened was the girls I wanted were never willing to deal with me, and the other ones I didn't care if they fell into a hole.

One girl who almost filled the bill came after me. She was going with another guy in my high school, but she decided she was going to be my girlfriend and set about to make things easy. We didn't go anywhere; our dates, such as they were, would be a cup of coffee at the coffee shop and a trip into Central Park to smooch. One night she had gotten herself good and drunk and made it very clear that now was the time. This wasn't any mighta-coulda got some; she was lying there, looking me in the eye, waiting for me to make the one move that was open to me.

But I couldn't follow through. After years of teen dreams and heartfelt fantasies, I just didn't want to lose it on the ground in the well-traveled darkness of Central Park to this girl who was hardly even a friend. I had always imagined sunset, soft sand, the warm breezes of a naked beach in Hawaii, and I was enough of a romantic to wait for my moment. When I finally did make love, right before senior year in high school, to a girl who knew every bit as little about the entire operation as I did, it was warm and affectionate but still bewildering. My mind raced for days and I told no one. Sometimes it takes years to unload the trash that guys talk to each other.

5

I felt strange heading back to high school that fall of 1964. All summer the world had opened up to me, as if I were a subway rising to be an el, but as senior year began I felt like I was plunging to a series of stops I'd made too often. The Power team continued undefeated; classes were just classes; I'd seen my name in print enough so that the thrill of publicity had been blunted, and I wasn't talking to the press because all they would have wanted was, Where are you going to college? and I just didn't know.

It is always nice to be in demand, but I didn't have a lot of respect for the people who wanted me, and that took the edge off the adulation. My summer of blackness had made me even more wary of strangers, and most of the new people I would have to be meeting were white. I maintained my school friendships, and once in a while I would go downtown and party with some white people

Kelly knew, but for the most part I wasn't very interested in meeting strangers, especially white strangers. I spent the autumn studying where I could be next year at this time. I was looking forward, nothing to be learned from looking around. Though I was quite literally pondering my future, my life was effectively on hold.

All I really wanted to do was get out. Since that was still a winter away I set out to change some of the rules. The high school jump from junior to senior is usually like being brought up from the minors to the bigs, and I extended even that, insisting that I was no boy anymore and didn't need so short a leash or so tight a curfew. I had things to do now and needed time to do them; my world was larger and it took many more hours than I had been allotted to walk from one end of it to the other. My parents, faced with the first intimations of my independence, eased up a little. Just a little, mind you; I was still a boy in their eyes.

I spent some serious time in the jazz clubs downtown, the Five Spot, the Half Note, the Village Vanguard, and when it got late I just stayed on. I would go with my friends, Kelly or Carl Snow or Johnny Graham, and with no Wilt around, I wasn't awed by the situation; it was beginning to be truly my element. Some of the musicians had known my father—Dizzy Gillespie one time said, "Oh, yeah, I remember he used to have a kid, this little baby with him. That was you, huh?"—and some of them knew me from the basketball headlines, so they looked out for me. I went to see Cannonball Adderley at the Five Spot and a guy who was traveling with the band, Lee Weaver, bought me a hamburger and a coke. That was a big time, that night. I wished at the time that I had caught him outside, because the Italian sausages they were selling out there on St. Mark's Place were smokin', but I took the burger.

I met some incredible musicians and heard some amazing performances. Roland Kirk, Sonny Rollins, Thelonius Monk. Kelly remembers us sitting at the Vanguard and Monk, when I wasn't looking, giving me the intense once-over, eyeing me up and down as if to say, "So this is the *big* dude."

I even got to know Monk personally. My friend from 150th Street, Tyrone, lived across the street from Jimmy Cobb, Miles Davis' drummer, and in the same building as Monk's drummer, Ben Riley. Tyrone and I would baby-sit Riley's son until Ben's wife came home, then we'd take the train downtown and make the second set. It was like a private community, and I was feeling stronger by the hour as I was welcomed into it. Records took on new meaning as I met the men who made them, and I began to hear music with a different ear as I got close to the people who played it. I even borrowed Snow's saxophone, took some lessons and learned how to play.

I ran with a pack of friends from the projects and nearby Sugar Hill. Kelly, Greg and Freddy Jewel, Gary Lucian, Donald Brock, Eric Engles and some others—we called ourselves the Colleagues. We were a social club, not a gang, and most of what we did was party. But this was no casual, street-corner wine-bibbing; we were smart and organized, and because we always had a good time when we were all together, we figured we should give our own parties. We none of us had any money but between us scraped up enough to rent out the Kappa House, a City College fraternity on 141st Street. We provided the house, the music on the record player, and the punch, charged ninety-nine cents at the door (a dollar or over and you had to charge tax, so we gathered up a bucket of pennies and beat the city out of its share), and, with a little word-of-mouth advertising, held our first great dance. We hit it. People from all over were looking for a good party, and the place was packed, a couple of hundred people, all on the look-out for new faces and hot times, jammed into the parlor floor of this big brownstone. We set up speakers and had a sensation on our hands. The overhead was low, we had the run of the place, and we managed to make some money.

Once we saw how easy it was, and fun, and profitable, the Colleagues became party-giving fools. We hopped around from building to building, one up on the hill near CCNY, another nearby called the Afro House. We had stumbled on a communal need—*everybody* was dying to get out of the house and rock. You could come to these blowouts in groups of six or by yourself and be sure of finding a lot of the kind of people you knew were around but couldn't quite hook up with. We danced, and people brought whatever stimulants they wanted to be stimulated by, and these parties were wild. We became the Dick Clarks of the black teen world; if you weren't down with the Colleagues you had some farther down to go.

We only had one "incident." We had found this nice dance hall right over the 145th Street Bridge in the Bronx. The first floor, where the party was held, still had remnants of that old-time grandeur, and the night of our affair its six ballrooms were all filled with people dancing and carrying on. It was a normal Colleagues extravaganza—loud music, dancing, and a lot of talk—until sometime after midnight a pack of hoodlum guys from Manhattan went around back and started coming through the window. They were a little older than we were, maybe twenty, and you could tell right away these were bad dudes. Some of them had knives, probably guns too. A couple of Colleagues went back to cut off the flow, but the locals went around front and tried to crash the door. We managed to hold the line, but soon the jitter-bugs who had made it inside broke off into two factions and started fighting each other. It was an indoor gang war between people we didn't even know. Guys were throwing chairs, fighting in close, slamming into walls and guests and anything in their way. It was chaos, people broke the doors trying to get out. The bouncers tried to gain control while paying customers ran from the apartment as if it were sinking, and finally the building security threw everybody out and shut the place down.

We hung around for an hour and a half trying to gather ourselves, then we split up the money and left.

But most of my free time was less tumultuous. Once I learned that the girls would say yes if you asked them the right way, I spent a lot of time looking for the right way. I dated, went to jazz clubs, played my saxophone. Kelly graduated high school in January and got himself a place down on West 28th Street in Chelsea. In exchange for helping out a bit with the rent, I got a key. This opened up new worlds. I still hear about the time Kelly, Bruce Ellis and this girl came home and found me and a young woman right in it, hip deep and telling the world. They backed out, "Oh, hey, what's happenin', 'bye," but they were grinning, and my stock rose that night.

My Mom didn't know about any of this. As long as I was going to Mass every Sunday and the other mothers were telling her what a nice boy her Lewis still was, she was happy. I had my own vision of what was ahead, but she wasn't a person from whom I could win a fight so I just tried to bide my time; I'd be out of there, I realized, soon enough.

As national champions, Power was the team everyone in the Catholic leagues keyed on. Teams who tried to run with us, we outran; teams who tried to shut us down, we either beat with outside shooting or got the ball in to me for the easy two. We hadn't lost since the end of my freshman year, though we'd had some close calls, and most games we played with the good intensity high schoolers give to their closed universe. Coach Donohue stayed on our backs, though he had become just a little gun-shy with me, and we kept on winning.

Our big showdown each year was against DeMatha, a Catholic high school down in Hyattsville, Maryland. They were a good, well-trained team with a winning tradition and the serious desire to beat our behinds. We didn't do a lot of traveling, but junior year, two days after Donohue made his slip of the lip, we went down and played them at the University of Maryland fieldhouse in front of 14,000 fans and beat them by three. I got thirty-five points and twenty-one rebounds that day, and we needed all of them. Senior year we went down there again, same fieldhouse, same overwhelming crowd (our gym held maybe a thousand).

DeMatha came prepared. They had two six-foot-eight-inch big men, Bob Whitmore and Sid Catlett, who both went on to play at Notre Dame, and they sandwiched me, tried to deny me the ball. One of their guards was Bernie Williams, who later played in the pros at San Diego. They slowed the game down, walked the ball up the court when they had it, and double- and triple-teamed me on our end. The game was close, but they played well, made the crucial shot at the end, and won it, 46–43.

After seventy-one straight wins, we took the loss with a decent amount of dignity. Sitting in the locker room, unwilling to take my uniform off and admit that the game was over, I was a little dazed. I'd gotten only sixteen points; it had been a hard afternoon, and I felt like I'd personally lost it. Coach Donohue walked over to me and said loudly, "Now wait a minute. It's very selfish of you to say you lost this game. What you're implying is that you won all the other games. If you want to take the blame for losing this game, you have to take credit for winning the other seventy-one. Are you willing to take credit for them? Yes or no?"

No, of course I wasn't. And if I was, I wasn't about to say it out loud right then. The coach was doing his best to soothe me, but I was past paying him full attention.

"I'm the coach," he continued, playing it to the room full of disappointed teenagers. "If I did, then I'd be taking credit for winning all the others, and I'm not going to do that because it's not true."

My teammates Charlie Farrugia, Eric Brown, Norwood Todman and I all sat around my hotel room. We weren't devastated, we were just glum. "Wow, we lost," somebody sighed. My parents had come down for the game, and afterwards my mother was in tears, but we all managed to keep it together. It had been almost three years between losses, we consoled ourselves, that was quite a run.

We didn't lose again, and in the spring Power Memorial was chosen national champions for the second time in a row. More All-City, All-American. I liked the feeling but I was ready to push it up a step.

I had proved to myself that I could make it on my own—late jazz nights, away games, a taste of passion: all the details teenagers read as life signs—but some obstacles remained. I had made some forays to freedom but, with a college to be chosen and the entire course of my life to be fashioned, my future was still being filtered through Coach Donohue, a man for whom I had lost all respect and much of my need. I was learning how to talk and deal with older men—Wilt had more power and authority in the real world than Coach Donohue ever had—and my black and independent summer had given me a measure of distance I'd never known. Until only a year earlier, I had never doubted Mr. Donohue's sincerity, his motivations on behalf of my best interests. When he had advised me I had listened and then almost invariably had done what he had suggested. He had molded me and I, in turn, had left myself in his hands. He had never steered me wrong. But after our incident I questioned everything; how could I allow the major decisions of my life to be influenced by a man who called me nigger?

I had long since learned not to look for emotional comfort from my parents—my mother was stifling, my father hardly there—and now the only other adult I had truly trusted had to be dismissed. With a lifetime of crossroads to be approached I was, I realized for the first time, quite alone. I thought about Curtis Lawton, but I hadn't seen him often enough for our relationship to deepen. I thought about the guys, but this was too sensitive a subject to allow them into. Norbert might have helped, but I needed someone with experience, with an overview, whom I could lean on and trust, and Norbert was just as confused as I was.

There was no lack of adults who would have loved to help out. Power was full of counselors, Brothers, and priests, but they had all played with me once too often. I knew there were guys on the street who would have some knowledge of my options, but most of them were sharks, and after four years' enforced separation I was in no position to sift through their sophisticated lies. Like most athletes, I had leaned on my coach, and with him proving soft support I had to stand by myself.

I could go anywhere. Large school, small school, Ivy League, Big Ten, established basketball program or up-and-coming, they had all written the requisite letters, sent the materials, stood ready to make their pitch. Did I want to go to Harvard? The University of Miami? It was up to me. Coach Donohue had culled the correspondence and offered up a cross section of choices based on his knowledge of the schools' basketball programs, educational qualities, geographical assets and liabilities, coaches, social possibilities, and overall tone. My parents and I pored over the candidates and weeded out some more. One thing was certain, I wasn't going to school in the South. My mother came from outside Charlotte, North Carolina, and Wake Forest recruited me very strongly, but my Easter in Goldsboro, plus the entire tenor of the times, eliminated all southern schools from my plans. I wasn't going to be anybody's nigger.

I wanted to play good, winning basketball at an institution that treated its athletes with an element of dignity, under a coach whom I could respect. I wasn't looking to turn anyone's program around, to save anything or anybody. I didn't want to be the first black athlete at a school, or the last. And I wanted someplace that was fun. I was looking to get out of the house and stay out.

The coach was undergoing his own pressures. With me going to college, Power's basketball future had never looked so poor nor his so potentially dazzling. With college coaches around the country dying for a few quick words to attract my attention, here was a guy who could make me run laps on a whim. Donohue was inside the blockade; his value soared—when would it be this high again?—and it was clearly time to make his move. He told me about some of the offers he received, and I heard later that one school even told him its coach was about to die and did Donohue know anyone interested in applying for the job soon to be vacated. Nobody, however, had heard about our racial standoff—I couldn't talk to the press, and he certainly wasn't saying anything about it—so the logical outside assumption was that wherever Coach Donohue went Lew might truly follow. Not likely.

What can a teenager really tell about a school from a letter full of superlatives and a four-color brochure? It's amazing to me that high school kids manage to make their choices at all; what it comes down to is a close analytical reading of advertising copy. I read what was presented, looked at the standings, asked around, and finally narrowed the field. My final four were distilled to the University of Michigan, Columbia, St. John's, and UCLA.

Michigan was a large school in an industrial state with a developing black presence. The university was placed in an urban setting without being grim, and there were plenty of black guys to hang around with. The perks that were hinted at sounded promising, and with Cazzie Russell making a lot of noise, the basketball program was in full swing. I had a good time on my visit there and thought about Michigan hard.

Columbia was New York. My father had gone to Juilliard and I kind of liked the continuity of our both being taught in and by the city. I could live near the campus which, at 116th Street and Broadway, was within walking distance of Harlem and only a subway ride from every jazz club I'd ever had to leave early. It was Ivy League and had that aura of hip, horn-rimmed cool—the Miles Davis of the educational world—that would have told everyone, without their asking, that not only was this guy big but he was smart. I could see myself ambling the campus in a tweed jacket with suede elbow patches, puffing thoughtfully on my pipe, humming "Straight, No Chaser" on my way to sociology class.

Unfortunately, the Columbia basketball program wasn't happening. They'd had losing seasons several years running but were beginning a new push. They recruited intensely, and their effort paid off nicely when Haywood Dotson and Jim McMillian chose Columbia a year later, but, much as I loved the idea of living the New York life, I finally decided to add my assets to a winner.

St. John's did a lot of winning, largely because of its coach, Joe Lapchick. I'd known his son, Richie, at Donohue's camp, and since I liked Richie I had to like his father. Joe Lapchick had played for the original Celtics and coached the Knicks and St. John's, and won everywhere he'd been. He knew basketball inside and out, fundamentals, strategy, the psychology of winning; his teams were adaptable and aggressive and smart. And he was an honorable man, I could just tell. He liked young people and set a hell of an example. There was a unique charisma about Coach Lapchick that I responded to the first time we met.

After a very short while, meeting with even the limited number of recruiters Coach Donohue permitted access to me, I became quite adept at intuiting out the phonies, the guys who had dollar signs or championship rings spinning in their eyes. Everyone I met with talked about how their concerns were for me and my education and my progress, but I knew quickly who was jive; it was something in the tone of voice—overstated authority or an air of desperation—and in the muscles at the side of the mouth that would pinch when I asked them about black players. But Coach Lapchick had obviously given some serious thought to me personally. He was the first man to put into words for me how the world alienates tall people. They expect more from a giant, he told me; they scale up their demands. You are larger than life and therefore less affected by it, as if it took more noise to get your attention or more pain to hurt you.

Joe was from New York, six feet five inches tall, a son of immigrants, and in his neighborhood full of newly arrived, rather diminutive people from Czechoslovakia, Yugoslavia, and southeastern Europe, he was a freak. "I'd go places," he told me, "and people would stare and say, 'Look, a gypsy!' " He proved right away that not only was his heart in the right place but he and I had the kind of simpático I truly needed.

There were other good reasons for me to go to St. John's. By scoring well on a daylong, statewide scholastic examination, I had won a New York State Scholarship, so that was $265 a month the state would give me on top of my basketball scholarship—I would have my own cash at last. Sonny Dove, whom I had played against in high school and become friends with, was at St. John's, so I would have immediate connections and no problems making friends. Johnny Graham was there on a music scholarship, and lots of black kids from Manhattan and Brooklyn went to St. John's, so I could definitely hang out.

But there were debits. St. John's was a Catholic school and I had had enough Catholic school. My mother, so close, would have kept after me about church and studies and just about everything else. In fact, St. John's was so close that I could have lived at home, which was not at all what I had in mind. That was one argument I would rather not have. Maybe I should just go far away.

Ultimately, St. John's eliminated itself. Coach Lapchick turned sixty-five, the school's mandatory retirement age. I had the sense that he would have liked to stay on, that basketball was in some way not only his pleasure but his sustenance, but he had been in college ball for almost twenty years and wouldn't fight the rule that retired him. He did go out in glory, however, winning both the Madison Square Garden Holiday Festival over Christmas and, that spring in his final game, the National Invitational Tournament.

But I had considered St. John's because of Coach Lapchick, and without him the school lost much of its appeal. Then I went and visited the University of California at Los Angeles, and that settled that.

UCLA was gorgeous. They showed me a twenty-minute walk I'd have across campus to my classes, and I saw that, if I wanted, I could stroll the whole way on fresh green grass. It was sunny and warm and open, and I couldn't imagine why anyone would willingly live anywhere else. Seemed like it was always springtime there, people in shorts moving from class to class like a fashion model parade, more pretty girls within arm's reach than I'd see all summer cruising the walkways of Central Park. Did I have to go back to the guys at Power? Couldn't I just stay here now?

I was shown around campus by Edgar Lacy, who was a starting forward on the UCLA team. I had met Edgar my sophomore year when we were both high school All-Americans and made one of those thirty-second, "And now on our big stage" group appearances on *The Ed Sullivan Show*. We had become friends then, and as Edgar pointed out the sights and laughed when I gawked at the ladies, he also gave me the lowdown on what UCLA was really like. The campus was cool; black guys hung together but the whites were okay; there was no problem in that area. Things were made comfortable for you—there were ways of finding more than the bare necessities of life—but not palatial. And you *would* work on your game.

The basketball inducements were not to be ignored, either. UCLA had just won the national championship for the second time in a row. The players themselves had become campus heroes. Pauley Pavilion, a mammoth new athletic arena that could hold 13,000 screaming Bruin fans, had already been erected and was standing there waiting for its convocation.

The construction of Pauley Pavilion had uprooted

the athletic department from its old haunts and temporarily relocated it in one of a series of Quonset huts that occupied the campus like a bivouac. The buildings were drab affairs not made any more attractive by even the slightest attempt to decorate them, and what was impressive about the place was the complete ordinariness of it all—national champions tucked among the file cabinets. If there was some pride in accomplishments around here, I thought as I looked at the cubicles, it certainly wasn't external.

But most of all, what UCLA offered was John Wooden. Coach Wooden's office was about the size of a walk-in closet. I was brought in, and there was this very quaint-looking midwesterner, gray hair with a part almost in the middle of his head, glasses on. I'd heard a lot about this man and his basketball wisdom, but he surely did look like he belonged in a one-room schoolhouse. He stood up, shook my hand, and invited me to sit down.

He was quiet, which was a relief because so was I. I am a great believer in my own snap judgments, and I am quick to find major fault in minor offenses, particularly in strangers who need me, but I found myself liking Mr. Wooden right away. He was calm, in no hurry to impress me with his knowledge or his power. He could have made me cool my heels, or jumped up and been my buddy, but he clearly worked on his own terms, and I appreciated that in the first few moments we met. His suit jacket was hanging from a peg on the wall, and he was working in shirt-sleeves, casual but not far from decorum. He called me Lewis, and that decision endeared him to me even more; it was at once formal, my full name—We are gentlemen here—and respectful. I was no baby Lewie. Lewis. I liked that.

There was a plainspokenness to Mr. Wooden, a distance from cynicism that my own teenage idealism responded to, and rather than gloss over the possible conflicts that might dissuade a recruit from deciding on the school, he told me what they expected from people at UCLA.

"We expect our boys to work hard and do well with their schoolwork," he told me in his flat yet not uninviting midwestern twang, "and I know you do have good grades so that should not be a problem for you. We expect you to be at practice on time and work hard while you're there. We do not expect our boys to present any disciplinary problems, but, again, we know you're not that kind of young man, and I don't expect you will have any difficulty here at UCLA.

"You've seen the campus. Do you have any questions?"

"I like the campus very much," I told him, "and I am very impressed with UCLA's basketball program."

"That's all very good," Coach Wooden said, "but I am impressed by your grades. You could do very well here as a student, whether you were an athlete or not. That is important. We work very hard to have our boys get through and earn their degrees. I hope all my student-athletes can achieve that. It is to both our benefits; your being a good student will keep you eligible to play in our basketball program, and your degree will be of value to you for the rest of your life."

I made a point of talking with all the coaches who recruited me about topics other than basketball. These were men, one of whom might have a profound effect on the course of my life, and I wanted to be as certain as I could that, basketball aside, I did not misjudge them. Again, Coach Wooden came through as a well-read, genuinely caring man. People would always tell me that they cared about me, but I felt Mr. Wooden really meant it. I came out of his office knowing I was going to UCLA.

My college travels broke up the end-of-high-school monotony, and I did a lot of agonizing as more information was thrown in my way. Out in the California sunshine choices were easy; at home it got harder. I had taken my College Boards along with everybody else, and although I was on the reverse end of the normal college entrance nervousness, the pressure was still considerable. Rather than have one's academic and (in a teenager's absolutist mind) entire future decided by a round table of strangers on the basis of 1500 of your most carefully conceived, if pompous, words, I had to weave my way through thousands of other people's grandiose invitations and decide my own. I was used to listening to and following advice, always too young, inexperienced, or essentially powerless to develop my own thoughts or put them into action. I had been taught obedience by the masters—parents, coaches, the Church—and, though I had begun to question a few of their dictates, it was still out of my realm of possibility to take a stand totally on my own.

Coach Donohue, meanwhile, had made his own decision. He had accepted the offer to become head coach at Holy Cross College the next fall, and he insisted I visit the campus in Massachusetts. "You owe it to me," is how he put it. I had no intention of attending the school, or anywhere else Mr. Donohue might have been coaching, but he had some people to impress, so I put in an appearance.

Mr. Donohue showed me around the campus. It was a pretty place, but there wasn't a lot of . . . color . . . around. It developed that there was actually only a handful of black students in the whole school, and Mr. Donohue had arranged for one of them to give me a Holy Cross sales pitch. "Go see him," Mr. Donohue had said. "He'll tell you what it's really like here."

I was introduced to my guide, and as soon as we got out of Mr. Donohue's earshot he made the good impression. "If you come here you're crazy," he told me. "This is the worst place for you to go to school. You won't have any fun at all. You'll be isolated, like I am. *Man, pick someplace else!*" I figured that about closed the book on my high school basketball career.

Second semester senior year is a great time for high school kids. Your final grades will be too late to affect any college's opinion of you, and if further formal education is not in your future, you're getting good and ready to get out into the world. It's warm outside; there is an unstated but acknowledged limit to how much power the teachers still have over you—What are they going to do, flunk you for mouthing off and then have to deal with your wise comments for all of next year too?—and, though the students don't know it, the teachers are looking to escape from the classroom almost as much as the kids. It feels like freedom and captivity are at war within your own body, a series of personal skirmishes fought out where everyone can see them.

Marking time as I was through all of senior year, by my last few months I was open for some stepping out and about. For years I had obeyed all the rules and come home when I was called. I even went so far as to come home when I wasn't called, because if I didn't, I'd have some explaining to do; often the time spent in the street was not worth either the words I'd have to hear about it or my own worry that I'd catch hell. I was so well trained that I had internalized my Mom's nervousness, given up my independence for her peace of mind. My mother wanted to protect me from what she saw as dangers in the street, but in the process she wasn't giving me the time or space to find the facts for myself. It was as if she didn't trust my judgment, wouldn't handle the fact that I could fend for myself. And, of course, the less I actually faced, the less I was prepared for. In her earnestness she made it, despite my size, hard for me to grow. At seventeen I was still a very good little boy.

But Cora didn't have the total stranglehold. Once in a while I'd strike out on my own, though even then I approached almost everything with a caution that bordered on suspicion. For instance, people had been trying to turn me on to marijuana since I was fifteen. A bunch of the guys I played ball with in Harlem smoked reefer, and since it had not been discovered by the media or distributed widely to white boys, there was still a very

111

deep mystique to the entire scene. Jazz musicians smoked it, and beatniks in the Village, and various uptown hipsters, but for years I passed on it. I had my basketball to consider, my wind; I didn't want to start messing with narcotics and screw around with my future. One puff and you're hooked. I didn't need it.

So it was amusing and ironic that, pot being a black cultural staple long before it found its way downtown, I should be brought to it by a white schoolmate from Power Memorial. Neil Chusid, who had turned me on to Bob Dylan, made me challenge my whole concept of marijuana as a dangerous drug.

"Hey," he said very happily, "it's not dangerous, it's not even addictive. It's fun!"

"Come on, man," I warned him, but being my good friend, he wanted all the best for me. I wouldn't smoke right away; it was December and the season was underway, and I wasn't going to risk my life on his good word, even if I did know he'd never do anything to hurt me. What I did was go and look it up. I researched marijuana as if it was an independent study project. I spent time in the library, thumbed through the card catalogue, checked the facts, followed the footnotes. I read the LaGuardia Report, a New York City government-sponsored drug-use study, and damned if Neil wasn't correct; marijuana was not a narcotic, it wasn't addictive. I was astonished. I had figured the street mythology was bullshit and the conventional wisdom was sound. Turned out I'd had it backwards!

Of course then I had to try it. If all the respectable citizens had been trying for years to keep me away from this drug and it couldn't do me any harm, it must certainly be one sure-fire good time. And I'd been too trusting for too long. One of my first major individual decisions was to smoke pot.

It took me a couple of tries to make things happen. Basketball season was still on, but, hey, I wasn't worried. By that time I'd canvassed my friends, and not one had a bad word for the weed. Guys who had tried to force it on me years earlier were pleased that I was joining the fraternity; it was such a hipster's bond, and such a fine feeling, that they would have been more than happy to roll a joint on the spot just to be there the first time I got high.

My marijuana induction was at a neighborhood party in February. We had the rolling ritual going and the couple of guys who were into it stepped into the bathroom and lit up. I had never smoked even a cigarette, so they had to teach me how to hold the joint, how to inhale and keep the stuff down. I knew intuitively how to be cool doing it; for all the hocus pocus there are some lessons you never forget learning.

But absolutely nothing happened. We got back to the party, and if there was anything different about my smoking partners, I couldn't tell. As for me, I felt normal, and more than a little disappointed. The party just went on as before, and I sat around thinking, "Wow, this is really nothing," and dismissed all this dope secrecy as one more in a long series of lies I'd been told by the brothers. I thought it was a hoax.

But the desire didn't go away, nor the opportunity. People did tend to socialize as springtime came around, and there was pot available, and I did go for it again. The second time was at a friend's birthday party in March. I had a wild night acting all spacey and goofy, but I just felt like having a good time for a change; wasn't any big thing, I just loosened up, that's all. People who saw me out there rocking asked me, "Are you doing anything?" but I was just having fun and didn't think anything of it. You're supposed to know when you're stoned, I thought; I'm just . . . relaxed.

The third time—Easter Sunday, 1965—was the charmer. I went to church early that morning, then headed over to a good friend's house. He had a pipe, and he and I had bought a nickel bag and plotted out the afternoon.

113

My compadre, who had some expertise and a friend's sense of style, let me go first.

I sucked on the pipe as if I could empty the room of air. Heavy, strong pulls that made the pot crackle in the bowl, then a pause, then, without exhaling, another long hit till the smoke was backed up my throat and all in my mouth and nose and eyes. I was determined to get high or burn my lungs out. I coughed and coughed, then passed the pipe to my buddy who did the same. But I was not to be denied. I took a couple more hits and started coughing again, and a drone all of a sudden set up in my ears, and I had to sit down before I fell. Then it hit me, this idea like a little chime ringing in the top of my head. *Ding.* I was definitely high! I stood up to try and put a record on, and my whole peripheral vision fuzzed up on me, like I was staring down a lucite tube at a living room far, far away.

We finally got the record on and started laughing and laughing. First I moved in slow motion, then we began running around the house chortling and cackling; if laughs could shatter glass, we'd have reduced the projects to rubble. My friend Little Bob was in the hallway and wondered what the hell was going on, sounds pretty silly in there. He knocked. Uh oh, who's there? Oh, it's Little Bob. Let's turn him on. We were laughing and shouting and getting funny and stupid all afternoon. This was too good not to last.

After that I'd get high on the occasional weekend or at parties every chance I could. I even did it one day before school. Usually you had to be inside the building at 8:45 A.M. but Power seniors had executive privilege and didn't have to show up till ten. My friend John, who was in my homeroom and biology class, met me at Columbus Circle and 59th Street at around 9:00 A.M., and with Power only three blocks away, we strolled into the morning greenery of Central Park, smoked a joint and then walked to class. New York in the springtime is beautiful, warm and especially colorful because you're not expecting such a brilliant glare, and we marveled at the day before sliding into schoolwork. By the time we arrived at the building we were more than cheerful. Every homeroom would begin with a prayer and the pledge of allegiance and all of a sudden we were giggling, standing there between these tiny desks, our heads bowed, trying not to blow it. We were dissecting our pig in biology that morning and just totally fell out, first a trickle of snickering, then uncontrollable dam-break teary-eyed yahoos. The Christian Brothers probably just chalked it up to spring fever, these high-spirited young boys.

Of course, I never found that marijuana did me any particular good. It didn't sharpen my hook shot or make my moves to the hoop even a fraction stronger. It's not vitamin B-12, and I'm not in any way recommending it as something that will improve anyone's life. I tried it because everyone was telling me not to, and I was just beginning to make my judgments for myself.

But if I was tasting the rare air of freedom, I was becoming anything but light-headed. If anything, finally finding out that the dangers my mother had warned me away from were mostly her fears and not mine made me sober and almost sullen. If pot wasn't bad for me, and life after midnight in no way threatening, what else had I been missing listening to this woman's regulations? I hadn't told her half of what I'd been up to because she would have called it out of bounds, but I had developed a strong guilt-by-proxy so that ultimately she didn't have to know about my experiments to make me scared of them, I did it myself; she had wormed her way in that far.

There wasn't any question that my mother loved me. But maybe because I grew up and away from her so young, was physically difficult to control and began hanging out with older boys so early on, she decided I needed her fierce protection. And having taken that task to heart like a jungle point man shooting anything that moves, she killed off a lot of encounters that would have made me strong had I overcome them and wiser had I not. I needed to go out on night patrol.

It was one in the morning when I called home from the subway. A bunch of the guys and our ladies had been hanging out and partying, stopping traffic and keeping the night alive. We were looking for someplace to continue the festivities, preferably one with beds and without adults, but the prospects seemed slim. My mother always insisted that I let her know if I was going to arrive home late, said it kept her from worrying, and although it embarrassed me to hold up our progress while I checked in, I dutifully put a dime in the phone box and dialed.

She was awake. It was late; she didn't want to hear about what I was doing; why wasn't I there yet?

I sagged by the phone. If I argued loudly, everyone would hear, and then I'd have to slink home like a whipped dog. If I told her no, I'd come home when I was ready, then I'd hear about it in aces whenever I showed up and for months after that. There was no way to win, and I was suddenly just worn out, as if I'd been racing and the night had slowed to a crawl. An express roared through, and I couldn't hear my mother or talk over it, so I stood and waited until it careened down the tunnel.

"All right, Mom," I said as the rumble faded, "I'm coming home," and hung up.

But when I dragged myself over to where the rest of the gang was standing, they had come up with not only some rather unique ways to extend the evening's entertainment but also a place to do them. I was in a bind. I didn't want to leave now that things were hitting their stride again, and I would surely look like a fool going home to mama—even turning around and calling her back would look bush—but there would be hard times forever if I didn't show.

There is always that shuffler's moment between planning and action, and I could have eased my way out or bolted, but, hey, I'm a big boy now, this isn't eleven-o'clock-lights-out anymore, if she can't handle it, that's hard.

The night's procession continued, and I marched in it with a vengeance.

My mother was in the window waiting for me when I got home at eight the next morning. From our living room you could see all the way down the block, and she watched as I walked from the subway station to our building, knew when I hit the elevator, and exploded when I let myself inside.

"Where have you been?! Do you know I stayed up the whole night waiting for you?"

"Hey, I didn't ask you to stay up," I started.

"Don't you get fresh with me, young man!" she shouted. "You were supposed to be home, and I want you to stay home!"

She was loud and sharp and piercing, and I couldn't begin to explain, didn't have words for it myself. I knew this was important right here, that she had no business talking to my vision of me this way, but I couldn't spit it out, and she was in a rage. I couldn't win, and I hadn't lost in a long time.

I raced to my room and threw the door shut. The whole house shook.

"Don't you walk away from me," my mother shouted. "Come back out here." I could hear her storming toward me. She tried to get in, but I put all my weight against the door, and it wouldn't budge. I'd never not faced her before, never denied her the direct line to me, and now, though I'd managed to keep her off me, I knew I had Al to contend with. There was a two-by-four lying on the floor, and I wedged it between the door knob and the closet just like I'd seen in the movies.

Cora didn't have to wake Al; we'd done that between us, but she told him what was doing. He called through the door, "Let me in, Son." No way. Al put his shoulder to it, but I had built an effective barricade, and even his considerable strength couldn't get past it. He tried a couple of times, then gave up. I knew he had to go to work, and I was counting on that enforced loyalty to save me. Sure enough, he and Cora had some words, he drank his coffee and went out. I waited a half hour after I heard him leave, then quickly broke down my home-made fortifications and beat it out of the house. Stayed away all day.

UCLA was on the other side of the continent, and that was fine with me. From the moment I announced my intention to attend, held my first press conference, and told them UCLA had "everything I want in a school," I was already out there. School was almost over; my stay at home was short-term. I had my own summer ahead of me for the first time since seventh grade, no Friendship Farm exile. I breezed through finals and said my good-byes to Power like shaking hands on the run; a month later it was a year behind me.

One of the first things UCLA did for me was get me a job. Mike Francovich, a movie producer and loyal alumnus, arranged for me to work at Columbia Pictures in New York. It was not much of a gig, mostly delivering interoffice memos or sitting around soaking up atmosphere, but I took home $125 a week, and that gave me the cash I needed to stay out of my parents' way. I saved what I could for the California days ahead and had some money for dates and music.

But the summer after senior year was really a treat because I could finally play in the Rucker Tournament. With no high school restrictions and not yet officially enrolled in college, I signed up and matched up against the legends. Had to see what I could do.

Just to be safe I played under an assumed name, as if they didn't know it was me. I was "El Khan," and I played with Charlie Scott, Earl "the Goat" Manigault, one of the playground immortals, Rick Cobb, and a guy named Onion who hung out with Earl. We did some intense warring with the other young street ballplayers.

We played Brooklyn, with Jim Tillman and Jackie Wilson, and they beat us. Bobby Washington dunked on me twice in a row, which was an intended humiliation. The crowd buzzed, and of course, then I had to do the big payback, so, with everybody on the other team trying to block my way to the hoop, I dunked over all of them. I could play this game!

The Philadelphia equivalent of the Rucker was the Baker League, and it was a matter of civic pride to beat their behinds when, after much preparation and arrangement, the Baker boys rolled into town. There were serious bragging rights at stake, so serious that I wasn't even starting; I didn't have the seniority or the game, they brought me in off the bench.

Philly had brought up two busloads of fans, and as the congregation fanned out, they set up this continuous wail that seemed to be coming from everywhere.

"Where's Jesus?"

"Black Jesus!"

"Where's Jesus?"

"I want to see him!"

We were shooting around, or leaning against the wire mesh fence, and what the hell is going on here? It's Baptist time, where are the folding fans and print dresses?

"Black Jesus!"

Then this dark character, six feet three in ratty shorts and a torn T-shirt, wearing one white low-cut sneaker and one black high-top, ambled onto the court. Supposed to be some kind of star. I'd never heard of him.

The game began. Tip-off. Shot. This guy grabbed the rebound. Strange, instead of pushing it up the court and showing what he's got, maybe putting it in someone's face, whoever this dude thinks he is started spinning with the ball—a herky-jerky, stop-and-go challenge in his own defensive end. One of our guards went after him to cut out this bullshit when, we didn't believe it as we saw it, this motherfucker with his own cheering section jumped into the air, did a 360 and, *while he was spinning* fired an overhand, full-court, topspin pass that bounced at the top of the key and, rising, caught his man in stride on the dead run for an easy lay-up.

The crowd went nuts.

"Black Jesus!"

"I saw him! I saw him!"

He just trotted back to play some D.

After a quarter I got in the game and ultimately our big guys were too tough for them, but the man with the bizarre sense of style played some basketball I had never seen.

Black Jesus. Turns out he was Earl Monroe.

6

I was shooting a lot of 35mm the day I left for college. I snapped my parents, the projects, some of the guys from the neighborhood. Maybe I was documenting my departure to prove to myself that I'd really made it out, or perhaps I was hedging my emotional bets by keeping some of the city with me. I was glad to be leaving, excited to be getting out of the house at last, but I wasn't saying much. After all the waiting, all the clocking in and marking of time, I made no false starts. Somewhere down inside I felt great, but I couldn't let anyone know. If I'd been all emotional in front of my friends, it wouldn't have gone over well. One, guys didn't do that, and, two, I might have offended them by flaunting my escape while they had none. I wouldn't wound my folks by telling them how happy I was finally to be free of their clutches. I could only kiss them good-bye, assure them I'd be all right, and walk out the door. School, the ladies, the streets—I was ready for a change. I went to California with no strings attached.

Everybody had always wanted to go to California. Back in grade school and junior high we'd all spend Wednesday nights glued to the tube watching Walt Disney and then replay it the whole next day. At St. Jude's, Michael Farrell had made us all happy-jealous by taking a trip to Disneyland, shooting some home movies and showing them to the class. From the Mickey Mouse Club through the Aquanauts and Lloyd Bridges on *Sea Hunt*, everybody wanted to go.

Kelly went with me. He had been a city champion in the mile relay and was supposed to run a year of track for Santa Monica City College and then switch over to UCLA. He says he remembers me looking out the window as our plane landed, sort of a faraway glaze on my eyes, but I only recall the air-conditioning chill down the corridors and then, as I stepped outside, the midday swirl, low skyline, and the rustle of those airport palm trees. You never saw the projects sway in the breeze.

I found the dorm and found that I'd been expected. The school newspaper that spring had run some big pictures, and it appeared that the campus was mobilized and ready for another year of great basketball. As I walked in and got the first of those bright California strangers' greetings—blond people clearly astonished at my height, each wanting to be the first to make contact, each with friendly words trying to say more than they could actually come up with ("Hey, welcome to LA, man")—I knew immediately that meeting people would be no problem. It took only a month until I was thinking of ways to avoid them.

An only child, used to the splendid isolation of my own room, my Cloister, never having had to share a bathroom let alone my entire daily life with anyone my own age, I was not at home in the public privacy of a dormitory. The guys on the hall were definitely curious, and I got more stares in one trip to the Student Union

122

than in a month of subways, but my first night in LA I didn't make any contact at all. Just ate my dinner, went back to my room, lay down and fell asleep.

The next morning it was Sunday, and I woke up to the ringing of my telephone. I didn't have the faintest idea who could want me this early, this soon.

"Hello?" I grunted.

"Lew Alcindor? Hi. This is the front desk. The athletic department has asked us to tell you, since you are Catholic, that mass will be held at the Newman Center this morning."

"Oh."

"We wanted to be sure you knew. If you need directions how to get there, we'll be glad to show you the way."

"Um hmm."

"Have a nice day."

I put down the phone and went back to sleep. I was eighteen, and that was the first Sunday in my life I'd intentionally missed going to mass. I never went again. I was out of the house altogether.

When I finally woke up, I went over and got some breakfast, picked up the paper, and took a walk around the campus. It was bright and beautiful. Classes hadn't started yet, so most people were just hanging out, sitting on the grass. This was, no doubt about it, not New York. First off, everybody said hello like they knew you. Pretty little girls in Bermuda shorts and short-sleeved yellow blouses, Beach Boy prototypes with streaked and wavy hair, Oriental guys who sounded the same as the beach boys, a couple of sisters—they'd all smile up as if expecting to tan from my sunny disposition.

At first I tried to be amiable. Who were these people, and, they didn't know me, why did they like me?

"Hello," I said as I passed.

"Hi!" "Hi!" "Good morning!" "Gee, you're tall." I was on parade.

In New York people had hardly looked up and, if

they did, had figured I was too big or too alien to mess with and had basically left me alone. I had either stayed on familiar ground or ventured out safe in the knowledge that in New York even in the street you are in your own world. You can bet this kind of nonstop sweetness and light wouldn't have happened at the NYU uptown campus.

Everybody wanted to know me. At UCLA, athletes were like movie stars, and in a town built on celebrity there were well-proscribed circles to run in. All this had been done by generations of starting ballplayers before me, so the way was well paved. While most incoming freshmen were going through their Indoctrination Week, I was escorted through mine. I had loved football since I was in grade school (never played it because my father was afraid I would get injured), had been a hard-core Giants fan, and spent more than my fair share of time in front of the tube for bowl games and playoffs. Now here I was at a school that was a perennial contender for the Rose Bowl; did I want to head over to practice? An adolescence full of running with the big guys had taught me how to maintain my cool, but though I didn't show it, I was very excited to get down on the turf and watch the team work out.

On the practice field the squad was broken into offense and defense, each in final preparation for the season opener only a week or so away. Power had never had a football team, and I didn't know the first thing about how a practice was structured or run. I was out there as a fan, picking up details with first-time-through eyes. Gary Beban was looking cocky running the team from quarterback. The linemen looked nervous behind their face guards, not as impenetrable as on TV. The coaches were white and yelling at everybody.

I walked over to the gym. Basketball practice hadn't started, but I was ready for a game. Some of the guys and I shot around. It wasn't 155th Street, but even that first day, everybody on the court had something to prove.

124

Four of us incoming freshmen played four guys from the varsity, full-court; we were going to get taught about class awareness.

We played to fifteen baskets and beat them three games running. It was the first time I'd seen Lucius Allen play, and I was very impressed. Lucius was a high school All-America guard from Kansas City, and he was my roommate. We had gotten to know each other in the past couple of days from talking in the dorm about girls and basketball and school, but I hadn't been able to tell much about what kind of a ballplayer he might be; guys will talk a lot of stuff, but you can't really judge till you see them on the court. Lucius, it was immediately obvious, was a player. He was extraordinarily quick, had the great shot, was driving around people; nobody could guard him. We'd beaten them twice, with Lucius burning them from the outside, when Edgar Lacy got tired of the unexpected humiliation and said, "Let me guard this guy." Lucius took the ball out, faked the jumper getting Edgar off his feet, then drove around him and lay the ball up nice on the other side of the basket. Edgar was an A-1 defensive player on the defending national championship team, and he could not deal with it. Right away I liked the chances of the class of '69.

The locker room was the athletes' meeting ground. On campus everybody had his own way of being a hero, and both the school and the students encouraged you to go for it. But the locker room hierarchy was higher still. There were the leaders' leaders, and it was pretty easy, even from the first, to see how things were run. Heroism was seasonal, and so football players ran the roost in the fall, into the winter if they had the New Year's date. After that it was our turn ... and not before. Which was all right with me; I was only learning how it was done.

I met Mel Farr in the locker room. Mel was an All-America running back on the UCLA football team. He was about six feet three inches tall, 220 pounds, great big shoulders and arms, slender waist, powerful thighs and calves. If you wanted an anatomy class to see a perfect male physique, show them Mel; the dude looked like Hercules. I looked at him, looked at me waiting to fill out, and said, "Holy mackerel."

Mel was a friendly guy from Texas with that slow southern amiability about him, and we got to talking, hit it off. One night he said, "Come on, we're going to a party." It was still a week before classes started, and there were lots of little gatherings, there was a mood to establish. I was from New York, I figured I knew about that.

What I didn't know was that football players are crazy. We got to the house, one of these condo complexes, and everybody got drunk in a hurry. There was loud music and blonde women, white guys, black guys, some serious bodies on all of them. I reached for my cola and found a seat. (No use in attracting attention when there's all this to be taken in first time.) Loud and beefy backslapping, very unhip. Boisterous, none of that carry-your-world-with-you New York reserve. Didn't anybody have any cools out here?

It was a UCLA party, but some guys from the University of Southern California showed up. This was a blood rivalry that I later came to understand. The schools are crosstown rivals and diametrically opposed to each other in theory and practice. USC is a private institution filled largely with wealthy white kids. It's situated in the middle of black ghetto Los Angeles. UCLA, on the other hand, is a public school filled with all varieties of third-world types as well as beach boys; it's open, it's not an elitist place, but it sits between the extremely high-bracket communities of Westwood and Bel Air, which is uptown to say the least. Football games between the two schools were like class warfare.

So these Southern Cal jokers showed up, and the UCLA crowd didn't like their looks. One UCLA supporter, home visiting his brother on a day off during the NFL season, made a point of picking a fight with one of the intruders. While they were arguing, another UCLA partygoer came up from behind and slapped the USC guy in the head. Sucker punched him. The whole damn place broke loose. It was like being back in the Bronx, except all of these guys ran 220 pounds or more. People were getting hit over the head with bottles, knocking over lamps, crashing into furniture. Somehow it got out the door; they were punching it out on the balcony. This was Los Angeles, so there was a central courtyard, and some people were still fighting when they fell into the pool.

I found a couple of black students from UCLA, and they said, "Think we'll go back onto campus," and we beat it the hell out of there. These people were nuts!

Apparently this kind of thing wasn't uncommon. I heard stories about how a whole bunch of guys had raped some girl, but she had consented far enough down the road, so it wasn't what they called "really" rape; just all of a sudden she had found herself isolated with a guy who wasn't going to take no for an answer, and she ended up having to give it up.

Strange fellows. In my dormitory they had this ritual. Our hallway was about four feet wide and fifty yards long, and all the rooms opened out onto the main corridor. They would flood the floor, get fire buckets or a garden hose and just lay a half inch of water over one whole end of it, then get naked, take a long run and kick up a wake sliding bare-ass down the hall. This is what they did on Friday and Saturday nights. Coming from New York this isn't what you wanted to see. I was a freshman, but as far as being streetwise or even vaguely adult, I was much older than these guys who were twenty, twenty-one, twenty-two. Living in dorms and acting like this, it was beyond me.

Here I'd thought I was going to the land of milk and honey—sunshine, big-time athletics, big-time academics, the intellectual elite of the country—but all autumn long I was in pronounced culture shock. In New York I had been hanging out with Kelly, going down to the Village and the Lower East Side to hear jazz, and I guess

I craved the bohemian look. I was running around Southern California with a tweed jacket, wire-rimmed shades, jeans—the real Village shot—and the rest of these people were into the California Ivy League, button-down shirts, chinos, penny loafers. We had a hard time connecting.

Everybody wanted to meet me, but I very quickly became less and less interested in meeting them. Fortunately, I found a small circle of friends, and among ourselves we did more commenting on the campus scene than participating in it. Edgar Lacy, the varsity forward whom I had met on *Ed Sullivan* several years earlier and who had shown me around on my visit, became a close companion. We knew we liked each other right away, sensed those intangibles about a guy's character that you just feel, like when you assume something strikes him as quirkily amusing just the way it does you, and you're right. But I was developing a special focus on being black, seeing the campus, the nation, the world as a black man first and foremost, and when I found we shared those assumptions as well—that whites were hard to read and harder to trust, that all blacks should be brothers, that you could expect trouble before you could expect peace—then we became really tight.

I also met an upperclassman named Jimmy Johnson. Jimmy was an A student, a brilliant young man who, aside from excelling in academics, liked to listen to jazz, read poetry, hang out, and make the rounds. When I brought out my record collection and played him some Archie Shepp, some Eric Dolphy, and some of the new things John Coltrane was getting into, I found I'd opened up new worlds for him and that brought us even closer. Jimmy, in turn, introduced me to black Los Angeles. He was from South Central LA, the heart of the ghetto that had burned just as I had watched Harlem burn. I didn't have a car, and some weekends Jimmy would invite me home.

I couldn't believe it. Harlem, with its weathered brownstones and abandoned brick buildings, is the prototype American ghetto. You could feel anger on the streets, watch hopelessness blow by like empty cigarette packs off tenement steps. In South Central L.A., people had their own houses with more than two bedrooms and front yards full of grass. Lawns in the ghetto! There was anger, but it seemed somehow more focused here. Where New York lived in rage and futility, LA combined wrath with pride. Black people here didn't brush their hair hard forward into ripples like buckled concrete, they flaunted its kinky curls, turned fact into beauty. People wore their Afros with defiance: That's right, I can walk around with all this on my head *and you will pay attention to me*!

When I met Jimmy I found the person I needed to know. We talked seriously for hours at a time about the pride we *should* feel in being black, about how little we had been taught about ourselves, and how much there was to know. I told him about the Schomburg, and we talked long and hard about Malcolm X. Seems like Jimmy and I were always talking, and the longer I lived in Southern California the more we had to talk about.

At UCLA I very quickly got the impression from some of my teachers and fellow students that not a lot was expected out of me in the world of academics. Either because I was an athlete or because I was black—probably both—there seemed to be a clear assumption that I wouldn't be up to the work. The school conducts what it calls a Subject A test, basic fundamentals of English, which one is required to pass in order to enter freshman year. All new, foreign, or transfer students are required to demonstrate that they can competently make themselves understood in English. We were put in a big classroom, given several alternative topics and a three-hour time limit, and asked for an essay of four or five hundred words.

I knocked it out in about thirty-five minutes. I said to myself, "Wow, this is all you've got to do to get into college?" I walked to the administration table at the front of the room and asked, "Is that all?" They said yes, and I turned to leave. A couple of the guys on the basketball team watched me get up, and I guess one of the instructors saw me about to leave early, probably thought, "He thinks he's getting away with something," because he went and snatched my blue book off the top of the pile and began to read it. I must have done reasonably well because I never heard from them again, and I didn't have to take Subject A.

I started college as an English major, and among the courses I enrolled in freshman year were English Composition and History of the Theater. The theater arts course began with early man dancing around campfires in animal costumes and worked through Elizabethan times to the present. It was held in a large lecture hall, and then the three hundred enrollees were divided into what were called quiz sections of about twenty students. You had to be on the ball because they'd throw a quick exam at you in a second, but I liked this stuff.

One day early in the first semester the teaching assistant who was running our section was laying down a long and involved discourse about the nature of man, and the theater as the first control of aggression, when she pointed to me and said, "Mr. Alcindor, what is your opinion on this matter?" There was the usual hush as most of the students glad-rushed that she hadn't called on them and then expected me to fall on my face. But I had done my reading and was ready, quoted the text, ran it right back at her. I didn't think much of the confrontation, figured, hey, this is college, everybody gets treated like that. Years later one of my classmates, Dave Thoreau (*Henry David Thoreau*, his parents did that to him), told me, "I always liked you after that, you really put her in her place." But I wasn't being hostile, I was just trying to handle whatever was thrown my way. And bit by bit I think I gathered some respect as my teachers found out I was at least a competent student.

In English class the instructor, Mr. Lindstrom, told us to write a descriptive essay on anything we pleased. I was in a bind; there was nothing within my immediate line of vision—the dorm, the campus, the state—that I really felt inspired to describe. I had some music on, and I started daydreaming about New York and the scene and the clubs. . . .

In my essay I tried to bring the Village Vanguard, the quintessential jazz club, to life for me. Max Gordon is at the door ushering us with a brusque warmth into this basement grotto below Seventh Avenue. The ceiling is low even for a person of normal height, and I can never stand up fully, making the small, stuffy room even more of a cocoon than it would already be. The red walls are covered with autographed photos of the greats of jazz— Charlie Parker, Thelonius Monk, Sonny Rollins—all of whom have made this room come alive with their music. The Charles Lloyd Quartet is wailing on the bandstand, which is only slightly raised from the floor as if to empha- size the spiritual closeness between those who play this music and those who truly dig it. . . .

The next week my essay was the one selected for reading and analysis by the class. I was surprised, and very proud. I had never doubted my facility with the language, but I was glad to find out that the step from the academic confines of Power to the vastness of UCLA was one I could take in stride.

My major classroom revelation was my constant contact with young women. I hadn't been in a classroom with a girl since eighth grade—Power was all boys and male teachers, the only women in the school being these gargoyles in the lunchroom and a secretary—and I had not really been Mr. Personality on the social scene. I'd never been around girls on a daily basis, and I'd always had basketball, school, and my parents to overcome. I had no idea even how to talk to them as if they were people. I did a lot of looking—at UCLA they came in all shapes, colors and sizes; it was like being in a candy store—but I had a very hard time with the most elemen- tary conversations. Every one was like breaking new ground. It wasn't only that I wanted to grab all the pretty ones, though there was that too, I just didn't know how to begin to make contact.

So I was more than a little pleased when, after the bell rang and the period was over, one of my classmates, Lynn Parmitter, came up beside me and asked, "Would you like to go have some coffee?" Lynn was a dream: brunette, tall and leggy at five feet nine, a great figure and a lovely, lovely face. A real knockout. I was sitting there in my literary afterglow and felt it pale next to the unexpected warmth of her invitation.

"Uh, sure," I swallowed, then couldn't find more to say. I palmed my books, stood, ducked my head as I went through the doorway, and we walked on down the hall. What did she want with me?

I had gotten used to being looked at in corridors, on the street, out of doors; it had been a constant since third grade, and most times I had learned to tune it out. But now, as I walked eyes ahead waiting for I didn't know what to begin, I was peculiarly self-conscious, as if everyone knew I had this extremely attractive white girl at my side and were staring their disapproval. Outside the building I picked up my stride. Lynn trotted to keep up. When I noticed, I slowed down.

"I enjoyed your essay," she said as we walked, "it was a really good piece of work. It made me feel like I was almost there."

"Oh, good," I answered. Should I go further? Was she interested in hearing about how I wrote it, my daydream? Or would that be too egotistical, telling her the roots of the story as if it had won some kind of prize? Or not cool enough? Boring? I said no more.

We sat over coffee and talked. She had that charmer's ability to overlook silences and assume a warm interest even if none was really showing. She had read my story and knew there was somebody home inside me and made an unthreatened effort to find out who that was. She refused to let the conversation drop, to let me slide into my discomfort; without being foolishly chatty she talked to me until I began to talk to her.

We stayed there for an hour, and I knew she liked me, felt she liked me for the right reasons as well, which was important. She wasn't just some locker room mama, she was the real deal. But I was eighteen, and I didn't know how to keep up with a real woman on my own. I'd always had to go home and be someone's child. I didn't have any grasp on how to act with confidence, be entertaining, let her see me. Girls were for getting some—I'd gotten some; I knew—not for being friends. Certainly not for both.

I'm sure Lynn would have gone for a walk with me, maybe a movie that evening, but when finally in the late afternoon the conversation did lag, I got nervous. "Oh, I . . . I'll see you later," I told her and headed back to the dorm. I must have been quite a strange type of guy to her, but all I could think of was negative, the reasons why we would never get along. I thought it was hopeless. She was ideal for one of the white guys who picked up these surfer girls like riding a wave, I figured, and they were ideal for her. Hey, if I couldn't keep a conversation going with her for an hour, how was I supposed to handle a date? I wasn't disappointed, because just getting her to sit with me over coffee had been an accomplishment. I'd taken a few steps on the verandah of the Taj Majal. Fool, why didn't you go in? I'd thought, "Gee, I got this far, I'd better just ease."

Lynn and I saw each other in class, but I never went out with her. Even to this day I regret it. If there ever was a Miss Wonderful, she filled the bill.

As soon as basketball practice started, it tried to take over my life. UCLA had had a successful recruiting year, with five high school All-Americans on the freshmen squad, but with all this talent there were still fundamentals to be taught, discipline instilled, a team to be formed. Gary Cunningham coached the freshmen, but he ran it strictly by Coach Wooden's dictates. All the drills were on file cards and timed almost to the second. While the varsity was going through their paces behind a giant partition at one end of the gym, we would have two minutes of lay-ups, two minutes of reverse lay-ups from both sides, five minutes of ball-handling drills, fast foot drills, passing the ball for the open jumper, shooting drills, bank shot drills, ball handling on the fast break for lay-ups, ball handling on the fast break for jump shots, shooting drills combining everything up and down the court. Everyone did everything: The guards took the big man drills, the big men worked at the guards' drills. Every big man wants the short man's versatility, just like it drives the little guys crazy to get the tip-in off the rebound, and Coach Wooden gave us those exercises as both a rehearsal and a treat. The entire workout was timed to the minute, day in and day out. You could videotape practice from one day to the next and not have them run out of sync.

I also had some special instruction. For intensive mental and physical conditioning, Coach Wooden had brought in a former Oregon State player and coach, Jay Carty, to make a point of running me through the more subtle and demanding parts of the game. Jay put me through agility drills, throwing a ball up off the extreme right-hand side of the backboard, which I would rebound, then throw it to the extreme left and run to rebound that, back and forth, to strengthen my lateral movement. He chalked a mark eighteen inches over the rim (eleven-and-a-half feet off the ground) and had me jump and touch it twenty times in succession with either hand every day. He made me dunk the ball from the free throw line—a running start but no foot allowed in the lane, a fifteen-foot flight for the stuff. I could never quite get all the way; eighteen inches in was my best leap. I've got a lot of respect for Bob Beamon, who holds the world's long jump record at over twenty-nine feet. (Of course, he didn't have to make the stuff at the other end.)

134

Carty also played me a lot of one-on-one, shooting me a knee here, a hip, a jolting elbow there. He taught me the ways I would get beaten on, how to avoid it, accept it, respond to it. He and the coaches thought basketball might be too easy for me and that I might stop concentrating. They had nothing to worry about.

From October to April I was tired. My stamina in high school had been excellent, but now every day after practice I had to go back to my room and sleep for a while, or I was no good to anybody. It cut down on my hanging out, but it definitely made me stronger and tougher. I was still growing—from seven feet when I entered college to a little under seven feet two inches when I graduated—but I was putting on muscle, and I needed it.

My hook shot was coming along by itself. I practiced it during the free shoot and in scrimmages. Coach Wooden did not work with the freshmen, but when he looked in on my private practices with Carty he called my shot a "flat hook." I never understood the term, but I must have been shooting it on a low trajectory. Mr. Wooden suggested that, because of my height, I shoot my free throws on a flat trajectory as well, so as to ease the ball in and give it a higher percentage chance at a friendly roll if it caught the rim.

I did learn to shoot a high-trajectory hook shot at UCLA, however, and it proved a valuable lesson in the pros. One of my teammates, forward Lynn Shackleford, had this ridiculous-looking left-handed jump shot that came off one shoulder like a shot-put and mooned almost straight up until it dropped down with amazing accuracy into the hoop. He'd can these from twenty feet out in the corner, all net, all night. We'd joke about it, the weirdest shot on earth, but when I turned and tossed up this rainmaker hook, and it started to fall in like it was going down a funnel, I liked that a lot.

Freshman basketball season was all about one game: us against the varsity. UCLA had won its second consecutive NCAA national championship only six months before, was returning a sizeable portion of its squad, and was ranked number one in the preseason polls. We had heard a lot of talk about what was expected of us, and as cocky kids fresh out of extremely successful high school careers, we thought we could take them, but we never really took it seriously. The other side of the partition was the big time, so the only big game would be the first one, and we were ready.

UCLA fans are rabid, and they were jammed in for the first game played in the new Pauley Pavilion. The freshmen in the stands were screaming with class pride; everybody else was just very curious. So were we.

The game was never close. Wooden teams thrived on the zone press, each player aggressively defending his area with help from whichever teammate was nearest, making even bringing the ball upcourt a difficult adventure. But these were *two* Wooden teams, and not only could the varsity not handle our press, we could break theirs at will. I would position myself at the free throw line, take the inbounds pass, and get it quickly to Lucius Allen who was cutting. Lucius either found the other guard with his passes or used his speed and finesse to bring the ball across midcourt; he could break their trap all by himself.

The varsity had no one able to guard me in close, so they had to sag their defense to prevent me from getting the ball. When they did not get there quickly enough, I scored. When they sent two men at me, I passed the ball back out to Lucius or Lynn Shackleford, and they killed them from outside. When the varsity ran back out to cover our shooters, I was open again. There was no defense against us. I scored thirty-one points, and we won by fifteen.

When we beat the national champs we said, "We must be *pretty* good," but we never got a chance to test it. Our schedule called for us to play other freshmen, junior varsities, and junior colleges in Southern California; we never got further away than San Diego. It was a lark, like a year off. We won all twenty-one of our games and not one of them was close.

So basketball was not the most important element of freshmen year. Getting out of the house was. And when our season was finally over I had, for the first time since St. Jude's, my life to myself. My only obligation was to do decently in class, and schoolwork was taking care of itself, so I had no worries on any score. No parents, no coaches, no church—I was free! I became extremely independent, probably in an exaggerated way. Mainly what I did was try and have as good a time as I could.

Coming out of an all-boys school and landing at UCLA, which is central casting for the Miss Wonderful contest, I must have seemed very strange to the ladies. All through basketball season, as visible as I was, I never really made contact. I had never known girls as people, and I had such crazy ideas about them—the Saints or Whores syndrome, where if a woman lets you like and touch her, she is forever after unlikeable and untouchable— that the whole process became a learning experience. Though I went out with some very nice young ladies, I didn't learn much. I basically hung out with the guys.

That spring, 1966, the new rage turned out to be LSD.

The white guys had the acid. They were over at some guy's house capping it, putting the drops of liquid into capsules to be sold, when I dropped over.

"What's this all about?" I asked.

"We gotta make our money so we can get up to San Francisco this summer," one of them told me. "July first, everybody's gonna be in San Francisco." This was May so they were deep into the production cycle. They were also very high. It was warm, and their hands were sweaty, and the acid would melt as they parceled it out and get into their pores, and they'd just be sitting there sopping up that acid, getting royally blown away. What was this stuff?

Tabs were two dollars and fifty cents apiece, so I bought two. I got back to my dorm room, and a friend and I took a little nibble from one of them. We got off—we were definitely not sober—but we didn't get *off* off, so we decided that the coming weekend, since we had some time, we'd do it right.

That Saturday we dropped a whole tab each and got crazy. It was a gorgeous clear blue day that had shimmered even before we started, now it was simultaneously dead still and shaking like mad. We called another compadre, and he came with his car and chaperoned us up into the mountains. There were jet-stream trails behind everything that moved—my hand, my friend's whole body, cars that passed us on the road—and we rushed and tripped and somehow found more than an earthly significance to it all. We sat on rocks high above Los Angeles and wondered aloud among ourselves about where the sun came from, what life really meant, where was Lynn Parmitter? We talked about race, the difference between black and white, cosmic realities, cosmic myths. We were nineteen and I loved it.

I got friendly with one of the hippies who was into this bizarre new substance, and three weekends in a row I went out driving with him while he made the rounds: At that time Wolfman Jack was broadcasting on a pirate radio station out of Mexico, selling hash pipes and mail-order roach clips. We were bombing around one night when we turned on the Wolfman and started to laugh. We listened to him and roared for three solid hours, this raspy lunatic who knew we were stoned, just *out there*, and talked in this growling be-bop language all night long. In between he'd be playing James Brown and all this really great rhythm and blues you'd never hear anywhere else, but it was his voice that kept cracking us up. Weeks later when we found out the Wolfman was not black, my friend wouldn't believe it. "I don't want to hear that shit!" he insisted. "This man is not white!"

But after four or five trips, what I ultimately learned

from acid was that I did not need to take acid. When you're high everything feels unnatural, all your central perceptions are heightened to a point where they are not simply being received by your brain but are assailing it, a constant information overload. It can be frightening. I never panicked because I never did that much of it—one tab was my limit—but at a certain point it can get depressing: like, when you've been in that state for forty-five minutes and you say, "Wow, this is enough," and it's going to be that way for four more hours. It's hard to cope with; you can get very anxious. I understand how people would freak out; here you are with this stuff coursing through your body and no end in sight.

I didn't do much acid after freshman year. I found that I'd learn enough just by living in a normal state of consciousness and concentrating, applying my intelligence to what I wanted to know. Plus, I didn't want to worry about my chromosomes. By junior year I'd stopped tripping altogether.

More significant than any mind-altering drug was the overwhelming change in perspective I found when I read *The Autobiography of Malcolm X*. I'd been aware of Malcolm in New York, heard his name called during the riots, listened when he would call the black AM radio station at the top of the dial on Sunday nights and declare all white people devils. I also knew he had broken with the Black Muslims and, little more than a year earlier, been murdered by them. Jimmy Johnson, whose opinion I respected in all matters, had spoken very highly of him as a man who was proud to be black, but I was unprepared for the effect his life would have on mine.

I couldn't put the book down but didn't want it to end. All I did the week I bought it was go to class and come home and read. It was exhilarating; all the things I had always assumed, he was saying out loud. His life was like a primer for me; his growth from nigger to man developed as if he could be the race in microcosm.

From the start it touched me very personally. In his foreword, Alex Haley (who collaborated with Malcolm on the book) describes Harlem right before Malcolm's death. This was only fifteen months previous, and sitting in my dorm room, I had New York very fresh in my mind. Malcolm's mother was from Grenada; my people came from Trinidad in the same generation. Malcolm's father was a follower of black nationalist Marcus Garvey; my father remembered his own father and mother talking heatedly about Garvey in their home. Early in the book Malcolm described how no black people were allowed in his hometown of Lansing, Michigan, after dark; I had felt this in New York, seen it in North Carolina. He said black people had been segregated so far out of American life that black history in the American history textbook was one paragraph, but that Crispus Attucks, a black man, was the first person to die in the American Revolution and that black people's contributions to America were a lot more than just working in the fields and doing the hambone.

I knew this! My summer in the Schomburg had taught me some facts, some values, but while I had just pocketed the information and occasionally passed it along in conversation, Malcolm had lived his life by it. He had been born poor, had had to scuffle like most black folks, had gone from a white man's clown to society's outcast—thief, addict, dope dealer, pimp—then found the strength and vision to resurrect himself and, almost from scratch, create (there were no models) a *black man*.

Reading Malcolm made me examine my entire racial thinking. I had supported all movements toward integration—all men, I felt, were created equal—but in his Black Muslim days Malcolm had derided the integration movement's goals. Integrated rest rooms—Did we want to sit down next to white people on the toilet? he asked. Is that a *goal* for blacks? Get served grits by some low-life cracker? Did I want to be just like one of these air-head beach boys?

And were these misdirected goals even reachable? Black people were being denied all access to economic and political power. No jobs. No vote. Especially in the South, where poll taxes were still demanded and registration was made difficult and dangerous, and, beyond that, the black population was being effectively disenfranchised by gerrymandering and outright physical intimidation.

Malcolm said the white man he admired was John Brown, a man who made a stand for black people and was killed by whites. Malcolm was a black man who made a stand for black people and was murdered by blacks. That made it very clear to me that nothing was clear, that I had to look at everything and everybody long and hard. I had always had white friends, and I would continue to, but I now had new criteria with which to judge people. The really hot part of the Sixties was getting ready to start, and I had a unique perspective on it, kept it to myself, on the inside looking out. I'd seen black people betrayed from within and without; there was no one to really trust except Malcolm, and he was dead.

But Malcolm left me a legacy. He had discovered himself through religion, first the distortions of the Black Muslims and then the more compelling teachings of Islam. He made his pilgrimage to Mecca and had his entire life concept altered. He returned and declared he was not a racist; he was definitely opposed to what the collective group of white people had done to the collective group of blacks, and he would not tolerate the racism that had been institutionalized in America, but he no longer considered all white people devils, no longer believed them all inherently evil. And he had realized this through Islam.

I had been totally fed up with Catholicism since midway through my senior year in high school, and Malcolm's revelations made me want to look for my own. Alienated from what I had believed and ignorant of the alternatives, I found myself hungry at the core.

It was a confusing time. I had a very firm grasp of the concepts I didn't like—white authority, unbending rules, false-faced people—but was much less certain where to draw the line in real life. I was wary, and angry that I had to examine everybody I came in contact with—sort of an emotional frisking—because every touch could be a slap. All my reservations became conscious, each chance meeting with a stranger and every introduction by a friend became a potential source of pain. I read all gestures intensively and terribly often found them racially hurtful, therefore personally unacceptable. People who tried too hard to be friendly were being patronizing racists; people who didn't try hard enough were blatant racists. People I didn't know weren't worth knowing; people I did know had to watch their step.

The lecturer in my theater arts course, Hal Marionthal, took an interest in me. Basketball was a hot topic in the school, and here one of the players was in his program, spoke well in class, actually was a good student. He invited me to come to his home for a Sunday brunch. I wasn't sure why he wanted me over, but I held my questions and showed up.

Mr. Marionthal had a nice house in West LA, some greenery, a very pleasant setting for a morning meal. He introduced me to his wife and his son and daughter, and over orange juice and eggs we talked about New York and California, my interest in English, my debating background. A professor was learning about his student, but I wasn't saying anything I hadn't already said.

Later that morning his daughter, Penny, asked if I'd like to take a walk around. Penny was younger than I was, still in high school, and extremely pretty. We excused ourselves and took off on foot for an ambling tour of the community. A teacher's child, she liked having the chance to show off her surroundings and speak like an adult to one of her father's students, but as she was asking me about where I came from, I broke in.

"Hey, look, you don't have to talk to me just because your father asked you to." You're not going to impress me, I thought, just because you're willing to talk to a black guy. It's okay if you've got other things to do.

Her eyes opened wide, and she stammered a surprised denial, but I didn't buy it. No one out here would be friendly with a black kid from New York for no reason. I didn't know what was in it for her, but this had to be a setup. We walked back to the house, and a short while later I went home. She must have told her father, because from that time on he was noticeably cool and I was never invited over again. By the time the school year ended, I was glad to be going home.

I returned to New York and found out I was a neighborhood celebrity. My picture had been in the *Daily News* that winter, me scoring over Rod Taylor from USC, my body totally stretched and extended as I slammed a dunk home. Sandy, a fine piece of business who lived in my building and had not once given me an encouraging word, came up with a big smile and "Oh . . . Lew!" This was going to be all right. The guys hanging out on the corner let me pass by and, when I didn't see them, caught me on the rebound. I was dressed a little different, some light California colors, and they said, "Oh, we thought you was white." But I hung all summer.

UCLA had gotten me a job at Columbia Pictures doing errands. One morning my boss sent me on the train to Baltimore. I got home at six that night instead of five and gave him a bunch of talk about it in the morning. Next thing I know I'm working for Don Kirshner in the record division. But that was cool, because after a while they forgot I was there. I'd check in at the desk each morning, keep going to the freight elevator, go out the back way, head to the subway and go right on back home.

All summer I hung out with the Colleagues, drank wine, smoked reefer, played basketball. Every Sunday was gorgeous, eighty-five degrees, no clouds. My mother wouldn't fix me breakfast because I wouldn't go to church, but the guys and I would hit Riis Beach—all black people— and swim and fool around all day long.

7

I looked to sophomore year like real life was about to begin. The games would be for real; I'd be working with Coach Wooden; I'd get around town and know the ropes. First thing I did when I returned to LA was buy a car and find an apartment. I had been very thrifty with my job money, saved almost the whole thing, so I had the $1100 to plunk down for this great '58 Mercedes 220 two-door box top. Finally mobile, no longer having to rely on other people to make my entrances and exits, I got off campus in a hurry. Edgar Lacy and I rented a two-bedroom place in Santa Monica, a short ride from school, and set up housekeeping. My first attempt at the bachelor life. I didn't go out on dates at all; the girls I saw it was, Your place or mine.

The basketball team was primed for the season. Coming off an undefeated freshman year and finally under the direct instruction of Coach Wooden himself, we expected a great deal from ourselves—the whole team—and we were ready to have fun in the process. The talent on our squad was deep and intense, but even before practice started we found we had to make some adjustments. Edgar Lacy, who had been projected as our starting forward, cracked his kneecap and would be unable to play the entire season. Mike Lynn, another upperclassman starting forward, got busted for allegedly using a stolen credit card and was banished for a year. What had promised to be a team that blended speed and power, youth and experience, was stripped of its front court and its seniors. Coach Wooden was faced with the necessity of starting four sophomores and one junior, guard Mike Warren. We had to grow up fast.

John Wooden sees basketball as a very simple game, and it is his unique talent to hone that simplicity toward perfection. His whole idea is to run with the basketball, beat the defense down the court, play good defense yourself, and get the easiest shots you can get. That's it. We drilled just the way we had drilled the year before, by the numbers, but this season what had been learned responses became natural ones. Mr. Wooden believed in supreme conditioning and unwavering fundamentals, not only knowing which plays to run and how to run them but being capable of calling up the physical and emotional stamina at the precise time you need it to win. Application is his guiding light, being tired all the time, accepting whatever pain is necessary in order to achieve your goal.

Mr. Wooden had an eye and mind that saw the game as if from above. He would drill us fiercely and expect dedication; he accepted no less. Dressed like his players in T-shirt, shorts, sweat socks and sneakers, with his jacket that read "Coach" on the back and a whistle around his neck, he would find our errors, our indecisions, and correct them. He never rode people; he treated everyone the same and displayed no favoritism, but you didn't want to make the same mistake twice. When he'd get mad he'd say, "Gracious sakes alive!" and it instilled more fear than any other coach's tirade of obscenities. "That is *not* the way to do it," he would say forcefully, the words careening around the practice gym rafters, and whoever had screwed up would stand there as if he'd been slapped.

He would blow me away sometimes when he'd leave his usual spot on the court and walk all the way up to the roof, sit in the last row and shout down instructions to a coach, who relayed them to us on the floor. It took a long time for me to realize that his comprehension of the game was so thorough that he was up there checking out the dynamics of the whole court and needed exactly that long-shot perspective to complete his study. The game flowed in his mind, and he wanted to be certain he had made it flow exactly the same in flesh and blood.

Mr. Wooden taught self-discipline and was his own best example. His awareness of what was happening in all parts of the game was very acute, but his demeanor was always contained, as if by ordering himself he was controlling all elements. His philosophy, he showed us, was that if you needed emotion to make you perform then sooner or later you'd be vulnerable, an emotional wreck, and then nonfunctional. He preferred thorough preparation over the need to rise to an occasion. Let others try to rise to a level we had already attained; we would be there to begin with. He would smile and be happy when he won, but I never saw him truly exultant; about the only overt expression he would allow himself was the tight twisting of his program, rolled not so much into a weapon as into a handle on the situation.

Mr. Wooden had gathered a good group for his teachings. I had been brought up not to cause trouble, and I still had that inside me, so I was no worry. Mike Warren, a starting guard, had two years under his belt and enjoyed his unexpected seniority. Kenny Heitz and Lynn Shackleford, our starting forwards, were both guys who went by the book. Lucius Allen, however, was another story.

146

Lucius was a brilliant ballplayer—great moves, incredible quickness, excellent shot—but always looking for the easy way out. He was at UCLA to play ball and have a good time; an education would have to sneak up on him. Which is not to say he was stupid. Lucius knows all the openings, options, and strategies of the most extensive and innovative chess theories. Has them memorized and loves to sit down and kick your ass around the chessboard. You figure, nah, this joker can't know much, and then he slams the door on you. But discipline in a game like basketball, which came so naturally to him? Not likely. He gave Coach Wooden a very hard time, and Mr. Wooden responded in kind. The coach would expect us at practice on time—I always showed up early to loosen up and get totally prepared—so, of course, Lucius could be counted on to wander in late. We were supposed to do well enough in class not to endanger our eligibility, by the end of junior year Lucius was scholastically a first-quarter sophomore. Lucius wanted to do what Lucius wanted to do.

Lucius also had no kind of luck. He got busted on May 27, 1967, and a year later, *on the same day*, May 27, 1968, got busted again. The first time he left an ounce of weed in the glove compartment of his car and had the misfortune to have his paper temporary license plate slip from the back window and fall out of sight. The cops thought that the car didn't have plates, towed it away, found the weed, and waited for its owner. Lucius came back, found his car had been taken, and went straight to the police.

"Somebody's stolen my car."

"Oh, it's your car. Come with us."

The second time he was with some people and was holding some pot up high in his sock when their car was pulled over. The cops got him on the third frisk. May 27, 1969, nobody I knew would go anywhere near him.

Lucius just liked to have fun, but he got a reputation. Wherever we played, all the hippies would come out to see him; he was *their* player. He and I once got a letter from a stranger in St. Louis that read, "This is for you, hope you enjoy it." Inside was a fat old joint. We smoked it down.

Our comic relief off the bench came from Jim Nielsen and Bill Sweek. Both were very able basketball players and fun guys to be around. Nielsen was a junior college transfer from the East Valley who was always into a dare and ready with a story about him and the ladies performing unbelievable acts of passion in admirably public places. On one road trip to U. Cal, he challenged Sweek to dive into the hotel pool. It was January in Oakland, but Sweek stripped off his shoes and sport coat, dived into the unheated water, won twenty bucks and immediately brought down the wrath of Coach Wooden.

Sweek was a fun-loving, upbeat southern Californian with a lot of nerve. Always saw the bright side of life, had the good positive outlook. He'd do things like date one girl and then take out another in the same sorority and have them both go for it, keeping his flame and his secret. He was also kind of a social provocateur, like when he found out that Mike Warren had gone out the year before with the girl Jim Nielsen was now dating. Somehow he got a picture of them together, Warren on a couch with his arm around the young lady, and tacked it up on the locker room bulletin board and waited for the fireworks.

There was one fellow, a total creep, who wanted to rush for Sweek's fraternity. Nobody liked him, but he kept coming around and coming around and something had to be done. Finally, they let him take a tour of the frat house, guided, of course, by Sweek.

"This is the kitchen," Sweek informed him as they passed by the chrome freezers. "And this is the dining room where all the brothers take their meals. . . . This is the living room. . . ." They climbed the stairs to the first landing, and Sweek opened one of the bedroom doors. The room was musky and dark and there was this strange rustling. "And this is . . . oops." He rushed the visitor away from the opening, but of course the candidate broke away and peeked inside. In the middle of the floor stood one of the fraternity members, his chinos in a pile at his ankles. Next to him knelt another brother, on his knees.

Needless to say, the persistent rusher never came back. Around the fraternity they laughed about the setup for days. Another kink in the Sweek legend.

Sweek and Nielsen were white boys, but Mike Lynn was the Great White Hope. He started out as just another crazy Californian, member of a fraternity that was UCLA's real Animal House. These dudes were off the wall. They'd rent a yellow school bus to drive to football games, line seven kegs of beer along the back seat and, between twenty-five of them, leave only a keg and a half the next morning. They'd give parties and have a stripper give a floor show. One night my phone rang, but I wanted to sleep and didn't answer it. Found out when I woke up that a bunch of guys had been having a gang bang and had been calling to offer me a place in line. School days.

When Mike got put on probation and suspended from the team for a year, they pulled the plug on him. He got the full white society ostracism. All the people he'd hung out with were suddenly gone, where he once had been cool now nobody would talk to him. He had no status, he was no damn good. A black sheep.

But Edgar, Kelly, and I knew better. Edgar was very much a guy who would go his own way, no matter what Coach Wooden or anybody else would tell him. Eliminate all our friends who'd been busted and we'd have had a hard time getting a good conversation. I knew a whole lot of guys who had been to jail, and Mike didn't even come close. We made Mike an honorary black dude, and he turned out to be a great friend. He knew these crazy hippies, criminals, bikers who would drive a truck three thousand miles from Los Angeles to Oaxaca, Mexico, fill it up with weed and drive it back. With friends like that how bad could a fellow be?

We used to hang out together, take a bunch of controlled substances, listen to music. One time he said, "You know, there's this black guy, I kinda like the way he plays guitar." I put the headphones on and it was Jimi Hendrix, "Purple Haze." I said, "This is a miracle here!" Mike was *persona non grata* around the campus but to us he was "the Hope."

If off the court the team was divided between the calms and the crazies, on the court we were a blend of tenacity and speed. We ran Mr. Wooden's zone press with enthusiasm and had the ball handlers to break whatever defense the opposition threw at us. When the season began we thought we were good but had no idea, beyond our cockiness and unbeaten freshman year, how far we could go. We were ranked number one in the preseason polls, but so was the varsity the year before, and they had faded. People expected us to go all the way—and we talked like we would—but we couldn't really be sure.

I don't know whether Mr. Wooden and his staff had recruited especially hard in order to have a powerhouse team to inaugurate Pauley Pavilion, but he scheduled our first five games in our new arena and immediately established a tradition. Bruin fans had always been zealots, but for us things got fierce. I was astonished to see students lined up in front of the box office two days before season tickets went on sale, doing their homework, throwing frisbees, spending two nights in a sleeping bag. When the games began we wanted to live up to our potential, win, play the season for us and our fans.

Even if it hadn't been the first game of the season, with the national championship finally a real goal and national attention beading on our shoulders like sweat under TV lights, we would have been pumped up to play USC. Our elitist crosstown rivals were looking to smash our domination, to shock and offend us, but they'd never been hit by a team like ours before. Nobody had.

Southern Cal played us man-for-man, a big mistake. I took my defender inside and scored on him. Lucius,

Mike Warren, and Shackleford popped from outside. We took the ball away from them and set ourselves in motion. Our set plays worked when they caught up to us but most of the time we just breezed on by. I scored fifty-six points, a UCLA record, and we won by fifteen.

A couple of days later we played Duke, number seven in the country. They put three guys around me and tried to deny me the ball, but Coach Wooden had planned for that and, with two other guys always open, I passed off most of the night. I scored nineteen points; we won by thirty-four. Duke tried again several nights later, and I got my thirty-eight in a twenty-point victory. We swept our first five at home and headed on up the coast to open our Pac-Eight season. It didn't take long for me to appreciate and like John Wooden.

Coaches fan out over the personality spectrum. Some are disciplinarians who demand respect through fear, others try to be pals and gain it through affection. In all cases a coach's bottom line is respect because once a player is on the court, he must run his coach's plays, roll out his coach's system, with an overwhelming confidence. If the players do not respect the man and the intelligence that calls the shots, they will not perform at their peak. A player must perform for his coach; a coach must inspire performance in his players.

Coach Wooden made us unbeatable in one of the last games of our initial homestand. We were playing Colorado State and having a very hard time. They were big, they ran well, they had good scorers at every position. We were out there, four sophomores and a junior, and we could not pull away. The game was close from the start: We ran, they ran; we hit from the outside, they matched us shot for shot, We were being challenged in the gut, and they were tough. Late in the game we were only up by a basket. But Coach Wooden just took over. He had created the system that had made us a success so far, but this was the first time we needed him for some on-the-spot creativity, and as we listened he came through.

He was always a precise speaker, but in the huddle he enunciated just a little more clearly, spoke a little more loudly. His eyes seemed even more sharply focused; he was *all there*. He called a play and we ran out there, and it worked! He called our defense, and they turned the ball over. He took control of the game. We put ourselves in his hands, and he taught us then and there how to win. He guided us when we really needed it, demonstrated his confidence, then instilled it in us; we'd do it his way, and we would win.

This man was a killer! This mild-looking, middle-aged midwesterner, who could've stepped out of a Pepperidge Farm ad, was a cold-blooded competitor when it came time to put everything on the line. He used his mind, and he understood the game totally. The best he could do was the best there was. We won that game through a combination of technique and will, and for the next three years our confidence in him never wavered. He hadn't earned our respect, he'd defined it. Over the years there were several really tight games that he personally won for us.

We were playing California in a tough game my junior year, and we all wanted to win. There was never a casual attitude about victory; no point in playing if you were going to accept defeat. The game was tight, and with twenty-five seconds left, we scored to go up by two, and Cal called time out. Coach Wooden was speaking crisply and loudly: "All right, now. As soon as they come across half-court, foul them."

I said to myself, "What are we going to foul them for? They might . . ."

"Foul them," he repeated. "If he misses the one-and-one, we've got the game. If he makes it, that's the only two points they can get. They can't get the three-point play. We get the last shot, or we'll win in overtime."

We went out and followed his instructions. The guy made the foul shots, and we beat them by about seven in OT. But I wouldn't have thought of it like that. I would've said, "Try and D up and we've got the game won now." Coach Wooden saw beyond that; he eliminated the possibility of defeat. It was genius! I was tremendously impressed and felt a strong liking for the man.

Apparently he felt something similar because sophomore year he had invited me over to his home for Thanksgiving dinner. That was unusual; I think Lucius and I got the only invitations that season. We got very lost and arrived an hour late, embarrassed that he might think we had intentionally offended him. But he was friendly, talked about New York and school and anything but basketball. Though I never spent any purely social time with him after that—he would befriend athletes but not run their lives—he knew he had my respect.

I did see Coach Wooden shoot pool one time. I should have known he could hustle. We were on the road and, after eating our pregame meal in the student union, found our way over to the campus poolroom. A couple of the guys were trying to look sharp and Lucius put in a few easy shots, when Mr. Wooden said, "Ah, that's niche-picking."

"Oh yeah?" Lucius was shocked. "Well, show us something." He handed over the stick.

Coach Wooden surveyed the table, chalked the cue, and positioned himself for a two-cushion bank shot.

He sank it, drew the ball across the table and left himself a nice follow-up. He was deep! Mr. Wooden took six or seven shots, long angles, combinations, and made all but two. "That's enough," he said and walked away. A lot of raised eyebrows on the squad.

Confidence in the coach, plus our own drive and ability, plowed us through the schedule. We were winning like we were supposed to, and pointing toward the NCAA's. I should have been happy, but there were other pressures that weighted this first ascent.

* * *

My major difficulty was money: I didn't have any. My scholarship covered tuition, room and board, but the dollars that went for a dorm room were nowhere near enough to cover even the minimal rent of the modest apartment Edgar Lacy and I were sharing. Edgar is like a ghost; he haunts a house rather than really living in it, so he was never around. The rent, and the upkeep on my car—which is a necessity in Los Angeles—began to be a considerable financial strain. When the first quarter ended I moved to Pacific Palisades and then, a quarter after that, to Westwood, where I rented a maid's quarters in a condominium building. It was about as big as a small hotel room, with a bathroom, but I put my bed in there and my desk, and my KLH portable AM/FM radio/record player, and lived there for about a year. The room had good radio reception and, equally as critical, it cost twenty-five dollars a month.

Lucius and I were in definite economic distress, and we didn't like it. Here we were in Southern California, where money was status and one's personal value was measured as net worth; we were stars, and we didn't have shit. I had holes in my pants. We were saying to ourselves, "Hey, I'm successful, but I'm still poor. I don't like this." We talked about leaving UCLA, him back to his home state of Kansas and me to the University of Michigan, where some other hinted benefits might come my way. We were grumbling and griping, and we made some sense.

I felt then, and I feel now, that college athletes should be given at least a stipend in return for the services they render to a university. Walk-on athletes, those who pay their own tuition and try out for teams simply for the pleasure of playing, are one thing; they make their own choices. But scholarship athletes, who are recruited by the schools for the express purpose of playing ball, should be paid. A university with a winning team in a major sport like basketball or football is going to make tremendous amounts of money from admissions, concession sales, and television revenues. Alumni contributions rise substantially when the teams are winning, as a result of exposure and prestige. The athletes are in large part responsible for these huge influxes of cash yet not only are they prohibited from sharing in the fruits of their labor, as it stands now, they are often asked to put in both a full day in the classroom and a full day on the field. It's a tough load to carry, and being chronically short of cash doesn't help. That's why you hear of so many bogus jobs and under-the-table arrangements between players and boosters.

At the very least, scholarship athletes should be given a stipend that is sufficient for them to live comfortably, including room, board, and transportation. If you gave them what they deserve, you'd have to give them salaries; they put in a lot of hours and are highly skilled people in a high-visibility arena. Those few who go on to play professional sports have used college as a training ground for well-paying, if not necessarily extended, careers. Those who are not so fortunate—that large percentage of starting offensive linemen or defensive backs, or guards, centers, and forwards—have had their talents used by the schools to great monetary advantage, with nothing monetary to show for their efforts. A college education is rarely foremost in any of the principals' minds when a school's recruiter offers a high school athlete a scholarship. It's emotion on one side and dollars on the other. The dollars should be divided more evenly.

I felt the educational crunch and changed my major to history when I found that English majors would be required to write a paper every week. No way I could practice, study, concentrate fully on basketball, and write so frequently. I also found a way to ease my financial stress, and I met Sam Gilbert at the same time.

Sam is a builder who knew the whole town as far as business was concerned. He has in recent years gotten a bad reputation, which he does not deserve. But Sam was a very valuable and influential friend to me. He never did anything illegal; all he did was ignore the NCAA's economic restrictions about helping athletes. He was like everybody's grandfather, got us stuff wholesale, knew where to get inexpensive tires for your car or a cheap apartment. I was griping, and Sam tried to help me grow up. He said, "Listen, somebody should tell you this because, look at your situation." My father had never had any great amounts of money; he was a working man and his budget planning extended for two weeks at a time, from one paycheck to the next. I knew I wanted some serious finance but I had no idea where to get it or how to put it to work. Sam tried to tell me what it meant to construct a budget, capitalize on tax advantages, build an overview of financial considerations. He knew that pretty soon I'd be getting a lot of money, and he took it upon himself to get me ready.

He got off doing it, and he helped many UCLA athletes and others over the years. He orchestrated Lucius Allen's induction into the National Guard when Lucius was flunking out of school and they were warming up a spot for him in Danang. Sam was that odd combination, a cagey humanitarian with a lot of muscle. Guys would go to him when they were in trouble, and he would find a way to fix it. What he got out of it was an association with success; I got a man who helped me grow up. We talked for hours about the things that really mattered: racism, socialism, the human condition, sex (although he was at least thirty years older than I was, Sam considered himself a real cocksman and had to have enjoyed being taken seriously in what I at the time considered a young man's game).

Sam steered clear of John Wooden, and Mr. Wooden gave him the same wide berth. Both helped the school greatly. Sam helped me get rid of my tickets, and once the money thing got worked out, I never gave another thought to leaving UCLA.

One thing that never did get worked out during my entire college career was my relationship with the press. During high school Coach Donohue had made the decision that whatever contact I would have with sports reporters was to be very infrequent and always under his supervision. His feeling was that a high school boy would not benefit from the attention, distraction, and potential disruption the press would offer. I went right along with him. By the time I got to college I was more mature, but the demand had outleaped my ability to handle it. Nobody—not me, not the UCLA athletic department, not the press—had any experience with a situation like mine because nothing like this had ever happened before. Every sports writer in the area, plus all the national magazines, radio and television networks wanted time. I could have given an interview to a different writer every day for months on end and still not satisfied everybody. No way I was going to do that. I needed my own time just to practice and study, and if it came to choosing between an interview and a good time, there was no choice at all.

Coach Wooden never allowed freshmen to be interviewed, so I had a year's reprieve, but sophomore year some system had to be devised to deal with the copy crush. I wasn't totally disinterested—as a former English major I was appreciative of the written word, particularly when it was about me—but I approached my first interviews more than cautiously. Postgame locker room talks were simple, if boring: Hear the same questions, give the same answers. But the "in-depth" discussions were more of a struggle. My interrogators, screened by the UCLA athletic department and approved by me, were mostly white strangers, and it became clear very early in our relationship that we had differing ideas of what was important. The obligatory basketball questions got old as soon as they were asked, yet each reporter trotted out his share as if he had just discovered Socrates. I was more interested in talking about black people and our mistreatment by America, but most of the writers were not sympathetic, and even those who were found it difficult to say so in their articles. I was in no mood to play the good boy for all those white readers, and when I became impatient with a writer's banal sports bias, they took my boredom for sullenness and were personally offended. When I found a writer to be either an outright bigot or, more often, an unthinking or unfeeling fool, I responded to his hostility with a solid dose of my own. I started getting written up as an ill-mannered, inconsiderate, grunting colossus. To hell with this, I said, and shut down completely. My world was closing.

The basketball team won all of our twenty-six games in 1966–67 and moved through the NCAAs with little worry. We were expected to win every game, and about halfway through the season it was apparent to us that we would. Victories became routine. We beat run-and-gun offenses; we beat the stall; there was no game plan that we couldn't dismantle. Winning came so naturally that there was hardly any partying after home victories, and none on the road. We rolled into the championships and reached the Final Four in Louisville before any true sense of what we were doing caught up with us. Even then it wasn't overwhelming. We were so young and on such a roll, all of us winners for so long, that defeat was inconceivable. We played the University of Houston in the semifinal round, and although Elvin Hayes did a lot of talking and both scored more points and grabbed more rebounds than I did, we beat them by an easy fifteen.

It took the championship final to break through our composure, and even then we kind of had to do it by ourselves. When you dream of winning a national championship, you think of a titanic struggle, a battle for life-long ambition fought with the components of war: desire, courage, and fear. We played the University of Dayton, which had gotten there through a series of upsets, and it was by no means the toughest game of the year. We just sort of cruised through, led all the way, and won by another fifteen.

When you are totally involved in an effort, you rarely look up from it and savor just how well you're

KAREEM:
Shots of the Basketball Legend

I was the biggest baby born in Sydenham Hospital, and my parents, Big Al and Cora, wanted me to grow up right.

High school
basketball started out
as a whole lot of hard
days in the gym. You
didn't want to look
bad in front of
Coach Donohue.
(WIDE WORLD PHOTOS)

(WIDE WORLD PHOTOS)

(*Left*) Guaranteed: in every school picture there I am
in the last row in the middle like I'm standing on a box.

But after a while I grew into my body,
and, with Charlie Farrugia (#22)
and Joe Carluk (#41), we won 71 straight games.
(WIDE WORLD PHOTOS)

Donohue
challenged my pride, then
went too far.
(AL GIESE)

Wilt Chamberlain was the first star I knew, and I
stood in awe of him. He took Carlos Green, me, and
my date Sandy to the Latin Quarter. Sandy was the
finest looking girl I knew. If I was hanging with
Wilt, I had to be up to the task.

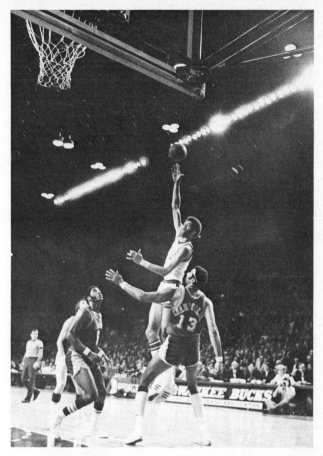

When you're going up against the best,
you've got to give it your best.
(UPI PHOTO)

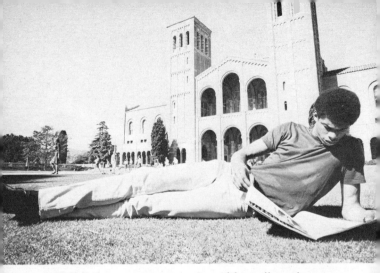

U.C.L.A. was gorgeous. I could stroll to class on fresh green grass. But it was also very insular, and by the time I got out I felt even more alone.
(WIDE WORLD PHOTOS)

Basketball took over my life. Coach Wooden preferred
thorough preparation over the need to rise to an
occasion. Let others try to rise to our level; we would
be there to begin with.

(WIDE WORLD PHOTOS)

Hamaas Abdul-Khaalis was the ultimate purist. He taught me Islam, cured me of racism and anti-Semitism, and showed me how to look at the world. But after his wife and children were murdered, he went haywire.
(WIDE WORLD PHOTOS)

Hamaas lost six members of his family and went into seclusion. . . .
(WIDE WORLD PHOTOS)

Bruce Lee showed me how to harness some of what
was raging inside me.
He was a close and valued friend.

Here's the
middle-eastern
version of
me (on the camel).

With the 1974 playoff against the
Celtics ticking away, I had my entire
concentration focused. I felt as if
everything was moving in
slow motion. The shot went right in.

(*Left*) Nate Thurmond consistently played me tough, and . . .

I always got up for the Knicks.

I like to win. I play to win. But getting intentionally pounded by 220-pound athletes 82 games a season, not including playoffs, is no day at the beach.

(UPI PHOTO)

The press figured my lighter public image, my "liberation," was by "Magic"—and he was very enjoyable to play with. But that was just the easy journalistic hook.

My son, Amir, is a real little dynamo,
and I love helping him grow.

working. It would spoil the moment, disrupt the pace and coordination of forces that are so smooth and effortless because they are not self-conscious. We had been cooking so naturally, each of us playing at top form day after day, that it wasn't until right after the game ended that it dawned on me what we had done. We won! National Champs! Coach Wooden had always taught us not to get depressed when we lost and not to get too crazy when we won. I half took him up on it; I didn't get depressed when things went wrong, but I got real crazy that night in Louisville. People were partying, and I prowled the city feeling a glow I wished I could have shared.

That summer I worked for the New York City Housing Authority, giving basketball clinics at projects around the city with Knicks players Fred Crawford and Emmette Bryant. Great job. I got to deal with black kids in the perfect setting for teaching and was able to talk to them about black pride and have a real sense that what I said was getting through. I also got $5,000 for doing it.

Junior year at UCLA we had a truly great team, the best of my three varsity years. Lucius, Mike Warren, Mike Lynn, Lynn Shackleford and I started, with Edgar on the bench. We were national champs, even stronger and deeper than we'd been the year before, tempered and more experienced. We weren't as hungry as we had been; we were no longer kids pursuing some idealized dream—each of us had been made to consider consciously what winning a championship so young and becoming part of a potential dynasty meant—but now we had a seasoned pride and the challenge that every game offered to our undefeated career. Our opponents may have been intimidated, but they all came gunning for us; we were the most important game on each of their schedules and had to face that kind of inspired intensity every time we showed up on the court. That never became wearing, in fact knowing that we were always in someone's gunsights helped us to maintain our own sharp edge.

I had been handed my own personal handicap. During the off-season the College Basketball Rules Committee had altered their regulations and made it a violation to dunk the ball. Clearly, they did it to undermine my dominance in the game. Equally clearly, if I'd been white they never would have done it. The dunk is one of basketball's great crowd pleasers, and there was no good reason to give it up except that this and other niggers were running away with the sport. It turned out all right—I was forced to develop a soft touch around the basket that I would use to good advantage in the pros—but that doesn't change their motives. The dunk, of course, was reintroduced into college ball ten years later.

Our season, and our entire team character, was determined by two games against the University of Houston. They had been NCAA semifinalists the year before and had an even stronger team this year, with Don Chaney and Elvin Hayes leading the pack. Elvin was a talker. Rather than be cool after we'd beaten them, he had mouthed off to the press about how I just stood around on defense, wasn't aggressive on the boards, and generally wasn't all I was cracked up to be.

Eight days before we were to play each other in the Houston Astrodome, I scratched the cornea of my left eyeball in a game against California. The pain was overwhelming but worse than that, I couldn't see. I had double vision, and those images that did get through were blurred and teary. That was okay, maybe, if you're playing keyboards or delivering a lecture, but for basketball it meant big trouble. I lay in a darkened hospital room with a patch over my eye for three days and missed two games altogether, which my teammates won quite easily without me. I could hardly move, let alone practice, and by the day of the Houston game I had lost not only a good portion of my sight but also my wind, conditioning, and the timing that was the key to UCLA's finesse.

But we were winners, and I couldn't possibly not suit up and play. I knew my depth perception was totally shot, but I thought I could make up for it by rebounding and playing good defense. Unfortunately, I overestimated myself, and so did Coach Wooden. When the game started I felt just like I had ten years before when I'd played my first game on a full court: I felt like I was playing basketball on a football field. The game wasn't five minutes old before I was exhausted, and I had no second wind. The week's lay-off had drained me to the point where the timing and coordination that I had drilled to come naturally were simply not available to me. I put up a turnaround jumper from the left side and shot an air ball. I was afraid this would be a very long night.

Meanwhile, Elvin was on fire. In my shape I couldn't handle him and neither could Edgar or Mike Lynn. He had twenty-nine points at the half until Jim Nielsen cooled him off some. I didn't have the strength or stamina to fight for my normal position on the floor or in the passing lanes, and with me out of the game as a major factor, the team had to struggle. Perhaps I should have taken myself out; I wasn't helping the team when we needed it, but I knew that what I would have intended as a team-oriented gesture would have been interpreted all across the country as a signal of my quitting. I tried to will myself into playing the kind of basketball I wanted to be able to play, but I came up short.

Coach Wooden saw the situation but left me in. Edgar Lacy, our prime defensive forward and an All-American, never got off the bench in the second half. I was out there unable to cope, and Mr. Wooden never gave Edgar the chance to play, neglected him, humiliated him. I ended up shooting four for eighteen from the floor, the first time in my college career that I'd shot under fifty percent, but Mr. Wooden never made the move.

For all that, we lost by only two points.

Immediately, our status fell. Instead of recognizing the obvious, that I was out of shape and our loss was a direct result of my injury, both wire services and most of the country's reporters and ratings systems shot down UCLA and replaced us with Houston as the number one team in the country. We were stung. We should have expected it, but we'd been winners for so long and wrapped in our cocoon of invincibility that we had forgotten how much people like to see the big guys take a fall. There was nothing we could do about it except beat the hell out of everybody we played from then on and hope Houston made it to the Final Four again. We knew we'd be there.

I never liked to lose, and I liked even less having to read about how Elvin didn't have much respect for my abilities. He won Player of the Year solely as a result of that game. *Sports Illustrated* slapped a photograph of Elvin scoring over me on their cover that week, and I cut the thing out and pasted it in my locker to keep me reminded of my mission. Not that I was going to forget.

Worse than losing to Houston, however, was the fact that we lost Edgar Lacy. Coach Wooden had humiliated him—our best defensive forward (in fact, our best forward entirely; he was a better ballplayer than both Lynn and Shackleford) benched for the whole second half of our most important game—and Edgar wouldn't take it. He had sat next to me on the bus back to the hotel that night and said, "Man, I'm gonna quit." He knew why he hadn't played. Coach Wooden, in spite of his tactical genius for the game, had a serious blind spot when it came to his players and their comportment. Mr. Wooden believed his athletes had to be not only physically and emotionally prepared but "morally" ready to play. Lynn Shackleford was his ideal: Shackleford studied hard, belonged to the Fellowship of Christian Athletes, took instruction and advice and criticism beautifully. Edgar was a better ballplayer, but he was his own man who would not alter his personality to suit his coach. He wound up fighting Mike Lynn, another "moral borderliner", for the starting spot both should have been awarded. This had

162

been eating at him all season, and getting left on the bench finally cut right through.

All during the week after the Houston loss I waited for Coach Wooden to smooth things out. In practice he'd say things like, "We all know that not every player can play every game, but that shouldn't upset them. There are a lot of things involved." Everybody knew he was talking about Edgar, but he never addressed him directly. Even a short statement like "I took Lacy out of the Houston game because he wasn't getting the job done" would have kept Edgar on the team where he belonged. Edgar had served UCLA and Coach Wooden well; he deserved at least that consideration. But no such gesture was made, and Edgar, a very sensitive and perceptive young man, just took a walk. He never played for UCLA again. He did play for the Los Angeles team in the ABA, but his basketball career was damaged and shortened by Mr. Wooden's refusal to give even an inch. It did not speak well for the coach, and I felt deeply for my friend who gave up so much for his principles.

My eye healed, and both we and Houston won the rest of our games. Our showdown was inevitable, and we were very glad when it came—in the NCAA semifinals, in Los Angeles, on national television.

The pregame locker room was quiet, no histrionics, no horsing around. All anybody said was, "We don't have any excuses. We've gotta beat them." It was the biggest game of our lives, bigger than the previous year's final because we were aware now of what was at stake, what the title felt like and meant; the championship had some body to it. But we didn't have much to say. Each guy in the room was at his highest point of preparation; wherever anybody's peak was, that's where he was at when we took the court.

We opened in a diamond and one, a pressing defense that Assistant Coach Jerry Norman had worked out the week before. Mike Warren had the point, with Lucius and Mike Lynn on the sides of the foul lane working toward the corners, and I closed off the inside. Lynn Shackleford took Elvin Hayes man-to-man. The first or second time down the floor on offense, as I posted low and looked for the ball, I felt Elvin lean on me and heard him threaten, "We're gonna beat you. We're gonna beat you bad!" I didn't answer, I was too busy.

From the outset we kicked Houston's ass. We stole the ball and blew by them for lay-ups. We hit from the outside. If they'd thought we'd let them anywhere near us, they were dead wrong. Elvin scored all of five points in the first half, got his other five in the second. We were pressing them when I stole the ball from their backcourt man and drove to the hoop. The no-dunk rule prevented me from slamming the ball down and making the crowd crazy the way I wanted, but I was so pumped up I must have had my elbow over the rim when I laid it in off the glass. We beat them by thirty-two points and settled *that* argument.

The championship game was again like an after-thought. We beat North Carolina by twenty-three and had our second consecutive national title.

8

All sophomore and junior years I'd been looking for something to believe in. Having abandoned the religious underpinnings of Catholicism senior year in high school and the physical trappings when I left my mother's house, and then been taught by Malcolm X that some central philosophy was necessary in order to live a meaningful life, I began my own study of comparative religions. I had changed my major from English to history and found myself in the happy position of being able to channel my studies toward my goal, taking courses in the history of India, the history of China, African and black studies. I read everything from existentialism to Buddhism, Taoism, Hinduism, Zen. Unfortunately, nothing I investigated seemed to make sense for all people. I was struck by the power of the originators of these philosophies, and was made to feel what it might have been like to be associated with such overwhelming personal magnetism

165

and charisma—the life-altering abandonment of an apostle to his master—but I was never made to share that passion. Taoism's eternal duality, the yin and yang, didn't move me. I was definitely into taking responsibility for my actions, but the rest of existentialism left me cold. Zen was just too subtle for me, and the Hindus bewildered me with their different gods for every day.

I was no longer a Catholic, but monotheism was still very much ingrained in me; it made sense to me that there would be one very complex superior source from which all the natural forces of the world would flow. In parochial school the sisters had taught me that there is one supreme being who is really three, or three supreme beings who are really one; they handed me some line of gibberish and told me to accept it on faith. When I looked in the Old Testament there was never any mention of three. In the Psalms of David: "I am One, my name is One." So I saw that Catholics believed in something that was contradicted by their own scriptures. When I studied further I found that the gospels were not contemporary eyewitness accounts of Jesus' life; they were written some seventy years after Jesus died and were third-party recollections taken from people who knew people who knew Jesus. Knowing men, and putting aside my faith in divine intervention, it seemed to me hard to pin down exactly what Jesus' life was about based on that kind of information. The Bible could be fact, but it could also be laced with a strong vein of fiction and mythology. It would almost be like trying to write a biography today of Woodrow Wilson; first off, you can't get the straight goods from Woodrow; he's gone and so are the people who worked for him. You've got to talk to the people who knew them, and while you might be blessed with some good insights, you couldn't be absolutely certain that you were coming up with the gospel truth.

Malcolm X, who was a profound influence on me, had himself been guided by his faith in Islam. He had turned to the teachings of Elijah Muhammad, with their burned-toast black people and white-devil Caucasians, while in prison and had preached that racist demonology until he'd made his pilgrimage to Mecca. There he'd found that true Islam had little to do with the mumbo-jumbo that Elijah Poole had concocted. He discovered that in that center of the Muslim world, people from all over the earth congregated to live in peace and share as brothers their commonly held belief and faith in Allah. The criteria for being a good Muslim was not your color or your cultural heritage or how much money you had but what you believed and what you practiced.

I read Malcolm and then read the Qur'an, and my friend Sadiq Benaissa encouraged me to read about the life of the Prophet. The Qur'an, I found, is the final Book of Revelations that started with the Old Testaments. In it I found there was a single god, Allah, and Muhammad was His messenger. I knew from my childhood Bible study that in the Old Testament, God had told Abraham that he would raise prophets from all his offspring, Ishmael and Isaac. Through Isaac came David, Solomon, Jesus—the House of David. Through Ishmael came Muhammad. I could see that Muhammad was confirming prophesies from the Old Testament. In Muhammad's life, I was told, there is the purest crystalization of Allah's message for mankind, and the prophet Muhammad is the seal of the prophethood. Moses was a lawgiver, as was Abraham. Jesus was not, Islam said; he told people how to live according to the laws that were already written. Muslims believe in Jesus' life completely, but they do not worship him. Muhammad, they believe, was the last messenger of Allah. As they described it, the messages of the prophecy—all the books of the Old Testament and the gospel—comprise an arch of which the life and teachings of Muhammad are the keystone. The prophet's words, I found, had been memorized and set down by people who were present with him. His teachings were contemporary, and conscientiously recorded, in no way removed from the prophet's life. If Muhammad was indeed the messenger of Allah, His words were getting directly through.

At first I was fascinated, then fully absorbed. Islam was a religion a large portion of whose believers were black and which touched on all of my concerns. I saw myself as a victim of racism, and here first Malcolm and then the religion itself are pointing out immediately that racism is wrong. It says in the Qur'an: "We created you from one parent, and we created differences so that you may know one another." The parent was Adam, the differences were ethnic and cultural variety and the one source, Allah. Not only was this preached, it was practiced widely, throughout the world. When I found this out, I said to myself, "Hey, this is the way people are supposed to live. This is it!" From that point on I was sold.

In New York that summer of 1968 I started to learn Islam in earnest. I had found through my studies that the two largest Islamic groups were the Sunnites (450 million) and the Shi'ites (30 million). The Sunnites live mostly in Arabia, Afghanistan, Pakistan, Turkey, North Africa, Indonesia, and India; and the Shi'ites live mostly in Iran and Iraq. Largely because Malcolm X had been a Sunnite Muslin when he died, I chose the Sunnites, and one morning I took my first step toward them.

The Sunnites ran a mosque in a building on 125th Street. The day was bright and warm, early summer New York before the heat and hopelessness become oppressive, and I was wearing my great loud African robe for the occasion. I had rarely put it on in public; that was exactly the kind of display that would have caused the hostile antiblack innuendoes I simply couldn't counter—"Lew Alcindor, looking like a Zulu warrior, led his teammates from the bus to the dressing room before UCLA ate Arizona State alive last night at the field house. . . ." I had pulled it out only once during the basketball season, when I was proud and exhilarated after we'd beaten Houston in the semis. Coach Wooden had seen it and smiled. My father had raised his eyebrows; my mother exclaimed, "My God!" It flowed all over me with big swirls and stripes of red, orange, and yellow, and made me feel African, or at least less of a slave to my surroundings.

I marched into the mosque, and the Muslims, dressed all in white, just kind of looked at me. There was an African Cultural Center in the same building and one of them glanced up and said, "Oh, you want the place downstairs."

No, no, I told them, what I want is right here.

I had a lot to learn. My reading had given me a rudimentary understanding of the workings of Islam, but I had no idea about the dedication involved. I had arrived on a Friday in the midst of preparation for the *Jumma* (or Sabbath) prayer, and one of the Muslim teachers gave me a booklet with several chapters of the Qur'an transliterated from the Arabic so I could memorize them. I took that home and started studying, learned those chapters and came back for more. They taught me how to make my ablutions, the Muslim cleansing process before prayer, and how to approach the rituals of the religion itself. I spent several Fridays at the mosque like a novitiate getting more and more deeply involved. Finally, after a month of intensive study, I felt prepared and committed enough to be a Muslim. I was taking my life in my hands, and I enjoyed it.

That Friday I went by myself to the mosque and cleaned and arranged myself according to Muslim law. Then, before witnesses, I pronounced my *shahada*, declared my faith that there is no god but Allah and that Muhammad is His messenger. When I stood up I was a Muslim.

A new man needs a new name. Having recognized a different aspect of myself beginning to control the way I lived, I wanted and deserved to have a new identity. My Muslim teacher, the man who had supervised my month-long training and had begun to know me, had the insight to name me Abdul ("servant of Allah") Kareem ("generous"). I find it interesting now, some fifteen years later, to note how I accepted his definition as my own. Very few people have the opportunity to define themselves—your parents name you at birth from their sense and hopes for what you are and will become—and when I was presented with this unique and significant chance to state who I was, I allowed my teacher to do it for me. I was out of my parents' house but had yet to fashion a physical or spiritual home of my own.

I told very few people about my conversion, only a couple of my friends, certainly not my folks. I thought of Abdul-Kareem as my religious name, much as a Janet Briggs could wind up as a Sister Mary Sebastian. I was still Lew to almost everybody, as if I knew them but they didn't know me.

I was in New York at the mosque that summer because I wasn't at the Olympics in Mexico City playing basketball for the United States team. I didn't see the point. In November 1967, a meeting of prominent black athletes had been organized on the west coast and presided over by Harry Edwards, a sociology professor at San Jose State College. Edwards was an intelligent, courageous black activist and he proposed a boycott of the Olympic Games by blacks to dramatize and protest the systematic discrimination we were all slapped with every day of our lives. After the 1960 Olympics a young Cassius Clay, not yet Muhammad Ali, had worn his gold medal into a southern restaurant and been refused service because he was black. As far as most of us were concerned, nothing substantial had changed since, and we pursued the idea of using the Olympics as a forum for making this idea more widely known. Pious denials notwithstanding, the Olympics has always been a highly political and politicized event, from Hitler's refusal to acknowledge Jesse Owens to the Cold War competition of "ways of life" between the USA and the Soviet Union. There were legitimate points to be made in the international arena. If white America was going to treat blacks poorly, then white America could win the Olympics on its own. We had all felt the effects of racial prejudice, from individual hurtful remarks to difficulties getting decent housing or good jobs, and while some of us were obtaining the privileges that athletic celebrity will bring, none of us had forgotten where he came from.

The meeting reached no final resolution, and no formal boycott was announced or carried out. I fully supported the idea; I felt no part of the country and had no desire to help it look good. I had better things to do. Playing in the Olympics would have meant losing a full quarter's worth of classes and not graduating from UCLA on time, and I had no intention of disrupting my education so that a country that was abusing my people could be made to shine for the world.

Kirk Douglas called me—collect—and tried to talk me out of it, said I shouldn't punish the United States, but I told him it wasn't my function to save the state. When the press attacked the athletes' meeting and played the threat of a boycott like we were holding the nation's honor hostage, I became even more resolved not to involve myself in their jingoism. I returned to my summer job, now titled Operation Sports Rescue by the city of New York, and went from Harlem to Bedford-Stuyvesant, Brownsville and the East Bronx teaching kids to play basketball and telling them to stay in school and make real people out of themselves. I thought then and think now that the pride I instilled in those hundreds of inner-city black kids by teaching and paying attention to them was ultimately worth more than whatever I could have contributed to the national morale in the way of an Olympic gold medal. I was fiercely proud of John Carlos and Tommie Smith when they made their black-gloved, victory-stand power salute. My passive gesture had cost me a lot—I was deluged by hate mail calling me an uppity nigger and a traitor—and I knew their active statement, in the public eye of that hurricane, would cost them much more. I think of them as patriots.

Apparently my opinion was in the minority. I was invited on the *Today* show to publicize Operation Sports

Rescue, and before I could begin to make a point, Joe Garagiola, one of the show's moderators at the time and something less than a political genius, began to bait me about my Olympic nonparticipation. He reminded me, in his enlightened way, that I was an American, I lived here.

"Yeah, I live here," I told him, "but it's not really my country."

Garagiola couldn't deal with it. "Well, then there's only one solution," he cracked, "maybe you should move."

Here's Joe Garagiola telling me and mine to go back to Africa.

Then we got cut off by a station break, and I never got back on camera. That's the way it works. That was the country I chose not to represent.

The next day my father got a call from an old acquaintance of his. Al had known the man from their days together in musicians' circles as Ernest McGee, a drummer, but he had given up music and become a Muslim and was now Hamaas Abdul-Khaalis.

Hamaas had seen my truncated TV appearance, noticed that I'd been wearing a star-and-crescent pendant, and told my father he would like to talk with me. I had told my parents nothing about my conversion; they certainly wouldn't have taken kindly to it, and I didn't feel I wanted either to share my new enthusiasm with them or get involved in some family holy war. But my father must have sensed something was up. He knew Hamaas was Muslim, and that he was trustworthy, and he passed along the message. So one morning a few days later, I left the house early and, before going to work, went to visit Mr. Khaalis.

Hamaas lived with his wife and four children in a tenement at 132nd Street and Lenox Avenue. I was welcomed inside by a man not much older than I was who introduced himself as Abdul Aziz, one of Hamaas' students. The apartment, in which six people lived, consisted of a kitchen, a bathroom, and one not very large room. An unremarkable looking place, no rugs on the walls or Eastern religious trappings lying around. It was a Harlem place to live; I had seen plenty of them. I was asked to remove my shoes before I entered, which I did without questioning, having learned at least that much at the 125th Street mosque.

Hamaas wasn't home when I arrived, already having left for work directing a local education project called the Street Academy at 116th Street and Eighth Avenue, so I spoke for some time with Aziz, who lived in the building. He told me that there were a whole lot of funny-time people involved in the religion just then; it was in vogue and many of the new "believers" really weren't schooled in Islam, that what was being promoted was often not Islam at all. Hamaas, however, took his religion as seriously as death, and, Aziz told me, I should come back and speak with him myself; I'd be convinced.

I was back the next morning, and Hamaas met me at the door. He was not a tall man, a stocky five nine, in his late forties, but he had an authoritarian, almost military bearing and my complexion. He took me inside and we sat at a small table.

"The first thing I want to tell you," he said sternly, "is, Don't ever say that this isn't your country." I was surprised by the power he could work up. We'd just met, and he was immediately giving me orders and definitely expecting to be obeyed. "Your ancestors lived and died in this country," he continued intensely, "and this *is* your country. You have to get all your rights as a citizen. Don't reject it, affirm it." I didn't know how to respond, so I just sat there a little stunned.

"Now," he said, "I hear you are interested in Islam. Are you a Muslim?"

"Yeah, I am," I told him.

"I see." He assumed he knew better. "What do you know?"

I recited the portions of the Qur'an I had memorized, told him what I had been taught at the mosque, summarized my college reading, and in ten minutes ran through my entire Muslim repertoire.

Hamaas listened, and as he peered at me, the more I spoke the less I knew I knew. When I finished, he asked me to comment on a specific passage in the Qur'an. I didn't know that? How about this, and he reeled off a paradox from the scripture. I couldn't respond. He very intensely posed several more esoteric yet significant questions, which only a serious study of the faith could answer, and when I was at a thorough loss for words, he said sternly, "You ought to be able to answer those questions if you're going to call yourself a believer. If you are going to accept Islam, you should really accept it in the proper way."

I had been proceeding on my instincts, finding in my gut the proper response to the religion and its filling of my needs. Hamaas reversed that, he wondered aloud whether I could, in truth, fulfill the needs of Islam. He wanted to know whether I was worthy of calling myself a Muslim. It was a measure of my devotion, and his. "There is an outer layer of religion that lots of people see," he told me, "but there is an inner core of Islam that only a few select people get to deal with. You want to find that belief, I can tell, and I am the only man in this country who knows where that core is and how to get there. I can teach you, as I was taught, but you've got to work at it. It's not easy, but if you come study with me, I will show you the way."

At six o'clock in the morning every day for the rest of the summer (except after I'd had a particularly hard night) I showed up at Hamaas' house for instruction. That meant I had to wake up at four-thirty, but I had to be at work by nine, so if I was going to get my two hours in, I had to make the sacrifice.

Hamaas had taught and converted his whole family, and they and a few other students comprised his "community," what in other religions might be called a congregation. They taught me the proper way to bathe before prayers,

174

how to make my ablutions. I already knew a couple of chapters of the Qur'an and had said my *shahada*, but Hamaas was not satisfied with what I had been taught. He taught five *kalimas*. The first is the declaration of faith; that's universal, but the rest affirm different aspects of Allah's presence and sovereignty. Hamaas felt that unless you knew the *kalimas* as he had been taught, you didn't really know too much about Islam; in fact, it was doubtful that you knew anything about Islam at all.

Hamaas was the ultimate purist. Even the name he was given, Hamaas Abdul-Khaalis, means "earnest, sincere, servant of the most pure," reaffirming the attributes of Allah his mentor saw most strongly in him. His mentor had been a Bengali mystic from a community of men whose faith allowed them the power to do things unexplained by science. One of Hamaas' co-students followed their teacher after class one day to track his mysterious background. He said the teacher met a man; they stopped and talked for a few moments, and when they left, the teacher went one way and the other man went and walked through a wall. I was a confirmed skeptic, but Hamaas believed it, and if Hamaas believed it, I had to take it seriously.

Hamaas could talk about the intricacies of Islam for hours, and all of it would be new and fascinating to me. We had to be totally clean before we were permitted to pray; you couldn't defile the presence of Allah, and true believers, he taught me, prayed five times a day, so what with a thorough bath and change of clothes each time, a true Muslim had little time for much else but attention to his religion. Most Muslims greet each other by saying *A Salaamu Alaikum*, but Hamaas taught that that was for the ill-informed and that we were to say, *Bismillah Ar Rahman Ar Raheem*, which means, "In the name of Allah the Compassionate, the Merciful," which is the opening of the Qur'an. There are minimum requirements to be a Muslim, and there are further requisites for those seeking more enlightenment and merit. For Hamaas nothing but the most rigorous obedience to the traditions was acceptable, the purest of the pure, and as a neophyte I found such devotion exhilarating, inspiring. In a very short time I became his most enthusiastic and hard-line convert.

But even more than the rituals and definitions of the religion, Hamaas taught me how to look at the world. He was a wise man with a world view, and the more he spoke the more I responded to him.

The first thing he did was cure me of racism. Ever since the Sunday bombing that killed four little girls in the Baptist church in Birmingham, Alabama, when a whole lot of white people died in a tragedy—say a fire or a plane crash—I'd be happy. When Bull Connor was on the Pettus Bridge with his police dogs and cattle prods, I saw them on television, and it left its mark. I was certain God was going to send some lightning down and sear all those bastards, and when that didn't happen, I wanted to do it myself. I would meet individual white people and like them on a personal level, but the race as a whole could die tomorrow as far as I was concerned.

"That's wrong," Hamaas told me. "It doesn't have to do with race. John Brown was a righteous man who put his life on the line for our welfare. And there are people like that today. If you saw them and they were white, you would turn your back on them, and you would be turning your back on someone who wants to do what is righteous and what Allah has ordered."

I was seeing things as too absolute, he told me. "Are all your black brothers righteous?" he asked.

I was personally involved with a large number of people who were less than model citizens, but I tried to run it by him. "Well, with the oppression we're in we don't know how to relate as a community."

"No," he said. "Being black just isn't the criteria, 'cause there's a whole lot of black people who work arm in arm with the forces of oppression," and he'd name examples from the few black officials in government to the guys snatching purses on Lenox Avenue.

Hamaas was strongly anti-Zionist, but he made me think away my anti-Semitism. I'd seen men like that Harlem pawnbroker strip and gouge the black community and, despite having Jewish friends, had developed a knee-jerk distrust for Jews in general.

"Now lookit here," Hamaas said to me, "what would you do if you were in Cleveland and you wanted to eat, to buy a hot dog, and there was no place to buy a kosher hot dog? You'd be in trouble, wouldn't you? One reason you're able to eat clean food, prepared or in the supermarket, is because of your Jewish brothers who believe in the law and practice according to what their beliefs are." The Mosaic and Muslim laws are not dissimilar, and he told me that many Jews became Muslims at the time of the Prophet.

Hamaas judged men and women by their sincerity and their convictions, and he taught me to deal with people not as parts of some blanket abstraction, like Jews or blacks or crackers, but as individuals with their own ideas. Not all Muslims were going to Heaven, he said, and not all non-Muslims will end up in Hell. We're all judged on what we do with our lives, our talents, our opportunities. Islam to Hamaas was a sacred moral order, and his entire life sprang from that purity. The foundation of Islam, he told me, was: Don't be a hypocrite; there are laws, live by them. I had thought of religious knowledge as a recitation of dogma, but Hamaas was applying common sense to my life based on an overriding religious philosophy. He made me view the world with a discerning eye, and he was good at it.

"Look how they use sex to sell everything in America," he told me. "They sell toothpaste, and they've got you thinking subliminally that if you buy this toothpaste, you're going to get laid. Hi-fi equipment, they have a woman lying on it. Tanning lotion, clothing, cars—if it's sexy, it sells. This is not what people should be worrying about when they buy things, they should think about the positive and negative effect it will have on their person. Is it good for you? Does it work? Sex is not recreation; it's not a sales tool."

As Muslims, Hamaas told me, we are culturally at odds with America. Alcohol, a legal substance in the United States but unacceptable under Muslim law, is involved in breaking up families, causing traffic accidents, robberies, murders. Its negative effect on society is overwhelming, but while Muslims have outlawed it, America makes money off it.

Sometimes he'd be reading the newspaper in the morning, and he'd comment on the headlines. I had never paid a lot of attention to the daily goings-on before. I was generally aware but had felt that most of what went on in the world was beyond my power to affect, so why give it much thought? It was Hamaas who started me thinking about Vietnam, about how we were sending people over there to die for no reason; and about how this government supported white racism in South Africa; and about how the government used all the poor people, black and white, to support the upper classes. He explained to me that there were certain people who run the government, and certain people who run the country, and that they weren't the same people! He showed me how industrial magnates, major oil companies, and international corporations get things they want done, whether they are to the citizens' benefit or not.

This was a total revelation to me. I had thought that in the United States the people did have the power. Hamaas showed me how that is more apparent than real; we have a lot of personal freedom, which is important, but the real power is held by some small number of men who don't ever have to run for election, who don't have to do anything but protect their interests.

I had heard some of this before, rhetoric from the Black Panthers, Black Muslims, and the radical left, but they had all seemed crazy to me. Hamaas backed it all up with facts and figures. He was a part-time consultant to the Ford Foundation, writing proposals for money to be spent within the black community, and was brilliant in relating facts to each other and drawing clear conclusions from them where I would have been at a loss.

Hamaas also had a lot of criticism of the Islamic world. American Muslims were very impressed with the Arabs because they spoke the language of the Qur'an; many teachers and mosques looked to the Middle East for examples and guidance. But Hamaas didn't buy it. "Islam is not Arabic," he told me. "Because those people speak Arabic, Americans think, 'Oh, man, they know it all.' They speak Arabic on their lips, but Islam isn't in their hearts; they don't practice it. They have all the wealth that Allah gave them; they don't use it Islamically. All those countries with Muslim majorities, none of them has an Islamic government. Even Saudi Arabia, where the most holy places in Islam are, that's a kingdom. They'll tell you how Muslim they are, but they won't live by the laws. You go to their country and it's oppression; people are locked in poverty and can't get out while these so-called Muslims have literally millions and millions of dollars to play around with."

One of the news weeklies had just run an article about all these Arab princes losing hundreds of thousands of dollars in Las Vegas. "What about all these dudes you see running around in their robes," he said, "with their white Cadillacs and gold shoes. They don't believe. That's a lot of hypocrisy; that's not Islam."

He had zero respect for the so-called Black Muslims, who weren't Muslims at all but had stolen a few cultural identifications, and the name, and tacked them onto a racist demagoguery. There was then, and continues to be, a great public confusion between Islam and the Black Muslims. The difference is between faith and mumbo-jumbo. Islam tells us that there is no god but Allah and Muhammad was His messenger; the Black Muslims believe that an itinerant preacher named Elijah Poole had

Allah's ear, that all white people are devils, and that all black people were created like burned toast on one of Allah's trial runs. They are not to be confused. Muhammad Ali became a Black Muslim. I am a Muslim.

The Black Muslims created a sense of unity for black people against a common enemy—whites—and operated as a unity. But they took the name of Allah and soiled it, and this above all else Hamaas could not tolerate. This was worse than hypocrisy, this was blasphemy. (Many years later, after Elijah Poole died, his own son, Imam W. Muhammad, rejected Poole's teachings and, as leader of the Black Muslims, declared that they now practice and adhere to the orthodox teachings of Islam. But that was not before many lives had been broken and many people had died.)

Every morning I spent at Hamaas' home I learned something important. No one had ever treated me this way—certainly not my father, nor my teachers, Mr. Donohue, nor Coach Wooden—and I soaked up his influences with a growing zeal. I had searched for an order, and now I had one with strict boundaries. Hamaas often quoted me one particular passage from the Qur'an: "In truth, the disbelievers are an open enemy to you."

Hamaas was an extraordinary mentor. I liked him as an instructor, but more than that, I liked him as a man because he was aware and he cared and he wasn't out for a whole lot for himself. He was living six people to a room! He was fully convinced, and said many times, that he was the only man in America educated and prepared to teach American Muslims. But at the same time he would tell me that when you truly understood what Islam was about, and what it meant to be alive in the world, you really wanted to get it over with so you could approach Paradise. This world, he said, is something you have to deal with; it's a struggle; this is where we prove ourselves. After we've done that, we get our rewards. When you think about people who would rather be in Paradise than here dealing with this stuff, that's Hamaas. You have to be dead to be in Paradise; he wouldn't have minded, he'd have left that day. I'd never met such a man.

At the end of the summer I pronounced my *shahada* again, this time before Hamaas. I shaved my head, then brought some fish and lamb that, after the ceremony, Hamaas' wife cooked and shared with the community as an *akikat*, or ceremonial meal. Then, Hamaas renamed me. I was already Abdul-Kareem but he added to my definition. "Kareem is 'noble' and 'generous,' " he said to me; "that's your first line, that's a good name. 'Abdul,' that's 'servant.' But we're missing your spirit, your spirit . . . Jabbar. That means 'powerful.' That's where your spirit is." Hamaas decided I was Kareem Abdul-Jabbar and I saw no reason to doubt him.

9

When I returned in the fall of 1968 for senior year, I was starting to outgrow UCLA. My concerns, religious and political, extended far beyond the campus, and I was beginning to come in contact with people who were having a serious effect on the real world. Basketball was my entrée into some of these new spheres, but for the first time it became a secondary source of satisfaction, and it stopped being fun.

We'd done the whole thing twice, lost one game in three years and avenged that in a big way, had lots of new talent this year but nothing left to prove. Every win was expected; every close call, a sign of weakness. We had added Sidney Wicks and Curtis Rowe, who had the size, speed, rebounding ability, and shooting touch of pro caliber forwards. The team was balanced and deep, but the urgency wasn't there all the time. Even so, we won every game until the last of the regular season when we came up very flat against USC and were beaten by two points by a stall.

All year long I had little social life on campus and expected none. My conversion to Islam and my concentration on black culture put a widening distance between me and all but my most intimate acquaintances. No longer simply put off by the Southern California lifestyle but, with the help of Hamaas, now able to define its deficiencies, I withdrew into an almost impenetrable world. The heat I'd taken about the Olympics, and the absolute unwillingness I'd found in the press, and by extension the general public, to accept what to me seemed so obvious—that the country was run by white people for white people, and that even the most powerful black men were still operating at a handicap—made me suspicious of strangers and even more jealous of my privacy. I was insulated and angry, surrounded by "disbelievers," and the more confined I felt the more irate I became.

In basketball, success had been obliterated; a third straight national title would not be a great triumph, just a lack of failure. Victory after victory we were in a no-win situation. On a social level I was enough of a celebrity that people wanted to be able to say they knew me personally, and was smart enough not to give them a chance. I shut out the hangers-on; unfortunately, I probably turned away some people who could have become sincere friends. It was my first adult contact with what I've since found is one of the true drawbacks of high-visibility success. Though I didn't think of myself as resentful—I was quite used to the splendid isolation of an only child with a private view of the Cloisters—I didn't have a lot of good times. Just as in senior year at Power, I was marking time until the next milestone, the pros.

My interest in the martial arts had been growing since freshman year. I had always had an interest in fighting—my father had boxed, and as a practical necessity, I had had to learn to handle myself just to live in the neighborhood—but my studies in Eastern thought brought it even more out in the open. As a kid I'd seen guys on television use karate to punch straight through a stack of maybe fourteen tiles, and Norbert Florendo had bought a karate book that we'd pored over. But what really turned me on was the first time I went to see a Zatoichi movie.

Zatoichi was a blind swordsman, the lead character in a series of Japanese martial arts films that combined great swordplay with Oriental philosophy and a dry sense of humor. Zatoichi was a masseur and a benign gambler who traveled from town to town in medieval Japan, but he was really just a guy with a problem: people always seemed to pick on him. He had a beatific smile and a remarkably gentle nature, the Stevie Wonder of the samurai world, but he was the best swordsman you'd ever want to see, and he was always being called upon to defend his friends or avenge a family's honor or protect an entire town from the rapacious henchmen of their villainous landlord.

Zatoichi would sit in the Japanese equivalent of a frontier saloon, and people would take him for granted, ignore his obvious decency, and offend him in that peculiarly Oriental fashion in which one slight implies a mortal disrespect. Finally, pushed one pace too far, he would beamingly, almost apologetically, slaughter all the bad guys they threw at him. I saw him—blind, mind you— take on a gang of twenty samurai thugs and, in a sequence that had everyone in the theater shouting with righteous vengeance and glee, slice them all up and leave them for dead. Four men would charge from all sides, and he would stick one, turn, cut another straight through and have his head topple over like ice cream off a cone, impale another as he raced in from behind, and then scare the fourth to flight by stamping his foot. The litter of corpses would at last lie silent before him, and the blind masseur would shuffle off, bemused, perhaps a trifle sad at the carnage, yet somehow avenged, satisfied.

Zatoichi was so great that I half believed this stuff and wanted to learn how to do it myself. The martial arts combined attack and self-defense, with which I was more than familiar, with the Eastern philosophies that I was finding more and more stimulating. I was in good shape, but the attraction of the martial arts for me was that it involved a discipline of the mind as well as the body. A victory here is your mind over somebody else's mind, as much as, if not more than, a simple physical mastery. The martial arts can teach you to use your body, make you do things you don't think you are able to do. The discipline also becomes a means of staying in shape mentally and keeping your entire inner self trained. I felt that need.

I had started to study Akido back in the summer of 1967 at the New York Akikai, and when I had returned to California that fall the publisher of *Black Belt* Magazine told me he knew a guy who had developed his own new style of fighting, very extraordinary, and maybe I'd want to go work with him. The guy's name was Bruce Lee.

"Oh, the actor," I said. I'd seen him on television as Kato in *The Green Hornet*, and he'd been terrific, so sure, I said, I was curious enough to meet him.

We were introduced, and I immediately felt like I was in a struggle. For Bruce Lee, I found quickly, every encounter was like a battle; it was a means of testing his philosophy and ideas against whomever he was dealing with. Here was a strong man, I thought as we talked, this guy doesn't play. After an hour or so of very strenuous conversation, I found myself saying, "Okay, you're the man with the knowledge, let's see what it's all about." I started training with Bruce, who was six years older than I was, and continued with him until his death five years later.

Bruce was a brilliant and unconventional martial artist, a total pragmatist. In many of the traditions the martial arts were used to develop character as well as prowess, but Bruce felt that was another job completely and concentrated entirely on aspects of fighting. Through training for combat, he believed, character would evolve.

His strength began with his amazing concentration. Everybody has it, that terrific strength and total calm you find inside yourself when you absolutely need it in crisis situations: the astonishing ability to lift a van off your pinned child or to control a car in an icy skid with four passengers' safety in your hands. Bruce showed me how to harness some of what was raging inside me and summon it completely at my will. The Chinese call it *chi*; the Japanese, *ki*; the Indians, *prana*—it is the life force, and it is incredibly powerful.

I was familiar with the concept of *chi*, but Bruce showed me how to direct it, to focus it for fighting. I extended this and used it in preparation for basketball as well. The most important element in dealing with stress is presence of mind. People get excited and forget everything. You have to be in full control; then it's a matter of concentration. In the original *Kung Fu* movie someone is throwing these steel, star-shaped discs at David Carradine, and the camera shows, in slow motion, how he avoids these weapons, has plenty of time to defend himself, is in no real danger where other men might wind up dead. I was quite amazed to find, after working with Bruce, that when I really had my presence of mind, when I did indeed control my life force, that's what I saw, things coming at me in slow motion with plenty of time to get out of the way. It sounds bizarre, and it can't be explained adequately except to those who have already experienced it, but it's one of the very few willable miracles.

It sounded mystical when he first told me, but I was becoming increasingly involved in matters of faith, and besides, Bruce grounded his philosophies in a good fight, which I could relate to. Bruce received most of his martial arts training in Hong Kong, where the differing disciplines often settled philosophical disputes by force. Over there, when you joined up with a martial arts school it was also a school of thought, as if you'd been adopted by a family. Students called each other "brother," and if any one of them was attacked there was the question of

186

face being lost, a matter of honor, you were expected to fight. The leading disciple of one school would challenge the best man of another, and a blood match would be arranged. You can lock off the rooftops in Hong Kong, Bruce told me, and as each school's followers lined the hallways to prevent foul play or interference, they would go at it. People regularly lost teeth and ears, got their noses broken or eyes gouged. It was serious.

Bruce Lee was an innovator; he had little use for the traditions. Many martial arts teachers enjoy the esteem of a system that supports them because of their continuity, though their teachings may be discredited. Bruce was a young man; he could outfight the old masters, and he could outargue them on paper. In a practical demonstration he could pinpoint glaring weaknesses in their fighting style, and in lectures he continually revealed big holes in their philosophical theories. He pared down what he saw as the cute, inessential mannerisms that had crept into the teachings, techniques that did not give you any real advantage in a fight. He described it as "learning how to swim on land," all these elaborate little movements you can learn that may be lovely but don't help you to swim. He had no patience for such uselessness.

As a result, Bruce made a lot of enemies. On a TV panel show in Hong Kong, he once told me, a master had said, "Look, I'm going to get in my stance, and you can't push me over," as if to prove a point. The man took his stance; Bruce walked over and punched him in the mouth to show him that the stance didn't mean anything, that fighting had nothing to do with parlor tricks.

Bruce and I were invited to observe a martial arts demonstration by a school he didn't have much to do with. When the display was over, Bruce spoke briefly to the class, was very polite, wished everybody good luck, told them they were very hard-working and dedicated. When we got outside, he said, "Those guys are turkeys. If it was necessary, all you'd have to do was watch my back, and we'd kick them all in the ass."

Bruce developed a revolutionary movement that he called the Six-Inch Punch. Teachings through the ages held that a blow with the front or lead fist was not very powerful; it had to travel from the rear area to the front in order to gain enough power to score a point or do any damage. Bruce said, "Why eliminate a valuable weapon? Why not use every source of power available?" He planted both feet and taught himself how to deliver a truly punishing blow that, through his concentration and technique, summoned his full *chi* and traveled like a piston only six inches from his body to his opponent's. When he demonstrated it on me, I became an immediate believer. His wife, more than a hundred pounds lighter than I was, hit me with it and rocked me.

Bruce and I sparred regularly. I presented a lot of problems to him because of my size and also because I was agile enough to move with him and use my reach advantage to tag him as he came in to attack. But we didn't compete; I was like a drawing board on which he could work out his theories, and he was instructing me how to deal with people and attack them.

I brought my friend Malek up there once. Malek played ball at UCLA and can definitely handle himself, and for a while, as they sparred, he held his own. He danced and moved, and Bruce didn't touch him. But the longer it took for Bruce to get through, the more Bruce's face hardened. Malek was concentrating so hard, was so intimidated by Bruce's dead glare, that before he knew what had happened he had been backed into the wall, and Bruce was all over him.

Malek also wonders how Bruce managed his spinning back kick. Bruce, he swears, jumped up, took his right foot up past Malek's face, then caught him a solid shot *from the other direction* with the same foot. And then landed. How he did it, Malek doesn't know.

Bruce was an amazing martial artist, but I responded to him for several other reasons as well. He had been hurt by racism and said so. After having played Kato on

The Green Hornet, he worked with the people who developed the *Kung Fu* character and was supposed to star in the television series. He would have been perfect, a master working his art before the national audience, but whoever it was that decided such things made it clear to Bruce that they didn't think a Chinese man could be a hero in America. They passed over Bruce and gave the part, and the stardom, to David Carradine.

Bruce was hired as a martial arts adviser on one Hollywood film and stunt supervisor on another. They wanted to exploit his expertise, and his martial arts cinematography was among the best ever directed, but having been told that his career extended as far as valet to the stars, Bruce was seriously motivated to go back home and work with his people. He returned to Hong Kong, gained some access to people in power, and made the movie *The Big Boss*. It was a hit, Bruce's acting ability and charisma immediately obvious. When *Fists of Fury* came out, his reputation grew, and he became a superstar in the Orient.

We had talked about my being in a movie with Bruce, and in 1972 he was finally in the position to call the shots. I flew to Hong Kong, and we shot my sequences, though that movie (*Game of Death*) was tabled for a time while he made *Enter the Dragon*. When *Dragon* was released here, he was finally an American celebrity. A year later I was traveling in the Orient, about to leave Singapore to meet him in Hong Kong, when I heard he'd died. I missed seeing him by twelve hours. I would like to have seen him even one more time.

I met Bruce when he was still developing his fighting style, but it wasn't really obvious to me that I was working with someone who was going to become a martial arts immortal. Bruce was, during this whole time, my friend, and I think we allowed each other to become close because I was as prominent in my field as he was in his. There wasn't any real competition, no clash of egos, and Bruce needed friends. Bruce, quite rightly, thought of himself as a strong person. He never showed any sign of weakness in his fighting persona, and he refused to show any vulnerability in his personality.

I was over at his house one afternoon. We'd just finished working out; it was sunny and warm, and Bruce said, "Hey, I have to go drop something off at a friend of mine's house."

"I might go with you," I offered.

"You want a ride?"

"Yeah," I said, "where is it? Is it far away?"

"No," he said, "it's near Lobertson."

He meant Robertson, an avenue off Venice Boulevard, but maybe two or three times a year his Chinese accent would sneak through.

Bruce's face went cold, like when he was stalking Malek. He thought I was going to mock him and, friend or no friend, he wanted to fight me. I saw him begin to coil, and I grabbed him, and hugged him, and we began to laugh. I couldn't tell anybody, of course; it was the kind of confidence that cements a friendship, but as I let go he punched me on the arm, real hard, just to let me know he was still Bruce Lee.

In spring 1969, after we'd won our third straight NCAA championship, after all the awards had been distributed and history recorded, it was time to think about the pros. Disabling injury had never occurred to me, so I had assumed since freshman year that this was where I'd end up. But now that it was right there over the graduation horizon, I knew the big stakes were about to get played. Even before negotiations began, some shady peripheral figure started making the rounds of everyone in the world who might possibly pay money to basketball players, from the National Basketball Association to the American Basketball Association to the Harlem Globetrotters and the Italian League, telling them he represented me, and for a little cash up front to "get the ball rolling," he could give them the inside line. He got found out pretty quickly, but I knew then that I had to find some business advisers in a hurry whom I could trust. The one man I knew I could turn to was Sam Gilbert. He was pleased to volunteer, and brought in a Los Angeles brokerage executive, Ralph Shapiro, and both of them stayed with me, unpaid, through the entire process.

I really wanted to play in New York. It was my hometown; I was sick to death of LA and its falsefacing, my friends were all in New York, as were Hamaas and other Muslims. Unfortunately, the Knicks hadn't won the rights to draft me, the Milwaukee Bucks had. However, the New York Nets of the ABA were in real pursuit, and all things being equal, I would have been more than happy to play for them. The ABA was a new league, without the tradition and composure of the NBA, but I was no great fan of tradition and composure and was not unaware of what Joe Namath had done in similar circumstances in professional football.

The ABA was serious about me. As well as sending a squad of doctors to check out my physical condition, they approached me with a team of psychologists who administered a battery of their own tests to see whether: one, I could bear up under the strain of high-pressure professional basketball; two, I was a flake who might dishonor or discredit their organization at a time when what they needed most was respectability. Apparently, I passed the exam.

Sam Gilbert, Ralph Shapiro, my father, and I came to New York to cut the deal. I've never been a very patient negotiator, and I was even less so then. We told both sides that, rather than get involved in a build-you-up/tear-you-down bidding war between the leagues, we would hear only one blind bid each and make our decision firmly. There were a number of benefits to this plan. First, it eliminated a lot of agonizing and anxiety; we figured I should get the best contract ever offered to a player coming into the league, but none of us was certain how much that was or how far we could push it. Second, we assumed that, rather than risk losing me, each team would put more money on the table than they might otherwise part with. We'd get the top dollar without having to worry about whether, if we'd only held out, more might have been forthcoming. Third, Sam and Mr. Shapiro felt that heated bidding might cause a lot of animosity, particularly from the side that lost, and in the long run that might not be good for my career. And fourth, it seemed to me the honorable thing to do.

We met first with Walter Kennedy, at the time the commissioner of the NBA, and the owners of the Bucks. They made an extremely good five-year offer. I left that meeting knowing, for the first time, what the numbers were. I could forget about holes in my pants or saving pennies at the gas pump; however these negotiations came out, I was solid on the bottom line. Until that morning the whole thing had been a concept—I could make some bucks here—but that afternoon I had left the working class. Somehow I had never let that thought get close to me before—I didn't need to be more removed from my surroundings than I already was—but there was no escaping it now: I was rich.

The next day we met with Arthur Brown, who owned the Nets, and ABA Commissioner George Mikan. They also made a five-year offer, but it was substantially below the NBA's. Sam and Mr. Shapiro were surprised; first, because the ABA was the less-established league, they had assumed it would have offered money in place of prestige, and second, several owners in the league had promised a significant sum of money as a signing bonus. Sam asked George Mikan if that was the total package. Mikan said that was it. He was quite adamant about it. Surprised, kind of let down after expecting to top the previous day's exhilaration, we told Mr. Brown that we'd have to decline his offer.

Back at the hotel I was a little stunned. That morning I had been wealthy and unconcerned, back in New York with the city spread out before me and no budget or curfew to keep me off its streets. By afternoon I had been uprooted. I loved New York, but I would have to pass up a great deal of money to live there. Basketball was a business, that fact was brought home to me my first day on the job. My first professional compromise: I chose Milwaukee.

Mr. Gilbert and Mr. Shapiro agreed, and we called Walter Kennedy with the decision. He asked if this was final, could he count on our word—and leak it to the press—and we said yes and asked him to draw up the papers.

By dinnertime word was out. Sam was stopped in the hotel lobby by two ABA owners. They had another offer. Sam said, Wait a minute, you guys knew the deal: one bid, one time. They said that Mikan didn't have the authority to make their final offer and asked if, please, we could hold off signing with the NBA until they could regroup and do some bargaining. Sam was surprised and angry. These guys had known the rules we had established but had bid low on the assumption that we weren't as good as our word and would abandon principle when it came down to more dollars. High-risk, low-smarts bargaining. But these were large figures being thrown around and, rather than reject them out of hand, he told these sportsmen he would double-check with me and my father.

I had wanted to sign with the Nets—thirty-second clock, three-point shot, multicolored basketball and all— but I was offended to be taken so lightly. If they hadn't taken me seriously when I was calling the shots, how would they treat me once I was under contract? Sounded like bozo business dealings to me. Besides, I had not three hours before given my word to the NBA. I was all tied up with respect and conviction and fairness. My religion taught me to abhor hypocrisy, and right off the bat I was faced with the choice between being where I wanted through double-dealing on the one hand and beginning a career honorably two thousand miles from nowhere on the other. I was pissed off. The Nets had had the inside track and had blown it. I signed with Milwaukee.

10

I graduated from UCLA in June 1969, and came home. That was a strange time. I was a devout Muslim, alive with the zeal of the newly converted. I had told my parents about that, but not much else. Hamaas did not encourage me to be close with them; in fact, he discouraged it. I'm sure he felt my mother did not approve of his influence on me, and he was right. She had brought me up Catholic, with all the strictures which that discipline implies, and she was very unhappy that I was no longer attending mass or even paying lip-service to her sabbath. I was growing up and away from her, and she hated Hamaas for what she must have thought of as his kidnapping of her boy's soul.

I was in and out of the house, a new man in my old boy's room, about to head off into the world without her. She didn't want to lose what little of me she still had, but she would not be disobeyed. I was twenty-two and no longer listening. It was a difficult summer.

I had given the city of Milwaukee no thought whatsoever. Pretty much all I knew about it was that in 1957, Warren Spahn, Lew Burdette, Hank Aaron, Wes Covington, and Eddie Mathews had kicked the Yankees' ass in the World Series, and for that I was thankful. I knew it was in the Midwest, and that the Milwaukee Bucks, an expansion team, had just finished its first year with the second worst record in the league and then won a coin toss with the Phoenix franchise to determine who owned the right to pick first in the NBA draft. I didn't appreciate having my major career move decided by two strangers in a coin flip, but there was nothing I could do about it. A professional compromise before I even became a professional.

They were glad to have me in Milwaukee, but I wasn't the happiest guy in the world to be there. When I arrived it was still warm from Indian summer, but that didn't last long. By October I felt like someone had slammed the freezer door on me. But more than intolerable weather, Milwaukee just wasn't a real city to me. I had lived in only two places, New York and Los Angeles, and this midwestern town had none of the excitement that I had assumed was always in the air like oxygen. For instance, I expected my friends to be the guys in the slick suits and shades because those were the people I was used to seeing in Harlem and Westwood. In my new home I was dealing with, at best, very square business suits; other than that it was the polyester set, which I just could not relate to, or farmers. Farmers!

My being a Muslim didn't help, either. I hadn't made a public pronouncement, everybody still knew me as Lew Alcindor, so I was leading a secret life on top of being from an alien urban culture. People thought I was nuts when I'd ask them to take off their shoes before they entered my apartment. (They knew about Wisconsin winters and minus-twenty-degree nights, and I didn't.) My

196

teammate Don Smith couldn't understand it at all. What's this Islam? Years later, after he had been traded to Houston, he converted and changed his name to Zaid Abdul-Aziz. When he tried to explain Islamic customs to everyone coming into his home and everyone down there thought *he* was crazy, he got the good empathy from me.

My religion wouldn't permit me to gamble or to drink, but I didn't tell them the reasons, I just didn't go out for a beer. And in Milwaukee that's mainly what you did for entertainment, in fact that's *all* you did. There wasn't the Vanguard or Five Spot to hang in and hear some music; there were polka joints. Serious culture shock. Milwaukee was a beer town; people socialized in bars, went there to meet friends and strangers and expand their circles. A tavern there was like a clubhouse. But, purist that I was, I wanted no part of it. Looked to me like a whole lot of red-necked farmers getting drunk.

But they liked me. When I walked on the court the first day I arrived for rookie training camp, I got a three-minute standing ovation. The Bucks were only a year old and had lost more than two thirds of their games in their first season, but all of Wisconsin and upper Michigan and even parts of Minnesota rooted for them as if they were a local high school. The fans came from all over—Delano, Madison, Eau Claire—to see the team play. New York and Los Angeles had the good ethnic diversity; in Milwaukee there were mostly Germans and Polish people, a lot of farmers. I found it difficult, outside of the locker room, working up a good conversation. And, being a Muslim and trying to live by the letter of Muslim law, I found little benefit in extending myself to these people. They were all "disbelievers," and therefore not to be trusted.

During the first weeks and months in this totally new environment, my religion became even more important to my identity. When I would think about Islam I would put on tunnel-vision glasses, and when I went out into the real world I'd take them off, the whole time thinking about what things would be like if I looked at them Islamically. I was constantly switching viewpoints, just trying to make an accommodation, to maintain some type of sanity. I was a devout Muslim, but I was still looking to go party or get laid. In New York I had drawn my commitment from Hamaas and the community, but now that they were not around, I had to make other connections. I would run all my reactions long-distance through their Muslim perceptions—What would Hamaas do in a situation like this?—and it slowed me down. It's hard to be spontaneous when you're operating by emotional remote control. I often faltered, but in my mind I always meant to get back to the ideal.

I was far from being a saint, and though I knew what I was getting into was Islamically wrong, I wasn't strong enough in character or faith not to chase the ladies. It is a part of my life I am still trying to deal with and correct.

About the only good time I had that winter was on the court. I had looked forward to playing in the NBA, and once the opportunity came, I did my best to play it to the hilt. I was not lacking in confidence. In a preseason All-Star game at Kutscher's Country Club in the Catskills, I had gone up against Wilt Chamberlain for the first time and played him tough. I was no schoolboy any longer, and though he tried to establish immediate mastery over me, it just didn't work out that way. By the time I got to the Bucks there was no question in my mind that I was going to make it as a pro.

The expansion Bucks had been a couple of men short, but as early as training camp we knew we were looking good. Jon McGlocklin was an All-Star guard and teamed with the excellent Flynn Robinson to form a solid backcourt. Bob Dandridge was drafted with me and impressed the coaches early as a quick forward with a nice shooting touch. Greg Smith, at six feet five, was an amazingly versatile small forward, a great leaper who could run with the guys who were six two and rebound with the six feet nine bruisers. The bench was serviceable, with Don Smith, my old New York Operation Rescue team-mate Fred Crawford, and Guy Rogers, one of the classiest passer-playmakers in NBA history. We were a little short on rebounding muscle, but we were young and fast, and all of us were ready to take a shot at the title.

Bill Russell had retired that spring after playing and coaching the Boston Celtics to another NBA champion-ship, so I didn't get the opportunity to go up against him. That's just as well. He was a brilliant player, and it's nice that I never had to work up the antagonism that would have been necessary to beat him. Wilt Chamberlain hurt his knee at the very start of the season and was out until the playoffs, so I didn't face him in my rookie year either.

The difference between college and the pros came to me fairly quickly. In college, playing two games a week before an audience with whom you have some personal connection, you can prepare and get up for the games emotionally. There always seemed some traditional pride on the line, like some maiden's honor, although maybe you're not the only one who's had her. In the pros you may play as often as four times a week, and the prepara-tion is less emotional than intellectual and physical. The best way to describe it is, overwhelming; you have to devote all your energy and time to your work. If you don't, you lose. It is your work; you are being paid to do this well. With more exertion and less emotion involved, you don't get the exhilaration that you can in college. The pros become a grind, a well-paying grind—you are being paid thousands of dollars a game—but a grind nevertheless. Winning is acceptable. Losing is costing some-body money. In the pros, I found, the game is very rarely fun.

As we made our first tour of the league, I found a lot was expected of me. The hype was enormous, and there was very little I could say that would affect it. I didn't have the slightest impulse to be cocky; it wasn't my style and could have been counterproductive if some teams thought I was figuring just to blow by them. I couldn't be silent; there were sportswriters scurrying around like cockroaches after crumbs, and my silence in college had created quite the mystique. Professional athletes are obliged to talk to reporters; it's a part of the working conditions, but it was a sad fact that the intelligent question quotient around the basketball beat was hovering near shoe size, and the interviewers were always underfoot. Combine this with my dislike for the white media treatment of blacks, my religious conviction that any but the most devoted Muslims were not likely my friends, and the almost total concentration I found necessary to play basketball on the level I wanted to play it, and it's not hard to imagine that I might have been a tough interview.

My adversary relationship with the press started during my second week in the league. It was after our third or fourth game; we had arrived in Detroit in the early afternoon after playing in Milwaukee the night before, and I was tired. I have insomnia after ballgames; all pumped up from the adrenalin and competition, I rarely fall asleep before three in the morning, and here I was at my fourth successive press conference confronted by the fourth mob of reporters and the fourth round of hot lights, cold faces, stale questions. I knew rationally that, yes, this was my first time around the league cities, and certainly, I'd have to deal with all these guys for many years to come, and of course, you couldn't expect them all to be Edward R. Murrow, but I'd been beat up on the court and then inspected like prime beef off it once too often that week. I didn't want to be there, answered questions brusquely if at all, and then bolted early.

The next day I took a whole lot of grief in the Detroit papers. They couldn't have known why I was uncooperative, but rather than press for an answer or get one next time around, one columnist wrote something like, "He may be a great big basketball player, but he's the smallest guy in the league." Genius insight, marvelously inventive imagery. I hadn't read the coverage of me in the sports pages very often, but there was usually something in it that I didn't like, and from then on I assumed the worst.

(Slights stay with me. I can remember the first really unkind words I heard coming out of the grandstand as if it happened this morning. I was a fourteen-year-old grammar school baseball outfielder, already six feet five, and I was pretty good. We were playing our neighborhood rivals, Good Shepherd, and I was adjusting my batting helmet and ambling up to the plate when two spectators got up to leave. "Let's go," one guy said to the other. "Wait a minute," said his companion, "let's see if this clown can hit." This clown! I lined the ball into the gap between centerfield and right, pulled into second with a double, and have kept that moment with me for twenty-three years.)

There are some good sportswriters, many more now than when I came into the league, but for the most part back then, they were wheedlers, little guys who derived great satisfaction from tweeking the tiger's whiskers or pulling the lion's tail. You could spot them a mile away, the striped-shirt-and-checked-pants set. I'm sure I intimidated them, as big and quiet and black as I was, and they used whatever power they could muster to make some impression on me or their readers by continually dwelling on the negative. It was as if anything good I performed was taken for granted; the extraordinary was expected, and anything less was abject failure. A great night for anybody else was merely okay for me. A great night for me had to be compared to the classic performances of all time, and anything less was hardly worth mentioning. Sitting by my locker after a game, I started to feel as if a swarm of flies was buzzing around my head; they couldn't really do me any harm, but they annoyed the hell out of me.

I wanted to get rid of them, but they were an occupational hazard. They did the same thing to a lot of athletes, mostly ones who weren't white. You never heard about how Mickey Mantle might be a jerk, just that Juan Marichal was a madman or Richie Allen a bad guy. I had seen them do it to Wilt for years. Nothing he ever did was good enough. In the days when he was averaging fifty points a game and leading his closest competitor by a couple of hundred rebounds they were still calling him a "loser" and a stiff. Back in high school, Mr. Donohue had pointed that out and said the same thing could happen to me. "Look how great Wilt is," he'd say, "and nobody's satisfied with what he does." Wilt would complain, get mad at the reporters, and tell them off. Then they'd write, "He's a crybaby *and* a stiff." So that first fortnight in the pros I knew enough not to talk about it.

What I did was give them as little as possible. I tried to keep my responses minimal, direct, removed. It would be hard to take quotes out of context if there was no context. I was making their job difficult, and they no doubt began to dislike me for it. But I didn't care, these hurtful little guys couldn't touch me; in fact, I kind of had fun pissing them off.

As I made my way from city to city, I found most writers were looking for an angle. Rather than establish some personal contact with athletes, they were forever searching for a weakness, some wound to prove or defensive lapse to score against. There was a lot of envy and resentment in the locker room: from the reporters because they were dwarfed by the athletes' stardom, and from the athletes because at the whim of these twerps they could be made to look like fools in front of several hundred thousand readers.

My response was to toy with them. I figured that being understood or reported on properly was out of the question so, once in a while, I amused myself by jousting. In high school I had worked out with the debating team before basketball practice, and now I put some of that training to work. Writers would pursue me, try to pose their questions so that I would have to give them a controversial answer, and they would have a headline for the next morning. (Question: "Wilt is thirty-three. He's getting pretty old, huh?" If I say, "Thirty-three, he's not a boy," I'd see it on the back page in fifty-point type: "Wilt's Over the Hill: Lew.") It was their job; they tried to make you say screwball things. I, however, played the game of semantics pretty well, and I wouldn't let them have their lines. We would go around for several minutes, them phrasing and rephrasing their bait, me stonewalling or evading. I knew what I was doing, and they knew I knew what I was doing. This was a little game we had going, and neither of us was winning and neither of us was very happy playing it.

For example, one guy in New York tried to provoke me because I had called someone a motherfucker. "What do you mean by that?" he asked. Pen poised, he stood in the hot crush of microphones, camera lights, and newsmen like he'd hooked a flounder. Nice question, the boys all nodded; Lew will cream somebody in print, and we'll all sell some papers and put another meal on the table. The guy didn't know he'd tackled a marlin.

"What do I mean by that?" What kind of stupid question was he asking? It wasn't like he'd never heard the word before. He knew exactly what I meant. I looked at him very long and hard.

"All right, man, you want some of this, I'll go through it with you," I growled.

"The black community is very much of a matriarchy," I began. "Has been ever since the days when families of slaves were broken up, the men sold all over the place with no regard for their wives or children, humiliated, made to feel like they were less than men. Lots of times the women had to take over everything, bring up the children by themselves, maybe bring up other people's children as well. That's lasted to this day; the men are still being humiliated, still being moved around, sometimes can't support a family, shamed. Black women are still raising most of the kids and running a lot of the culture.

The mothers are very important to black people. So anyone who would fuck his mother is thought of as the lowest type of person, and what I was saying was that this person is a very low type person.

"Now, you got that?"

The reporter kind of folded. I had answered his question directly, he could never accuse me of evading him, but he couldn't use a word of it. What made me mad was that I wished he could.

A couple of times around the league and the writers started to keep their distance. I was trouble, likely as not to embarrass them in front of their peers, so rather than take their chances in person they began sniping at me in print. I was "aloof," "distant," "taciturn." My game was limited, I was too skinny, not aggressive on defense, lazy, uninvolved. The truth was, I was just not going to be a stationary target for the barbs from the press table.

Over the years I did meet some good writers. I liked talking with Frank Deford, although I wrote him a stupid note telling him he'd written something racist about my family, which was my overreaction and wasn't true. I was interviewed by Roger Kahn at the same time he was writing *The Boys of Summer,* and as big a Dodger fan as I am, we hit it off very well. But for the rare enjoyable encounter I've had fifty that have been truly unpleasant.

It didn't take three days in the NBA until I started to feel under siege. Because I am taller than almost everybody, and more agile, there has always been the assumption that the rules, precautions and safeguards that apply for everyone else should not be applied too strictly to me because I have some sort of unfair advantage. Even back in grade school, the refs let me get pounded underneath the boards rather than call fouls because they felt they should "even things out." From grade school through high school, college, and the pros, that hasn't altered. I don't get the protection of the rules that everybody else gets. Foolishly, I had thought that would change once I got to the game's summit, the NBA. Another element of innocence dashed in a hurry; I took a quick beating, fouled out of my first game when my retaliation and jockeying for position was not subtle enough for professional standards. I was supposed to take it because I was large. It's been that way all my life; rather than appreciate my use of what I've been given, people consistently try to cut me down.

In the movie *One Flew Over the Cuckoo's Nest* the Chief, played by Will Sampson, talks about his father to Jack Nicholson. He says something like, "You know, my father was a real big man. But everybody tried to take a piece of him. He would drink whiskey, and every drink would take a piece out of him until there wasn't much left anymore." That's how I began to feel. Basketball had ceased to be fun. It was work, and with every game my abilities might have been growing, but the people who ran it were taking chunks out of me the way the white man had devoured the Indian. I had lived with everyone's exalted expectations, had tried to live up to them, but that wasn't what anyone wanted. It was like, if everybody could jump over one barrel, they wanted me to jump over five. If I did it, so what, I was a giant. If I made it over only three, I was a bum. On the court the officials never gave me the benefit of the doubt. "Either/or" always went to the smaller man. Players were allowed to hold, grab, and foul me because I was bigger and better than they were, and I didn't need the protection of the rules the way they did. Most superstars get the calls their way: Jerry West charged for years and was permitted to get away with it; Oscar Robertson jammed his defenders something fierce and was rarely called; Elgin Baylor could use his off arm to hold people off the ball, make the shot and get a free throw for his effort. It's one of the superstars' perquisites. Not for me. The pattern began my rookie year and has never been altered: There's a whole 'nother rule book for Kareem.

Sounds whiney, like sour grapes, but my rookie

year as a pro drove me pretty deep into myself where I couldn't be visited, couldn't be bruised.

The 1969–70 season itself went well. Though we started slowly, the team gathered a nice head of steam, and about halfway through, we really hit our stride. The Bucks were an expansion team, stocked with players not deemed valuable enough by their original clubs to "protect" in the expansion draft, plus me and Bob Dandridge from one year's college draft, and a couple of guys picked up in trades. Expansion teams never do well; they have a cast-off mentality and, at best, moderate skills. In this one season we became a team, developed an affection for each other and a collective confidence that started from absolute zero, and finished second in our division with the second-best won-lost percentage in the league. Our big match-up all season long was with the New York Knickerbockers, and mine was with Willis Reed.

Individual match-ups are not really of consequence in a team game like basketball, and one man cannot carry a team over an entire season. A player is definitely capable of going wild for a week or two, getting a roaring confidence and a hot shooting hand and personally pulling and willing his team to victory. Once in a while you see a guy on fire, and his attitude spreads to his entire team, and they're hard to beat. To put together a winning season over eighty-two games and eight months, however, a team needs strength in all positions, balance, health, and luck. Because I came from New York, and the Bucks and Knicks had the two best records in the NBA, a lot was made of our games together. We had a good rivalry, played in the same division, and went head-to-head in the Eastern Division Championship Finals.

We had beaten the Philadelphia '76ers, with Billy Cunningham, Hal Greer, Archie Clark, and Wally Jones, in the semis. We didn't know if we had the team to go all the way, but we were definitely going all out for it.

My game in the pros was much like it was in

college, only expanded. On defense I was generally much quicker and more agile than the centers who were playing me, and I didn't have a whole lot of trouble putting the ball in the hoop. I averaged over twenty-eight points a game. Also, both Mr. Donohue and Coach Wooden had taught me to look to make the good pass when I was double-teamed, and the Bucks' Coach Larry Costello encouraged it as well, so I gave out about four assists per game over the course of the year. But my major strength was on defense. I had closed down the middle at UCLA, but in the pros the zone defense was outlawed, meaning I had to stay with my man or guard somebody else. Because most big men posted down low, however, I could stay near the basket, and I made it my job exclusively to control the inside, help my teammates by blocking the shots of anyone who might have gone around them and tested the lane. My teammates could play their men tight or gamble for the steal, safe in the knowledge that I was going to reject any courageous soul who had the audacity to drive on me.

This system worked well, but we had a hard time with the Knicks. Willis Reed, their center, was about four inches shorter than I was but ten pounds heavier. He was thick, mobile, and aggressive inside, which was not uncommon for NBA centers, and he had a soft, accurate touch with his jumper from twelve to eighteen feet, which was. If you left him alone, he could hit with it a good portion of the night. That made the Knicks an extraordinarily difficult opponent for us. I could go out and stop Reed's jumper, but the Bucks had no strong forward to pick up the rebounds or cover the middle; so Walt Frazier would drive, Dave DeBusschere would post up, and Bill Bradley would be popping behind screens and hitting his jumper. I spent the whole series running back and forth trying to guard Willis outside and help my teammates inside. Though I could handle Willis personally, the teams matched up very much in New York's favor.

After every game the only thing the writers wanted

207

to know was, "What did Willis do to dominate you?" He didn't dominate me. I was scoring thirty points a game, going in for a lot of rebounds, getting a lot of assists; I played as hard as I could, but the Bucks were not good enough to beat the Knicks consistently. An individual's play never offsets a great team's play, and the Knicks had a great team from their starting five through Cazzie Russell and Dave Stallworth on a deep bench. Because this was the playoffs, I tried explaining this to the media. They'd stop writing and listen to me and say, "That's a pretty good observation." Then they'd go right ahead and write whatever it was they wanted their readers to believe, that Willis dominated Lew. I expected it in print, and they didn't disappoint me. Willis had a great year; he was chosen Most Valuable Player. I won Rookie of the Year. He did what he had to do to make his team win, but he had a lot of help. The Knicks beat the Bucks in five games.

The winter in Milwaukee was cold beyond belief, and I didn't have much interest in going out in it. I wasn't looking to be friends with anybody white, and I never really hit it off with black Milwaukee, my devotion to Islam keeping me away from casual strangers and their constant transgressions, and the absence of an active Muslim community making it virtually impossible for me to meet anybody. A built-in isolation factor. Don Smith (now Zaid Abdul-Aziz), had gone to John Jay High School in Brooklyn and was on the Bucks, and I'd hang out and have some chuckles with Greg Smith, but aside from dealing with my teammates on the road, I didn't have much going for me.

I knew I was in trouble when I got my first three-hundred-dollar phone bill. I spent all my money calling the ladies I knew in Los Angeles. The next month my American Express bill doubled from flying them into Milwaukee. It was a pretty lonely existence, and I didn't see it getting any better. I left Milwaukee right after the season ended and didn't come back till fall.

11

If my personal life was at a standstill, my professional life was taking the great leap forward. Tired of playing on a losing ballclub and willing to go to court to establish his right to become a free agent at the expiration of his contract, Oscar Robertson forced the team owners' hand and that autumn got himself traded to the Bucks.

I was ecstatic. We had been good but young, quick but lacking in the on-court presence that could command deference not only from our opponents but from ourselves. Last year every game had been a toss-up. Now, even before the Big O walked on the court for our first practice, we all had the feeling that this was our year.

Oscar Robertson is, in my opinion, the best all-around player in the history of basketball. A lot has been made recently of the "triple double," a player going into double figures for one game in rebounds, assists, and scoring. Broadcasters and commentators talk about it like it was the Holy Grail. In the 1961–62 season Oscar *averaged* a triple double: Over an eighty-game schedule he could be counted on for double-figure rebounds; he led the league in assists with 899, and he scored over thirty points a game. He is the all-time NBA leader in assists and free throws made, and third in all-time scoring.

I had watched him on television when I was in high school, but his greatness hadn't been obvious to me. Playing with the perennial also-ran Cincinnati Royals, he was deadly with that compact, ass-out jump shot, but he didn't impress me that much. It was when I started playing against him that I began to understand how he controlled the game, and when I finally played with him I really started to see what his game was all about.

Oscar Robertson was the epitome of the subtle, no-flash ballplayer. He had the game broken down into such fine points that if he got even a half-step on you, you were in big trouble. He kept the game very simple, which was his first secret. All the most effective basketball strategists and players have kept their technique honed to its most lean and essential parts. John Wooden did it in his coaching; Bill Russell did it in his playing, and Oscar was the same way. He didn't have blazing speed, and he didn't do a whole lot of pirouettes, all he did was score, rebound, and dish the ball off. He could handle the basketball well with both hands, using the crossover dribble, first the right hand then the left then back to the right again, to lure his man into going off-balance or leaning in the wrong direction, after which he'd go right by him, and then it was either time for his shot or a pass. If you were going to stop him, you were just going to stop the basics, and you would have to do it perfectly because he could take advantage of any miscue you might make.

At six feet five inches tall, 210 pounds, Oscar was the first big guard. It wasn't obvious because he was so smooth and graceful, but he had tremendous brute strength, and if he bumped into you, he'd knock you back on your heels. On defense he was quick and smart and solid, as easily slap the ball away from his man as be the wall that would not crumble before a drive. On offense he had the consistently effective shot and the absolute will to put it in. His whole thing was access to the basket. When he got ready to shoot, if I could give him even a glimpse of space to work with, he would drive past, leading his defender into my shoulder, which would stop the man, and once past me either hit the lay-up or have the court awareness to hit the teammate whose defender had momentarily left him free while trying to stop Oscar.

He was a master of the three-point play, and he was at his best against guys who played him tough. Oscar versus Jerry Sloan was always a great match-up because Jerry played very physical defense. Jerry would get great position, allowing for no movement, no first step to the hoop, and then let his man run into him and be charged with the foul. Oscar loved that because it played right into his hands. Oscar would always let Jerry set, then fake as if he was going around him. Oscar had the great move so, out of respect, Jerry would react, and as soon as he started, Oscar would bowl Jerry over, go up and hit the jumper, and be on his way to the foul line as the whistle was blowing and the ball was hitting the net. Oscar was so subtle he'd never get called for it. Meanwhile, Oscar was a truck, it was like getting hit by Jim Brown. But Sloan would bounce back up, complain to the refs, and get on with his game. I loved to watch them.

But Oscar was even more valuable as a leader than as a scorer. He was thirty-two years old and had lost maybe a step, but his total mastery enabled him to be just as effective as when he was averaging thirty points a game. By directing and inspiring the rest of us, he enabled the Bucks to play the game the way it was supposed to be played.

We had all the components in place. The Bucks had obtained Lucius Allen in an off-season deal with

Seattle—it was good to have my old friend and running mate with me again—and with Lucius, Bobby Dandridge, and Greg Smith, we had three guys who could get up and down the court in a hurry. I was in the middle, and Oscar controlled the ball like he was dishing out compliments. Bobby was deadly from fifteen to twenty feet, and Oscar could spot him the moment he came open. People wouldn't guard Greg Smith, which let him run free under the backboard where he was a terror. Oscar would find him. Lucius and Jon McGlocklin played off Oscar, and both of them could either put the ball on the floor or seem to be careening down the court and then pull up and shoot, which made our fast break effective. All the guys played D, and with Bob Boozer and McCoy McLemore coming off the bench for some board strength, we were a very powerful squad.

Coming out of three consecutive college championships and an NBA semifinal, I was used to winning and assumed it would continue pretty regularly, so I was not as overwhelmed playing with Oscar as I might have been. Had I known that what he added to my game would come only once in my professional lifetime, I might have stopped to savor the pleasure of working with the best. I'd never known anything but the best, though, so while I enjoyed playing with Oscar, it wasn't until several years later that I appreciated him fully.

What the Big O did for me that gave a quantum jump to my game was get me the ball. It sounds simple, and it was—for him. Oscar had this incredible court vision and a complete understanding of the dynamics of the game. Not only did he see guys open on the periphery for a jumper, he knew when each of us would fight through a pick or come open behind a screen, and the ball would arrive and be there like you were taking it off a table.

There is an exact moment when a center, working hard in the pivot for a glimmer of an advantage, has the position he needs for the score. You've run the length of the court, established your ground, defended it against the hands, forearms, elbows, trunks, and knees of another two-hundred-and-fifty-pound zealot who is slapping and bumping and shoving to move you off your high ground. You need the ball right then. It's like a moon shot: Fire too soon and you miss the orbit; fire too late and you're out of range, but let fly when all signals are Go, and you should hit it right on. Oscar had the knack of getting me the ball right at that place and time. Not too high, didn't want to go up in the air and lose the ground you've fought for. Not too low, didn't want to bend for the ball and create a scramble down there. Never wanted to put the ball on the floor where some little guy could steal in and slap it away. Oscar knew all of this, and his genius was, whether two men were in his face trying to prevent him from making the pass or in mine trying to prevent me from receiving it, in getting me the ball chest-high so I could turn and hook in one unbroken motion. No way not to score when Oscar was around. No wonder he has 2,500 more assists than anyone in NBA history.

One night he showed me the whole game. We were playing Golden State, and for some reason Oscar shed ten years and brought out the Big O one last time. Getting old in professional sports doesn't always mean losing your ability all at once, mostly it means only being able to do in unpredictable spurts what you once could call up at will; becoming a miler among sprinters. That night, maybe because he was challenged, maybe because he was angry, maybe simply because he wanted to, Oscar just dominated the floor. He crushed everyone who opposed him on the court; threw hard, precise passes that demanded to be converted; rebounded with a passion, made seventy percent of his shots and scored thirty-seven points before he was lifted. Total mastery. I envy the guys who played with him in his prime. Playing with Oscar was like working with Thomas Edison.

Oscar took the game seriously. All season long if

someone screwed up or didn't seem to want to play, he would chew them out for not doing his job. People who weren't rebounding, guys who weren't playing defense, they were in trouble around Oscar. You had to respect him; you were playing with a legend, and he was still doing all of his job; how could you not do yours?

That year I played with a legend and against one. I finally got to go up against Wilt for real. (As with the Babe, Willie, Duke and Oscar, for the greats one name will do.) He had injured his knee and was out my rookie year, but he was very much a presence my second time through.

Wilt held his position in the pro basketball hierarchy with total seriousness. He fought for it the way he went for rebounds, with strength and intimidation. It was his only identity. Finally out from under Russell's shadow, or at least no longer having to read the comparisons in every column and box score, he could have done without my interference. It would have been pleasant for him to rule the roost for a few years before some new young guy knocked him out of the box. And why did it have to be me, the kid he'd taken under his wing? After all, I was the boy he'd loaned his records to, to whom he'd shown the ropes. How could I possibly be threatening to take his place at the top? It took a special will to turn me into the demon threat to his kingdom who had to be defeated. But when the stakes are as high as identity itself, it's amazing what the mind can do.

Wilt had a lot to complain about because, from the start, he couldn't control me. Wilt's entire game was built on strength. He controlled the lane. (In fact, it was because of his dominance that the rules committee widened it by four feet the same way college ball outlawed dunking for me.) He had great timing and excellent spring, and he would routinely reject opponents' shots, either stuffing them while still in the guys' hands or batting them out of the air after they'd been launched. He was very big and very strong, and he would position himself underneath, and you could forget about coming near him. Nobody could move Wilt out of the pivot, and he was ferocious off the boards. (Over the course of his career he grabbed 2,200 more rebounds than Bill Russell and about 8,000 more than I have.) He was the dominant guy in there, with a personality to match.

Wilt has a place of special honor in the history of basketball. He personally made the game progress, brought the big man from clod to controlling factor. If it weren't for Wilt, people wouldn't believe some things were possible—one hundred points by one man in a single game, a fifty-point-per-game average. He led the league in scoring seven times and was the only center ever to lead the NBA in assists.

Wilt was not perfect, however. He wasn't the best competitor; he didn't have the most savvy as far as how to make his team win. Russell seemed to get the more crucial rebounds, and though Wilt won all the scoring titles, Russell came away with eleven championship rings to Wilt's two. (Admittedly, Russell was playing with a superior team around him.) More importantly to me, Wilt was stationary and I was mobile, and I found out fast that he could not handle me on offense. I was eleven years younger than he was, and quicker to begin with. I found my first time down the floor against him that if I let him stand in the pivot and didn't move before I got the ball, he would destroy me. The next time down, however, I saw that if I got even a little movement, I could either fake him left and go up the other way with all the time in the world for a hook, or fake the hook, get him up in the air and drive the other way for a stuff.

Early on, he didn't play me tough, figuring, I guess, that I was just a kid and he could intimidate me with the backboard growl. When that didn't work he tried his usual bag of tricks that had worked on a generation of NBA centers. He'd go for my hands, but find himself a split-second too late, the shot was gone. He'd lay back and try for the in-flight rejection, but I'd get up too high and shoot it over him. That's when it got to be fun. You could see him getting frustrated as my shots kept falling. He would coil and make this tremendous jump, his arms extended like a crane, but I had gauged it, knew exactly how high his outstretched fingers could reach, and put the ball *just* over them. He'd grunt, and it would drop for two.

I worked on a special trajectory shot just for Wilt. I'd start right under the basket, then lean away a tiny bit, and put the ball at the top of the backboard. Wilt would go after it every time. He was determined. It would go past his reach, and I'd know from his body language he'd be thinking, "That's not going in, it's up too high." The ball would squeak against the top of the backboard above the rim and fall right through. Frustrated the hell out of him.

At first, when he would back off me I'd sink the hooks from eight to ten feet. Made it seem like he wasn't playing defense. He hated that. Then the coaches tried to have him muscle me, get all on my back. For a game or two he was reaching up under my armpit and knocking me off balance or batting the ball from my hands. The referees pretty much let this go, and it was fairly successful until I found a countermove. When he threw his arm under my armpit, I'd clamp down on it with my bicep and pin it to my side, then I'd go to the hoop with him. If he pulled it out, it was a foul. If he didn't, I would hold him there while I shot my shot. If he yanked it out while I was shooting, I got my three points. It made him crazy. Jerry West, at the time his teammate on the Lakers and later my coach, told me Wilt would yell at his teammates and complain that they weren't helping him guard me. Jerry says this was the only time he'd ever seen Wilt break down and ask for help.

I never took Wilt for granted, however. You can't ever say that Wilt didn't give his best, or that his best wasn't superlative. Wilt was one of the great centers to play the game, and the next three years we had a very fierce competition. In the years since, he has said I played extra hard against him, as if I had something to prove. He is right; I did play extra hard against him—if I hadn't, he would have dominated me, embarrassed me in front of the league, and undermined my whole game and career. I'd seen him play too long to think I could just go out there and play and not be overwhelmed. Wilt demanded my best, and I gave it to him with a vengeance. I was definitely aware that I was posting up with the man against whom all comparisons would be made. (In airplanes and subways, on movie lines or in the street all big black guys were asked not "Are you Bill Russell?" but, "Are you Wilt?") He was the standard, and because part of his game was intimidation, I had to work especially hard to overcome him.

I think, though, that Wilt feels that beyond playing hard I tried to embarrass him, somehow to build my reputation at his expense, pull him down from his greatness. Make him look small. Wilt's only identity was basketball; it was what made him a man, and he must have seen me—young, full of the future, capable in areas where he'd never been—as a very deep threat. And sometimes, on the court, I did embarrass him, though never intentionally. Toward the end of his career, when he was thirty-six and I was twenty-five, I had it any way I wanted. The Bucks would play his Lakers at the Forum, I'd be getting fifty points against him; he'd try the fadeaway, but I'd be there to block it, and he'd storm out to half-court. With his career, and to Wilt that pretty much meant his life, being closed in his face, he must have taken the defeat to heart. I definitely meant to beat him—I play to win at all times—but never to show him up. From Mr. Donohue on, my coaches had been emphatic about not hot-dogging, and I agreed fully. I try for the victory, and while I'm achieving that I don't try to make anybody feel bad. I'd looked bad for my first fourteen years, and while that might have led some people to inflict it on others, I knew what it felt like and wouldn't dish it out frivolously. Certainly not to a man as important to me as Wilt.

Wilt and I have had our falling outs, however. I started to lose my reverence for him when he supported Richard Nixon for president in 1968. Harlem was in an uproar; black people were struggling for basic human rights, and Wilt was throwing his weight behind an obvious crook who had no regard for us. I became very suspicious of him. As I began to form my own personal philosophy, I found that he and I disagreed on some basics. He was a high-profile, jet-set, trickle-down Republican, and I was a private, community-oriented, share-the-wealth Muslim. Some of the people who hung around him were not my kind of folks, and he wouldn't have had a lot to say to the people I took seriously. We had our own little generation gap going.

Our differences were made perfectly clear when he published his autobiography and in it declared that black women were inferior sexual partners, were generally socially inferior because they were unsophisticated. I knew that was bullshit, and though I should have assumed it would cause trouble, I said so in public. When it got back to him, Wilt was less than pleased; he apparently said I didn't know what I was talking about. But I did know what I was talking about. I would never have criticized Wilt unless I felt extremely strong in my beliefs; he was not a guy to cross lightly, but I couldn't let that one ride. This was sexuality and capitulation and racial abandonment all in one piece. Wilt was a powerful black man, a symbol to a generation (I had looked up to him myself) and to an entire race; there was no way he should have denigrated his people, particularly in front of a white public guaranteed to seize upon this racist assertion as another means to divide and control us. Wilt the lover had gone too far. I stopped seeing him as a political crossover and began thinking of him as a traitor.

At that point we broke contact. Wilt has a large and very sensitive ego; you just don't put him down. He felt slighted or worse, as if I was repaying his kindness with betrayal. I hadn't betrayed him; I had disagreed with him. To Wilt that was the same thing. From then on he took every opportunity to downgrade my ability, put me on a secondary level in the history of basketball that he found so sustaining. For my part, although I remembered having fun with him and his being a charming and generous man, each slap made me angrier, then calloused. Let the guy talk; I knew what it was about.

It took almost ten years for Wilt and me finally to reestablish communications. We had both been hired to do a television airlines advertisement, and when we entered the studio there was a terrific tension, him and his entourage in one dressing room, me and my friends in another. When we came out, there was an awkward silence. He broke it. "Nice suit," he told me, fingering my lapels. We giants have a hard time getting fitted—forget about buying anything except T-shirts off the rack—and clothing turned out to be a mutual concern. I gave him the name of my tailor, and we started talking.

Turns out he thought I didn't like him. I always liked him, just hated his politics. Thought he was a nice guy. Still do. We shook hands, started joking, got a little loose. The ad, him sitting in his seat, me dwarfing him by three-quarters of an inch, showed our restrained ease with each other. I left the shooting that evening exhilarated and relieved, as if we'd both been battling for a rebound that had never come down.

I'm still glad I kicked his ass on the court, and I would have been perfectly pleased to have gone up against him in his prime. In 1971, my second year in the league and my first against him, he was still playing great. We beat the Lakers in the Western Conference Finals, but after the last game, in Milwaukee, the fans gave him a standing ovation for his performance.

The 1971 All-Star Game in San Diego showed me a lot about how the NBA works, and some of it I didn't want to know. It was one of only two games in which Wilt and I played on the same side. All-Star games are closer to street ball than the regular season allows because usually the squads, drawn from teams around the league, are only together for a couple of hours' practice, and all the guys rely on one-on-one skills and natural ability rather than the patterned play that a well-drilled team can pull off. Unless someone comes on the court in a particularly generous mood, or is out to prove a specific point, you don't see a whole lot of assists (except the occasional spectacular pass) or a great deal of helping out on defense.

I was starting at center for the West squad, and I was pleased to see that Willis Reed, captain of the Knicks, had been selected to start at center for the East. I kind of felt I had something to prove. From the playoffs the past year into the 1970–71 season, all I'd heard about when I'd gone to New York was how Willis was dominating me; I was agile but he'd shut me down, I was big but he was the best. Willis had been MVP; he was an excellent and inspirational ballplayer, but he had never dominated me. When he had a good game against me the writers would crow about it in the papers; when I played well against him, however, you couldn't find a whole lot of column inches on it. The All-Star game, on national TV among the NBA's most celebrated players, was my shot.

One-on-one I matched up very well against Willis. He tried, but he couldn't muscle me under the offensive boards. Without the collapsing Knick defense to help him out, he couldn't handle me alone, and I scored on him easily. On the other end of the floor I followed him outside and blocked several of his shots. This wasn't the Knicks running set routes, and I had a whole team of All-Stars, each of whom could cover his man very well without my help, so I didn't have to worry about running back and forth to shut down the middle. I played Willis tight, and he made only five of the sixteen shots he got off, while I grabbed fourteen rebounds.

The game was close all the way. We led by four after the first quarter, by two at the half, and were down by one at the start of fourth quarter play. The game seesawed, and there was some fine ball getting played out there. But when the game was on the line I took over. My teammates looked for me down low, and, over Willis, my hooks were falling. I made the last six points, blocked a shot, came down and made a three-point play with less than ten seconds left to ice the game. We won 108–107 and I was stoked! This was great, high-level In Your Face, and I came off the court cheered and cheery, like I'd just hit a home run in Little League. I knew I was the game's MVP. I knew it and I wanted it.

They gave the award to Lenny Wilkens. The voting had been done before the game ended. Lenny had played well; I had won all those awards in college; I didn't need it like he did; we could change the voting but it's a hassle; let's give it to Lenny.

I heard it but I couldn't believe it. No way anybody was the MVP of that game but me. It sounds petty, but that is a valuable award. Forget money, it's about respect, prestige. I had fought through Willis in the teeth of the media and then watched as they effectively ignored it. Complaining wouldn't help, it would only sound sour and ungracious. What could I do? Be small about it, and they'd nail me in video and print; be big about it, and they'd do it over and over again. I tried not to grumble. After all, the players saw what had gone on out there. I had done my proving to them, and they were most important. Your reputation adds to your game, and I had just showed everybody who knew how to watch that I was no longer a year away but right up there right now. We had won, I had shown my stuff, I was happy. So why was I so upset?

Maybe the people who influence the public thought I didn't need their applause, was unaffected by their approval. I certainly wasn't letting them see my emotions in the locker room all season long, perhaps they thought

I knew I was the best and didn't need them to tell me. Maybe, power being only as strong as the will of those underneath to accept it, they needed to dominate me and could only do it through denial. I was a bad interview, they could reward someone who would give them a pay-off. Short-term smarts. If they wanted me to talk, this was no way to warm the relationship. Fuck these guys, I thought, and went out and got some dinner.

We beat the Lakers in five and sat around waiting to see who we'd be playing for the 1971 championship. Baltimore was playing New York, and we had a serious rooting interest in the Knicks. They had knocked us out of the playoffs the year before; they were defending champions, and we wanted to take the crown from the king. I wanted to do it in New York in front of my Mom and Pop and all my friends. I knew we were going to win—we had lost just sixteen games the whole year and only two out of thirty-six at home—and I wanted to see how the New York press was going to explain our blowing the Knicks away.

Unfortunately, the Knicks lost by two points in the seventh game, and we had to play in Baltimore. A bad break; Baltimore is hardly the media center New York is, and our championship series immediately lost about forty percent of its impact.

The Bullets were pretty well spent by the time we got at them. The New York series had been emotional and grueling, and dethroning the champions may have seemed like accomplishment enough for one week. They had a strong team with Gus Johnson, Wesley Unseld, Earl Monroe, Jack Marin, and Kevin Loughery, but the Knicks took a lot of running and pounding and thinking to beat, and when the World Championship round began, they seemed just a little bit drained.

Then, Fred Carter made a drastic mistake.

Fred "Mad Dog" Carter had come off the Bullet bench against the Knicks and made himself into a hero.

He'd shot; he'd driven to the hoop; he'd gotten the points when the Bullets had needed them and no one could have expected that he'd deliver. Stardom was new to Fred Carter and, maybe a little filled with himself, he said something in the first game I'm sure he wishes he could take back.

"Give me the ball," he shouted as he ran down the floor and found who was guarding him, "I've got Oscar, I'll score easy!"

Oscar Robertson was already keyed up. Until that day he had been the Ernie Banks of basketball, the best player never to play for a world championship, but when Carter insulted him he became incensed. He was determined to crush anybody in his path to get to that title. We were all ready, but Oscar had this rage to win.

The whole series, any time he had Fred Carter on him, Oscar took him down on the baseline and misused him. Oscar had been a forward in college, and when he got his man low he'd back him in, back him in; if the guy gave him half a step he'd take it, then bump him and have the man give up another one. It was like Bruce Lee cornering Malek, like something inevitable. The next thing you knew Oscar was seven feet from the basket. Then he'd pump, get Carter up in the air, jump into him to draw the foul, hit the two, and make the free throw. He had Carter in foul trouble and talking to himself. We swept the series in four games. My second year in the league and here I am playing on the World Champions and named the NBA's Most Valuable Player. I was ecstatic for two days. Then I was home in Milwaukee.

Outside of basketball, that winter all I had given any time to was Islam and women. Just as Oscar Robertson had been the team leader and me the willing and necessary producer, Hamaas read me and fed me the strict guidelines of the religion while I gave him my support, which came in the form of obedience and money.

In the summer of 1970, after my rookie year,

Hamaas had decided to establish a formal Muslim community. Living six to a room in a New York tenement made that difficult, so he took his family and some students and moved to Washington, D.C. I was totally in favor of the project. Hamaas had taught me the wisdom I respected most in the world and continued to be the major influence in my life; I was in touch with him regularly and saw him whenever possible. As lost and isolated as I felt in Wisconsin, I felt grounded around him. I found solidity through the faith and the faith through him.

Surrounded by hostile forces, as I felt myself to be, I needed someone to believe in. Allah was a source of comfort, and the teachings of Muhammad gave me inspiration in an otherwise extremely boring home life, but what I didn't have near me, and what Hamaas provided, was a sincere and trustworthy friend to tell me what to do. I was twenty-four years old, making more money than I knew how to deal with, was suspicious of everyone because I knew about Joe Louis and an entire generation of black athletes who had made millions and kept peanuts. I was a Muslim in a culture that I felt resented and despised me, a city man among farmers, a purist among the compromised. Hamaas was the sincerest man I had ever met, the "servant of the most pure," and I used to bounce everything off him.

Hamaas encouraged, in fact demanded, commitment. "We've already gotten down on the Arabs for being hypocrites, and all other people who say they're Muslims but don't live it," he'd tell me. "You say you are a Muslim but are you *living* it?" I could be a Muslim, because that means understanding and believing in the religion. But Hamaas wasn't interested in anyone, myself definitely included, unless he was a true believer, which meant not only understanding but practicing Islam in its strictest and most traditional form. He was constantly testing my personal commitment, and I was made to confront myself intensely and often. I would get off the phone with him exhilarated.

The community needed a center of operations, and I bought it one. Hamaas found a three-story townhouse in a middle-class, interracial section of Washington, and when I went down and looked at the building, I was fully prepared to buy it and give it to the community. Hamaas didn't want it. He said, "You own it; it's a valuable piece of real estate. If anything happens between us, if we split, you can sell it, you'll probably make some money."

The house cost $80,000, and I put up the down payment and opened the building to the community. It was a mosque, home, community center, and everybody used it. Hamaas and his family lived there along with several others, and every time I was free or nearby I would visit and participate.

I was the only one with any money, but I contributed gladly. Others taught or proselytized or ran the center, giving what they were capable of giving. Hamaas had been taught by his own mentor that a teacher ought to be supported by his pupils, that the revelations of the Qur'an were of great value, and any man who was actively pursuing and expanding the religion ought not to have to worry about the basics of food, clothing, shelter. Students were to provide that by paying a *zakat*, or stipend. We had a difference of opinion over the amount I should be sending down there, money could always be used by the growing community, but my donations did increase. My *zakat* wasn't exorbitant, never got to be a burden, never interfered with my ability to live the way I wanted or to support my parents. I had lots of money left to invest. In fact, he hooked me up with a good lawyer from a reputable firm with whom I still work. Where money is concerned, I was and still am very skeptical, and at the time I saw the potential for being ripped off, but Hamaas never once misused me. I declared my donations with the IRS, and all that money was used for the community.

225

Hamaas always accounted for every penny—receipts, forms in triplicate, he was that kind of guy. He didn't take me and go to Rio. If he regularly wanted more money from me, it was because there was more work to be done.

This was a very special community because Hamaas was an extraordinary man. To Hamaas, who believed that he was the only person sincere, educated, and immersed deeply enough in Islam to lead the entire population of Muslims in America, all other communities were a joke. There may have been occasional righteous individuals, but as far as he was concerned, there was no one as fully prepared as he to lead Muslims, and no community that was on the right path. We all looked to him for guidance, and as he considered all compromise failure—you don't negotiate with Allah, you live by His word or you are tainted—we became more and more isolated. From Wisconsin I did not pursue any of my old friendships and let many of them die. I didn't stay in contact with my parents. It was just basketball and the people directly in my path.

I wasn't dead, however; I still liked the ladies. I found a way to suspend some of my prohibitions as, city by city, attractive women presented themselves around the league. (It's no secret that celebrity and athletics and big black guys will bring out the parade.) But right after I'd declared my *shahada,* while I was still in college, Hamaas had challenged me. He'd never said, "Now that you've become a Muslim are you going to stop fucking?" which is morally, in terms of Islam, what I should have done. He knew that wasn't likely. What he'd said was, "If you're going to do it, do it right. . . . You should be married."

Then he'd asked me if I wanted to marry his daughter.

"Ahhh, no," I'd said quickly, "I don't want to marry your daughter." I doubt if he'd thought I was worthy of her. She had been raised as a Muslim all her life; I was just a neophyte. I also was not in love with her. He never brought it up again.

But it had made me think: Why am I fucking? Am

I doing it for selfish pleasure, or am I doing it to bring more people into the world and raise them as Muslims and show them the righteous way to live so that they will extend the word of Allah? Now I knew the answer, and I knew I had to change it.

"You should be trying to find a woman who loves you and who can accept Islam," Hamaas had said. "When you do, have her come here, and we'll train her."

I'd really seen only two girls seriously senior year in college, and since I was in no frame of mind to meet anyone in Milwaukee, these were the women who were special to me. I'd met one at a Laker game. Lucius Allen knew one of the Lakers, Cliff Anderson, and when Anderson took us to the Forum one night, he dropped by and picked up his date, an attractive woman named Janice Brown. She was bright, pleasant, a senior at Cal State. But she was going out with Cliff.

Several months later, completely on a whim, I took a chance and dropped by her house. (I remembered where she lived from our having picked her up.) We talked; I invited her to come see UCLA play, and she said okay. I started calling her, and we began going out. By the end of the school year, which was my graduation, we'd gotten pretty close. One night, though, we'd headed on over to the kind of campus good-bye celebration that tries to cap off a college career with a whole course load of extra-curricular activities, a final exam in debauchery. It was one of those loud, boisterous parties filled with my wildest friends smoking dope and sniffing drugs, and I got real crazy and felt right at home among the madmen. Janice got fed up, didn't feel like that was where she belonged, asked me to take her home. I figured, she likes me but she doesn't like my friends, so maybe we should just forget about it.

I didn't see or hear from Janice until the end of the summer. She had gone to school with a guy who lived in the Dyckman Street projects, and when she came to New York to see him, we found each other and almost immediately got close again. My first winter in Milwaukee, she visited me a few times and, lonely as I was, I found myself thinking in nonfrivolous future terms. Hamaas had told me a Muslim should be married, and since any woman I would even consider marrying would have to be a Muslim, I asked her if she would consider looking into the religion. She said yes, though I'm sure her interest was more in me than in Islam, and that summer she studied in Washington with Hamaas and his wife. Very quickly she responded strongly to the religion, moved permanently to D.C., got a job and became part of the community. Hamaas named her Habiba.

At the same time I was seeing Habiba I met another young lady. I had been on campus, just out for a stroll, when this very pretty girl came walking my way. My eyebrows went up, but I was cool. We made eye contact—the closer she got the better she looked!—I kind of half smiled and gave her the subtle nod, and she did me the same. We both kept on going. It was all I could do not to turn around and check out the fadeaway. College is full of that kind of lost opportunity—"If only I'd said . . ."—and that night I cursed my reticence.

The next time I saw her I didn't let her get away. I stopped and tried to talk with her. She paused, and we introduced ourselves, and I found myself chatting in a way I'd never conceived of mastering as a freshman. We went out, phoned each other often, started building a relationship.

Let me call her Benavshad, though it's not her name. She was tall and slender, built like she might have been a distance runner, and she had this madonna smile. She was subtle-happy, as if something was glowing inside that always seemed to please her. I'd ask her about it, how she could seem so peaceful even when everywhere you looked there was trouble, and she'd just laugh. She was warm, and she warmed me. We'd drive to the beach at two in the morning when the surf was up and walk on the sand, fall asleep in the car at dawn. I took her to the clubs and turned her on to jazz. We had fun, and what had been an immediate rapport deepened as we grew together. I could tell her anything, from dumb jokes to new ideas I'd heard in class to my own personal revelations, and she could do the same with me. Slowly I realized I had found not only someone I admired but a very special friend.

By semester's end we had grown very close and made a commitment to each other. I had been moved so far as to go down and visit her parents. That winter she too came to visit me in Milwaukee and, eventually, said she was interested enough in Islam to go to D.C. and see for herself what was happening. She also became a Muslim.

So during my second year in Milwaukee, while my outside contacts were being erased or abandoned and my home life was hotel rooms and prayer, when I decided that I wanted and needed to get married, I had a terrible choice to make. I liked Habiba; we had become comfortable together, and she was home-minded and stable, a firm and devout Muslim woman. She was like a buddy. But I loved Benavshad; there was a depth of emotion that enveloped us more deeply than I'd felt possible with any woman.

I went to Hamaas. He had offered me one course of wisdom that had changed my life, and I wanted to talk about another major decision. I trusted his judgment, I think, more than I believed in my own. The prime force in my life was Islam; I relied on it for moral foundation, spiritual guidance, and a means of dealing with the physical world, and Hamaas was not only thoroughly schooled in the faith, he had incorporated it into his gut. He was so deeply involved that his every move was intuitively Islamic; he had the kind of devotion I could only admire and wish one day to approach. On top of that he knew my needs, had himself either suggested or created them. Who better to ask how to have them filled?

Hamaas had trained both ladies, renamed them, come to know each in a way even I wasn't able. He had also taken me from an angry boy searching for something to believe in to a devout and passionate follower of what he taught me was a strict and rigid faith. He was accustomed to being asked for direction and more than willing to give it. I told him my feelings for both women, and he sat me down and issued his advice.

The conversation took about half an hour. He spoke about marriage to one as opposed to marriage to the other, balanced the benefits of love versus devotion. I knew when we began that he wasn't going to tell me what I wanted to hear, and though I tried listlessly to tip the scales, Hamaas was working with his own logic, and he was conclusive.

"You may find Benavshad attractive now," he told me, "but is that enough? Should your love for a woman be stronger than your love of Allah? If you are to be a true believer, shouldn't Allah be first in your heart and first in your mind?"

I would not argue with him. After all, I thought, he is so much closer to the faith, has so much more vision than I do. "You want to be so pure and righteous before Allah. I know you do. Benavshad will never understand you," he said. "Habiba will. You should marry Habiba."

I can't say that Hamaas made me take that step. I had my free choice; I could have done whatever I wanted. But I didn't do what I wanted, didn't even really go off by myself and ponder this major question. As wealthy and powerful and celebrated as I was, I was still not capable of taking my life in my hands. Where was my strength, my confidence, my self-esteem? I permitted—encouraged—Hamaas to weigh a decision I was supposed to weigh. How could I expect anyone else to understand the crosscurrents of my desires? How could they possibly know when I was so unsure myself? I never questioned Hamaas. Finally, I did as I was advised.

When I told Benavshad my decision I felt like I had died. How could I possibly explain? I love you; I'm marrying another woman. There wasn't a lot of talking that got done. We were both hurt and confused, torn between an ideology that was only now being tested for the first time and a vision of emotion that everyone I had any respect for always carried with him, between Islam and true love.

The conversation was brief. She thanked me for introducing her to Islam and helping change her life. She said she saw in Islam the proper way to live. She said she'd always care for me.

I've regretted that day since the moment it began. Two weeks later she married another man.

12

I married Habiba at the townhouse mosque in Washington, D.C., a couple of weeks after we'd won the NBA championship. The ceremony was held at dawn in accordance with Muslim law as Hamaas interpreted it. I was almost in a trance, full of impulses I had always before been able to control. It was as if someone were simultaneously pumping my emotional throttle and standing on the brakes. I had made my ablutions and said my prayers, and dressed all in white robes, I was taking a life step that was serious and traditional and binding. I might have been marrying the religion itself.

We were married in the presence only of Muslims. There were occasions when Hamaas would not be in the company of unbelievers, and apparently he felt the ceremony and the commitment itself was so sacred it could not be shared. Hamaas hadn't told me this beforehand, but I was not so fully studied in the Qur'an to know whether it was forbidden to have outsiders at a Muslim wedding, even if they were family, and that morning I was not looking to challenge Hamaas on a point of doctrine or anything else. Hamaas presided, and having exchanged vows before Allah, Habiba and I became husband and wife.

There were sharp words in the hallway. My mother and father, who had left New York at midnight and driven five hours to get there, had not been told in advance that they would not be permitted at the ceremony and were being barred at the door. I hadn't known that they would be denied entrance. This wasn't the kind of wedding I had fantasized about in my room in the projects, so I had kind of followed the ritual as it was laid out for me. I wanted to do it right in the eyes of Allah and hadn't given a lot of thought to its effect on Al and Cora.

Hamaas came and told me, "Kareem, your mother is here." Somebody else said, "Your parents were here, but they came too early." I went to the door.

My mother was furious. "Come on inside," I told her. "No," her voice could etch glass, "I will *not* come inside."

"What happened?"

"Your father and I drove all night to get here, and then whoever runs this place sent a man out to keep us from coming in. I said, 'May I come in and use the bathroom?' He said, 'They're all in use.' 'Then who's at the ceremony?' I went down and found a service station and used the facilities, and when I came back the ceremony was over. I don't accept that; I don't accept any of this, and I'm not going in and showing my respect."

Cora stayed outside. My father came in for a few minutes while I made them a reservation at a hotel, and they left. A half hour later I followed them.

In her room my mother was very upset. I tried to explain the reasons in terms of Muslim law, but I wasn't convincing because I myself wasn't fully convinced. Cora wasn't buying it at all. She had come to see her son get married; she had been prevented, and people had been rude to her on top of that. Her son had not come to her aid and now was not only not apologizing but was defending her enemies. There were no raised voices; the hotel room so early in the morning absorbed the sounds and deadened them in the used carpet, but my mother felt abandoned. When I left, nothing had been resolved. We held a reception that afternoon, open to everyone, but although Al came for a little while, Cora didn't appear. I was stunned by her anger. As much as I wasn't able to argue with Hamaas, I agreed with her. I didn't see why she couldn't have been invited to the ceremony. True, I had become pretty distant from my parents, but a wedding had always seemed as much a family event as a religious one, and if I had thought about it, I'd have wanted them at mine. Sometimes, I would have felt, you could uphold the letter and spirit of Islamic law and also accommodate people. Hamaas was not about to make any accommodations, and, I had to admit to myself, I had gone along with him.

I was numbed all day. Accepted congratulations, praised Allah, felt like I wasn't there. As soon as the reception was over I left. Didn't spend the night with Habiba. I spent my wedding night driving to Cherry Hill, New Jersey, to my friend Archie Clark's house and stayed there. I had to be alone. I had very successfully incorporated my religion into my daily life, but it had never made the kind of exclusive, conflicting demands that had backed up on me on what I had always been told was supposed to be one of *the* memorably joyous days.

I didn't sleep well, and the next afternoon I drove up to New York to try and placate my mother. It didn't work. I was angry at Cora for not giving an inch, angry at myself for allowing this to happen, upset with Hamaas for creating this collision course, and angry at myself again for daring to question my mentor.

A week later Habiba and I went on a State Department tour of Africa. We made a pilgrimage to Mecca, came back, went straight to Wisconsin and started married life.

That autumn, 1971, I changed my name legally from Lew Alcindor to Kareem Abdul-Jabbar. I had lived two lives too long. I knew I was going to take some heat for it, but Muhammad Ali had established a precedent and borne some of the brunt of the attack. There would be the jokes, the unfamiliar Arabic being too difficult or threatening for some people to accept without a fight. There would also be the confusion between my religion and his. This was very important because Ali's religion was a sham to me, and I took mine very seriously. The Muslims and the so-called Black Muslims have very little in common. Rather than go out of my way explaining, however, I chose to make brief, concise statements and insist upon the attention I thought I deserved. I didn't want to be some clown engaging in religious debates with ignoramuses; you didn't hear sportswriters discussing Protestantism with Jerry West. I simply wanted to be called by my legal name and be given the same respect anyone else got. I knew, however, that I would be taunted from a distance. As far as I was concerned, the more distance the better.

My faith in Allah and Hamaas, and my continuing perception of myself as a black man first and an American somewhere down the line, made me increasingly withdrawn. Habiba's religious devotion and stay-at-home nature added to my isolation, and my residence in Milwaukee didn't open me up to the outside world. Also, the more I read the papers the less I felt compelled to be connected to the country.

America in 1971 was defined by Vietnam. The war was killing young men in record numbers; any fool could see that the politicians had been lying for years about body counts and "winning the hearts and minds," and about how and why we were there. It wasn't my war, wasn't my cause, and I didn't want to see any of my guys get shot up in it.

I wasn't about to go over there to begin with. You were supposed to register for the draft within three weeks of your eighteenth birthday, but I had waited four months before finally sauntering down to the Selective Service Center. I would have waited longer but UCLA had to know my draft status.

The place was crowded that day and I was looking jaunty in my beat-up racing cap, standing in this puke-green formica-tiled bullpen waiting to go through the process when I heard this vaguely familiar voice coming from four rows down.

"Hey, Schwartz!"

It was Joseph Traum, from Power. "Weiss, my man!"

"How you doin'?"

"Great, man, what's happenin'?"

We were chattering into the dread silence across the whole place, other guys on line beginning to look around for more conversation, when this sergeant came busting out from behind the battery of desks. He stormed up to me and said, "You, take off that cap, be quiet!"

I said, "Hey, man, what's this shit . . ." and that soldier had me in the express lane to Khe Sanh.

"I want your name, son, you're going in." He was talking to me like I had already died.

When I finally got interviewed I was sent to my local draft board. I walked in there, and they sent me to the doctor who said, "You know, if you're over six feet six inches, you're too tall for the service." I was looking down on the top of the measuring stick, but he wanted to see how tall I was anyway. Two or three weeks later I got my 4-F.

A lot of my friends did go in, though, none of them happily. Johnny Graham had his 2-S, but after he graduated from college he was drafted and shipped to Vietnam. He survived. Vino, always looking for the angle, knew he was dead infantry meat, so he signed his raggedy ass into the air force and did his time in Arkansas, Tennessee, and England, and lived to tell. A Californian named Fred, who had been a senior at UCLA when I was a freshman, had been shipped to Vietnam and hung out with all these brothers from New York and Detroit and Philadelphia, and came back with a whole new outlook. He'd gone over there a pretty straight-A guy and came back smoking dope and talking a whole lot of crazy stuff, telling me how they were sending smoke back by army transport from Nam to San Francisco, sewn into the chest cavities of the corpses.

I had a friend called "the Dab," after the Brylcreem ad, "a little dab'll do ya," because he was so slick. The Dab made certain his superior officers knew this was one black draftee who was not cut out for the military. The Dab was both smart and educated, and from boot camp on he made himself a professional disciplinary problem. He had no respect for the animals who were training him or the killing work he was being trained to do, and he wasted no opportunity to let everybody around him know about it. He rarely obeyed orders, he questioned everything—the thinking man's prerogative, the citizen's right—he argued and nagged and complained. Every day he was in the sick bay with an upset stomach. It took him eight months of intense battle, but he was finally given a general discharge that was ultimately upgraded to honorable. It was the middle of the winter when he knocked on his father's door. His father looked through the peephole and there was The Dab, who he'd thought could be dead before springtime. The man grabbed him and growled, "I knew you'd make it."

My friend Carl from the projects also got drafted. He had been deferred because his father had died and Carl was the sole support of his mother, but they canceled that and were about to send him to Nam. I came home one night and saw Carl sitting by himself beside the Harlem River Drive. The Drive is a beat-up four-lane highway that ends right at the grounds of the Dyckman Street projects, down by the Harlem River, and Carl was all alone on the benches watching the traffic crawl downtown. I went over to him and he was despondent. He had only two months, maybe less, before he had to go in the service. He didn't think he was coming back. A bunch of us tried to cheer him up, because other guys had been drafted, but it wasn't working. About all the help I could be was to tell him to make the best of it and stay alive.

Carl survived the Tet offensive. He had been stationed ten or fifteen miles outside of Saigon, and one day he just decided he'd had enough. Walking back to the city as it was starting to get dark, he saw he wasn't going to make it, so when he found a bombed-out ambulance with nobody around—no enemy activity, no troops, nothing—he climbed in and sacked out. That night they hit his unit, hit Saigon, but Carl was in between. He woke up alive the next morning. I don't think he ever got over it.

Carl made it all the way through his tour of duty without getting shot or wounded, without catching the clap. When he got home he fell apart. I couldn't believe it. He'd survived the worst, now when it was time to rebuild his life he was a total failure. The war completely broke him.

My man Munti, who had lived in my building, went to Vietnam all gung-ho. He was a point man on patrol in the jungle and loving it. Then one day his squad walked right into a horseshoe, a classic Viet Cong ambush where they let you move forward until you're almost encircled and then open fire from 270 degrees. Most of the guys in his unit were hit, and Munti got a flesh wound, some shrapnel in the mouth. They were pinned down, some guys dying, when the VC stopped shooting and yelled to them, in English, "Why are you fighting us, soul brothers?" As quickly as the ambush had begun, it dispersed.

Munti went wild after that. His political awareness

had been magnified a thousand times; his life had been spared. From then on Munti decided he just wasn't going to fight anymore. He kept his rifle with him at all times, but he said he just wasn't doing any more combat duty. He had only six weeks left on his active tour, so they said he had "combat hysteria" and sent him home. Munti came back and lived in New York for seven or eight years. Then one day he checked into a hotel, left a letter, and blew his brains out.

Fat Charlie lived in my building when I was eleven years old, and whether it was about punchball or a game of tag, we always used to generate a lot of friction. He would slug me. He was fat but strong; he could throw you around, and though he was shorter than I was, I didn't think I could whip him; so every time he hit me I would run and tell his mother. One day there was a blizzard. It was snowing so hard we couldn't go to school, couldn't even go outside. When you're living in a fourteen-story building with twelve apartments on each floor, that's not so bad; you could just go visit people. I could have gone up to J.J.'s house on eleven but instead I went down, and when I walked past Charlie's floor there was Charlie, in the stairwell, with some kids. I wanted to get past him, so immediately we got into it.

I was in the concrete stairwell fighting Charlie, and I was losing. I wasn't losing bad, didn't take any real hard blows to the head or the gut, but Fat Charlie was wrestling me, wearing me out. He got me in a headlock on the ground, and we were scuffling, and my ear got folded over and mashed against one of the stairs, and it really hurt. Finally, I pulled free and jumped up. Now I was enraged. Fat Charlie rushed me, but somehow I caught him with a great combination—a left with a right following right behind it—and when I hit him in the eye, it made that squishy sound I knew mostly from the inside.

Fat Charlie jumped back. Oh shit, I thought, I've gone and done it now. He looked like he was going to pound my ass for sure. He felt his eye and said . . . "Let's go have some lunch." Fat Charlie took me to his house!

After that I was all right with Fat Charlie. He'd never liked me because I'd always been such a weasel and run to his mother, but that one time I fought him he respected me, and from then on we never had any serious friction.

Fat Charlie joined the marines. He died in combat on the Plain of Jarres.

My connections to mainstream America were either atrophying or being severed. Although my wife was with me, my family and friends were at a distance; I was living in a midwestern city that supported me without sustaining me; I had few acquaintances and wasn't spending time with those I had. All I had was my work, and I threw myself into that.

Throughout my life I've found the people I've played ball with to be, on the whole, excellent men. It's an insular life for the professionally outsized, but we develop a camaraderie your normal office worker doesn't usually get to. There are a lot of guys I know only from having played against them. Larry Costello, the Bucks' coach, told us, "Don't talk to the players before a game, they're your enemy. Don't let them think you're going to give them any type of a break." I went along with that for a couple of years, but after a while I realized his reasoning was a little far-fetched. I could be pleasant without being a pushover, and I enjoyed meeting these people. Some of the guys who will talk readily, the real talkers, you get to know them and you can't help but like them. Doesn't mean I won't pin them to the glass if they try to come inside on me.

Some guys go through total personality changes once they hit the floor. Tiny Archibald is a pretty friendly guy off the court; you get on it, and he doesn't even want to say hello. JoJo White was worse. You go around to shake hands before the opening tip-off. "Hey, JoJo, what's happenin'."

"Fuck you." It's like you're trying to take advantage of JoJo just by speaking to him.

It's mostly the guards who are the talkers in the NBA. Among the centers and forwards it's life and death around the hoop. Talk? About what? You'd better be watching where the ball is and who's got the rebound and who's trying to make a lay-up, and should you block or should you box out? Or is the ball going to hit off the rim and come smash you in the face? There's a lot to be thinking about; you can't be thinking about talking. The dudes outside, the guards, they can just bring the ball up the court as slow as they please. They've got more space to work with, more time to run their mouth. They can quip it up back and forth and then throw the ball to the middle and yell in, "Kill 'em, Moses."

Most of what I hear is when I'm standing around waiting for the refs to put the ball in bounds, or walking to the bench for a time out, or at the foul line. Usually it's pretty quiet because guys are working on what they're doing—"What side do you want to take the ball out?" "What play do you want to run?"—but sometimes you get some conversation. Calvin Murphy of the Houston Rockets is a talker. Calvin is an outstanding ballplayer, quick, good shooter, one of the all-time great foul shooters, who has been at an extreme disadvantage his entire career because he's only five feet nine inches tall. I've got the good seventeen inches on him, but he'll come stand next to me on the free throw line and tell me all his problems. He went to high school in Connecticut, but twelve years in Texas have given him a twang, and he talks very fast and choppy. "They keep trying to find someone to replace me, but they can't replace me; you know they can't replace me, but they keep trying to replace me, Abdul." I'm always his confidant. "They can't do that. I'm the only one who can shoot these jumpers.

"And I want to remind you," he'll look up at me

with an angel's sincerity, "don't block mine. Don't block the jumper. Don't want you blocking my lay-ups, either. Got to have those lay-ups."

"Tell you what, Calvin." He's got me laughing, but I know his game. "I won't try to block your jumpers, but don't you even think about trying to come in here with that weak shit. I don't want to see you in here trying to shoot any lay-ups."

Cazzie Russell was another guy who would let you know what was on his mind. I played against him and on the same team, and he was always ready for a good time. In practice he'd stand with the ball twenty feet from the basket and say, "You wanna try and get this?"

Stu Lantz, a guard on the team, would always rise to the bait. He'd say, "Cazzie, I don't have time to get out there."

Cazzie wanted company, and he'd say, "You've got time, you've got ample time, the time you have is perfectly sufficient." Stu or I would run out there to try for the block, and just before we got there Cazzie would shoot it right over our fingertips. He'd be laughing, and with the shot in the air he'd shout, "The bank is open!" and the ball would bank off the glass and into the basket for two.

Once in a game we made a steal in the front court and the ball was passed out to me, and there I was, in the middle of the floor handling the ball on the fast break. Cazzie was on the left wing, so I faked the pass to my right, drew his defender, and hit Cazzie for the open shot. Cazzie pulled up, and as he was about to let go with the jumper, I shouted, "The bank is open! The bank is open!" Cazzie was laughing when the ball left his hand, laughing when it banked home. It was one of the few times I've gotten to indulge in some little-man chatter.

Cazzie was a great guy to have on a team; he was loose, and he clearly enjoyed what he was doing. We'd get on him about his funny-looking run, and he'd shake his head in disbelief. "You know," he'd tell us, "I'm the only guy here inflicted with white man's disease." He couldn't jump. Once at practice, the ball got stuck, jammed underneath the level of the rim between the rim and backboard. "I'll just go up and get it," said Cazzie. He jumped, and missed it. Jumped. Missed it. Kept jumping till he couldn't jump anymore and the entire team was doubled over on the floor with laughter.

Some guys are silent and deadly, like a fog. George Gervin will be dropping in his forty-eighth and forty-ninth points of the night saying, "Please don't block it, Kareem," and I know I don't have a chance of getting anywhere close to him while he's shooting it. It doesn't matter where he is on the court, if he has to shoot a jumper, he'll kill you with it, and if you're going to let him drive, he'll kill you with that too. One time George was playing a little forward and got Jamaal Wilkes inside and, as fine a defensive player as Jamaal is, just misused him. Before he put up his shot, as he was taking his last steps to the hoop, Earvin Johnson and I were yelling, "George, don't *do* that to Silk!" Didn't matter, he hit it anyway.

The late Terry Furlow was a fun player on the court because he displayed a real joy for living, and to him every game was a challenge. He would taunt you, but you had to smile. He'd take you out deep and shoot jumpers from thirty-five feet and make a couple. Terry was from Flint, Michigan, which is close to Lansing, where Earvin Johnson became "Magic," and every time Terry would make a basket, he'd turn, catch Earvin's eye, and make sure he knew about it. I stole the ball from Terry in the backcourt once and shocked his behind. He had just gotten the ball in bounds, was about to switch from right hand to left and head up court when I ran around the left side, made the steal, went up and hit the hoop from the baseline. Hubie Brown, his coach at the time, was apoplectic at having the opposing center steal the ball from his point guard, but Terry was impressed. "Hey, Abdul," he called, protecting the ball with his chest now and pointing at me, "that was deep, man, I didn't know you could do that." Later, after Hubie had chewed him out, he found me on the free throw line and said, "Kareem, *please* don't make any more steals."

Though I have been known to vent my displeasure on the occasional referee, there is a whole war of words I'm in no position to get involved in. Some players do a good job provoking their opponents into the kind of verbal displays that get them chased. I've only done that once, and even then it wasn't on purpose. The last regular season game the year we won the championship in Milwaukee, we were playing Baltimore. It was a hard game, and Earl Monroe was trying to play the tenacious D, and he fouled someone in the backcourt. The referee, Richie Powers, was right there and called it. Earl turned away from Richie and I was standing between them. "Stupid ass," Monroe grumbled to himself, "stupid motherfucker. I didn't foul him."

"Yeah, you fouled him, Earl," I told him.

"Shut up, stupid motherfucker," Earl exploded at me. "I *didn't* foul him, you stupid ass."

Powers heard the stream of expletives, thought Earl was cursing him, and ran Monroe out of the game.

Some guys you just get a good feeling about. Dan Issel is a big white guy, solid player, competitor. I've never spent time with him socially, but I know him. And like him. Dan is involved in the game, but he still has the awareness and the perspective to stop and wonder at people doing marvelous things on the court, and he'll talk to me about it. At the foul line or when we pass in the locker room hallway, we'll always have something to say, little things that are immediate and you're dealing with right there but that show some character. Wisecracks about the coaches or quick player critiques. One time I almost got him in trouble because I couldn't stop laughing at George McGinnis' foul shooting. I was standing at the lane grinning—George had a very weird shot-put motion, and when he looked like that and missed, it just struck me funny—and I got Issel going too. Dan didn't want to shake George's confidence, or get the coach down on his own back, so in between giggles he was trying to shut me up.

Another time we were running down the court on a fast break, our three against their two, Norman Nixon had the ball, and Dan picked me up on the wing. When whoever else was on defense faked at Nixon and then dropped back to pick up the other side, Norman stopped at the foul line, and when a third defender came at him from behind he faked, let the guy dive by, and put up the jumper. I closed in for the offensive rebound, and Dan went through his entire repertoire of grunts and grabs and holds to keep me away. The jumper fell straight through, and Dan sighed. "I don't know why I went through all that effort to box you out," he said, "seeing how Norman shoots," and we went back to the game.

There have been some good guys in the league. Micheal Ray Richardson is a warm, friendly person who loves to play basketball. He's like Ernie Banks; he'd play two games in a day if he could. Armond Hill, Jack Sikma, Artis Gilmore—you get a chance to speak with them, and they're nice people.

Sam Lacey was a chronic complainer. Any time he got fouled it was a capital offense. He'd be at the line getting his free throws and still be going on about how he'd been abused. Once Sam was in the middle of one of his tirades, and I looked next to me, and Leon Douglas, one of his teammates, had his chin buried in his own chest, looked like he was convulsing. "Leon, what's the matter, man?" I leaned over to him.

"Don't say nothing, don't say nothing." There were tears on his cheeks; his arms were at his side, but he was shaking his hands for me to be cool. "I'm trying . . ."

Lacey had given Leon the giggles. Leon was trying to keep his job, and he didn't want the coach to think he's out there with a frivolous attitude, but it was all he could do to keep from busting out laughing. Didn't want to be having too good a time out there.

Walt Bellamy used to crack me up. He was a big, crazy center who would always be talking to himself whenever they called a foul on him. "You're always looking for me," he'd say to the referees, whether they were in earshot or not. "Never anybody else gets these fouls, just me, number eight, got to give it to Dr. Bellamy." He'd call everybody "Doctor." You spoke to him, you'd call him "Doctor B." He wasn't slick, but he was a riot. Somebody would drive the lane, he'd slap them in the face, then pick them up off the floor and ask them if they're hurt. Trip some guy on the way to the hoop, then bend down and ask, "You all right?"

Dr. B's commentary did a lot more running than he did. The second game I played against him I was boxing him out in my defensive end, and we got the ball and started the fast break. I didn't get the rebound and was tangled up with him, and as I tried to get unscrambled and get down the court, he grabbed my trunks and whispered, "No, man, don't run, don't run. 'Cause if you don't run down the court, *I* don't have to run down the court!"

Everybody has his favorite secondhand coach story, and this is mine. Jerry Chambers told me about a game Dolph Schayes was coaching at Buffalo, and the team they were playing against was putting on a half-court press. Chambers says Schayes came in at half time and was yelling. "You guys can't handle the press!" he shouted. "It's quite obvious they're beating us; you guys can't handle the press; this is how they're pressing, so this is what we're going to do." He drew a diagram on the blackboard, folded his arms, assumed a pensive position, and for the whole rest of the halftime all he did was stand there and stare at the board. The team waited for their instructions, but Schayes was glassy-eyed, slack-jawed. He was just gone. Finally, the guys had to get up and go back on the court to start the second half. When they left, he was still standing there staring, lost in his own zone.

The basketball season, from training camp through the playoffs, runs eight months, and players spend half of that on the road. When you're home it's for, at most, a week at a time, generally only two or three days. Basketball players are young, physically healthy guys, usually unmarried, always on the lookout for action, and the in-and-out nature of the schedule—often we stay in a city less than twenty-four hours—makes for a frantic social life. It's life in a bubble. You come to town late at night after playing elsewhere, or in the morning off an early flight; you go to bed; you go to practice; you go to sleep again, then you go to the game. After the game you have some time to hang out, and every now and then you can do some partying, but basically it is very physically demanding. You spend a lot of your time being physically drained. But on the prowl anyway.

I was newly married, so my activity level, which had been right up there, was all the way down, but that made the locker-room chatter and off-court camaraderie all the more important to me. I met a lot of crazy guys, and we'd trade lies like high school kids, and now and then I'd get displays that pushed the stories to the wall.

We got to the hotel on one road trip, and I'm carrying my travel bag to my room when I hear, "Pssst." I look to my right, and there's one of my teammates, his pants around his ankles, sitting on the crapper with a beer in one hand and a joint in the other. You can see him from the hallway! "Hey, Abdul," he took a hit off the spliff, "what's goin' on?"

Another of the NBA's true madmen was Mickey Davis. He was out there. We got on a bus to go to Chicago one morning, and he had a bottle of wine in his pocket, the pint blast, Mogen David, "Mad Dog," MD 20/20. He said, "I had to get this, it had my initials *and* my number on it."

Mickey had some nice friends, too. We went over to somebody's house one time; they had all these bales of marijuana, and they were using it for furniture. We sat on them, threw a tablecloth over a big pile in the middle, and it was a table. We had to get out of there; Mickey got the serious paranoia.

Charlie Yelverton was the league's only black hippie. On the road he'd use his hotel room like a crash pad, take the mattress off the bed and have people sleeping on it, on the boxsprings and the floor, in the tub. Charlie was an adventuresome soul, the league's countercultural pioneer. He'd come out during warm-ups and sit at mid-court and meditate. Wore dreadlocks, so that when he went to have his hair trimmed, the barber told him he'd have to cut it all off. Made the good impression on the coaches.

My good friend, the late Sonny Dove, played with one of the truly bizarre characters in the NBA, Reggie Harding. As Sonny told it, Reggie was a serious badman. After practice he would come back to the locker room, wouldn't shower just towel off, put on his clothes, take up his gym bag, pull out his pistol, flip out the chambers, spin them to see if he had all his bullets, close it up, stick it in his belt and leave. Reggie was born in Detroit, went to the University of Detroit, was drafted by the Pistons, and unfortunately never really got out of the urban black gangster subculture.

Reggie was rooming with Flynn Robinson, and once at four or five in the morning, Flynn says, Flynn heard Reggie come in, then didn't hear anything else. Flynn got kind of anxious. He dragged himself out of bed and hit the light. As he turned around, there was Reggie with the gun at Flynn's temple. "Yeah! I would've got you in the dark!"

One morning at seven, Reggie and Sonny Dove were just getting in when their teammate, Terry Dischinger, was getting up for breakfast. They ran into each other in

the parking lot. Reggie took out his gun and told Terry
to "dance."

"What are you talking about?" Terry sneered.

Reggie shot in between his feet a few times, then
ordered him to crawl back down the hall to his room.

Reggie was six eleven, and legend has it, he stuck
up a grocery store in the neighborhood where he lived.
He was wearing a stocking mask as a disguise. The man
behind the counter said, "I know that's you, Reggie."

"No, it ain't me, man. Shut up and give me the
money."

Ended up somebody killed Reggie. He must have
owed somebody money for something; he was sitting on
his front porch, and they came by and shot him. Definite
Hall of Fame madman.

But that's the outer fringe. Cazzie Russell was enjoyable to be around and a lot less dangerous. Cazzie was
from Chicago and was a lifelong White Sox fan. Myself
with the Dodger blue in my veins, we spent a lot of time
rehashing the '59 World Series. Cazzie was a good catcher,
probably wanted to be Earl Battey, and could do a perfect
Harry Carey. His main man for all time was Orestes
"Minnie" Minoso, the White Sox great outfielder. Never
called him "Minnie," always "Orestes 'Minnie' Minoso."
He'd tell me, "He could do everything; he could bunt, he
could field, he could run the bases."

"Caz," I'd tell him, "they never went anywhere."
He wouldn't listen.

Cazzie and Don Ford would try and top each other.
Ford was a blond, blue-eyed surfer type, and Cazzie kept
calling him Chick Hearn's "son" because Don had that
Southern California image, and Chick, the Lakers' play-
by-play announcer, was a big fan of his. An announcer
can heavily influence the fans' feelings about a player by
the way in which he presents and comments about him,
and Cazzie was sure that's what was keeping Ford on the
team. Cazzie would tell a story and end it with a trademark cackle, and Ford would mimic the laugh, and that

would burn Cazzie up. He'd start talking about "power forwards with no power."

On the court you judge a guy by his game: Has he got the moves? Is he smart? Is he generous or will no one see the ball? Will he back down? Color makes no difference among players if you can play. Off the court, color does come into focus. When I joined the league it was still largely white, but since then the ratios have changed, and the NBA social world now revolves around blacks.

The majority of players are black, and on the road we do tend to stick together. White players aren't excluded from parties or gatherings, but very few of them finally fit into the social circle. If they've done it before, they do it now; it's hard to grow up playing basketball without being exposed to, or immersed in, black street culture, so unless a guy has gone to school in South Africa, he'll at least know some of the ropes.

If white guys haven't hung with blacks before, they rarely start in the pros. It's a hard scene to crack, with a whole new vocabulary and set of assumptions. For instance, I've had people say, "Hey, man, your legs are ashy," which means I've got a lot of dry skin. Dry skin on dark-skinned people turns up gray, looks like ash. I've had to explain that to certain white guys. When I tell somebody I look like Arthur Ashe, I want them to know what I'm talking about.

Even on the team bus the coaches and press sit up front while the black players go to the rear. White players are often left somewhere in between. Some guys were funny about it. Mickey Davis, Chuck Terry, and Terry Driscoll, all Caucasians, used to go out for a few beers or a couple of distilled beverages, and sometimes Jon McGlocklin would hang with them. They were a fairly raucous bunch, and McGlocklin was sort of a straight arrow. He used to sit farther up in the bus than they did, and the guys used to say, "Jon McGlocklin thinks he's white."

*   *   *

250

Women don't have an easy time with ballplayers on the road. They make themselves available, which is always pleasant, then expect some commitment in return, which is unrealistic. Ballplayers are proud people, many to the point of egotism, that's how they become such good ballplayers. Women are attracted to the celebrity, the glamour, the wealth; what they often don't learn until it's too late is that there are twenty-two NBA cities, and guys are in and out of them all year long. The regard for womanhood in concept is very high around the NBA, in practice it's less than enlightened. Wives and girlfriends are not encouraged to tour with the teams. First, they could be a distraction from a player's concentrating on the game, and, second, they might see some things they're not supposed to see and go report it back to the rest of the wives. That kind of team disruption is deemed not worth the risk. Divorce suits *will* detract from cohesive team play.

One of my teammates made himself a dubious reputation one evening when a prostitute trying to hustle him decided she would give him some of what he wouldn't pay for and then shame him out of the money on the other end. They had their time, and when he was done he said, "You gotta leave."

"Aren't you gonna pay me?"

"No."

She started to get loud, so he slapped her up and threw her, half-naked, out into the hallway. The woman went and banged on Earvin Johnson's door. He opened it, looked at her and said, "Can't help you, baby," and as he was speaking, he saw the door down the hall open and the rest of her clothes come flying out. Earvin calls it "The Case of the Cash Bobos."

What you get on the road is periods of boredom followed by the intense adrenalin rush followed by a desire, sometimes turning to a need, not to fall back to the boredom. There are various options on how to fill that time, chasing women being the most widespread and the most fun. You get a lot of this back-of-the-bus braggadocio, but being performers, sometimes the guys will prove it in public. At training camp my rookie year we were at a Holiday Inn in Janesville, Wisconsin. Our rooms were at ground level, and if the drapes weren't drawn, you could look in from two feet away. One night after practice a bunch of us were heading out for a little dinner when we casually glanced to our right and were transfixed. The bedside lamp was turned on in one of the rooms, and from the gathering darkness the place seemed lit like a stage. Inside, one of my larger teammates, must have gone at least two hundred thirty pounds, was plowing into this woman who herself had to have run one eighty. They both had their clothes on—we'd spotted this quick consummation just in time—him with his pants around his knees, her with her skirt up, underwear around one ankle, legs in the air. Four hundred pounds of passion. We gave them a standing O.

One of my teammates, I'll call him Jackie, had a lady in his room, and they were at it for hours. You could hear it from the hallway. When the guy finally got finished with her she was half unconscious, and as he got up and left (he had other things to do that afternoon), he passed his friend in the hall. The friend was a notorious stutterer, used to be the butt of unkind jokes behind his back, but he was nobody's fool. The door was open and when he entered the room, all the lights were out, and the woman was still lying there in a daze. He took off all his clothes and slid in beside her. The woman stirred. "Is that you, Jackie?" she asked.

"Y-y-y-yeah," he answered, "it's J-J-J-Jackie."

Another time Jackie and a teammate were orgying with a woman, and she passed out. Big fat woman. They panicked. She wouldn't wake up, and she was much too big to put her clothes back on, so they dragged her down the hall and dumped her and all her belongings on the fire stairs. Not cool.

Life on the road isn't all abusing women and sating

252

lust, however. Guys have loved and married ladies they've met through the NBA nightlife, and many of the attending women are welcomed as supportive friends, familiar faces who can make the traveling life less frantic and more fun.

The road is also where you really find out about the people on your team. Basketball is good that way. In pro football there are forty-six players on the squad, in baseball it's twenty-five; it's hard to know them all. In pro basketball there are only twelve, and with so much time spent together you can really get to know each man. Some guys are all basketball, that's all there is to them, and away from the court the conversation dies fast. Others have more to say.

From adolescence on, good athletes tend to hang together. It may be as simple as a confident gait, a soul strut, or as complex as the ego itself, but there is an understanding and emotional coordination among athletes that people who have a harder time coping with the physical world can't share. At this level, though, it's not the starting five that keeps together, but those guys who have picked up a little something more along the way.

My best friend on the Bucks was Greg Smith. Greg not only played a smart game, he was a smart man. He was the quietest guy in the world when I got there, which I responded to, but a year with the wildmen and we started calling him "Killer," after Flip Wilson's character. I found I could talk to Greg about most of what I couldn't tell anyone, and he could do the same with me. Women, homelife, being black and lonely—we talked it all out and got to be true confidants. In the middle of the madhouse he and I would know there was more to it than playing and partying.

Greg was Captain Video, a total video junkie. If he wasn't at the movies, he'd be watching TV. We were on a trip in Seattle, there for two or three days, no practice that afternoon, Greg said, "Come on, let's go to a movie." I said fine, so we went and saw a double bill. We came out after four hours; the sun had been shining when we'd gone in, but now it was as dark outside as it had been in the theater, and there was a movie house next door with another double feature that was going to start in fifteen minutes.

"Come on, let's go to this one," Greg said cheerfully.

"Greg . . . I'll see you later, man." He was going to be there until midnight, and he loved it.

I enjoyed having Greg on my team. He was totally selfless on the court and a sensitive, sympathetic man off it. He gave some balance to trips away from home.

Twenty-eight games into the season the Bucks traded Greg and McCoy McLemore to Houston for Curtis Perry.

I was very upset. I'd never had a friend forcibly removed before by some management whim. It was typical, wrong-headed owner thinking: Somebody tells you that Curtis has more of the basketball skills necessary to play the position, so get Curtis. What they didn't understand was that Greg was a key ingredient in the special chemistry that had made us champions. His selflessness, his continual movement, his leaping and defense, all were blended into a team that knew exactly how to win. We had become close as a team on and off the court largely because of his bright and affable personality. We'd just become champs, why break us up?

I tried not to care, but Greg's absence left a real gap where I needed a friend. I didn't realize how much I'd miss him, how close he had become, until he was gone. I played hard but I grew wary. The deal didn't turn out well for anybody. Greg was traded from Houston to Portland, where he played for a few years, but he never found the magic combination again, was never treated with the degree of respect for his special talents that he deserved.

The Bucks won the division and beat Golden State in the 1972 Western Conference Semifinals, but Oscar got injured and we lost to the Lakers in six. I was chosen the league's Most Valuable Player for the second year in a row, which I appreciated, won the scoring title with a 34.8 average, and was third in the league in rebounding, but I would have traded it all for the championship and Greg's return.

13

Three weeks after our playoffs ended, my first daughter was born. I was right there in the delivery room, scared and thrilled as I watched her come in. What a great day. The anesthesiologist saw this fat little face appearing and said, "Oh, it's a boy! It looks just like you." Everything from the hips on down was still inside Habiba, so I said, "Yeah, it's a boy!" Then they pulled the baby out, and it was a girl, and she did look just like me. She was healthy and I was proud.

It is Muslim custom to call the *adhan* at every baby's birth. The *adhan* is the basic declaration of faith and praise to Allah, and one must call it in the baby's right ear to begin a child's righteous life. The nurses cut the umbilical cord, cleaned her and wrapped her in paper, and the whole time she was crying and fretful, you could see her struggling in this new world. They handed my daughter to me, she was only minutes old and so very tiny, and I held her in my arms and raised her to my face and started to call the *adhan* very softly. As soon as I started praying, she got completely calm. She could feel me, and I could feel a bond growing that I'd never dared hope I could feel. As I spoke, she stopped her struggle and was quiet and restful, and so was I. When I finished the prayer I gave her back to the nurse, and the baby started wailing again. I was totally in love.

Hamaas had named me and my wife and everyone in the community, and he named my daughter. He felt that because he had the most complete Muslim training he had the best insight into each person's spirituality, and Muslim names being a more overt means of connecting a person with Allah than Christian ones, it would be best that he name her. I loved my daughter tremendously; this great intuitive pool of emotion had been tapped, and I would have liked to have searched my own heart to define her, but I didn't argue with Hamaas. I didn't feel I had the right.

He named her Habiba.

The baby was wonderful, and for a while my wife and I loved her and made the best of each other. My wife did everything she could to make me comfortable. She learned how to cook the things I liked to eat; she became aware of and tried to practice the spiritual discipline as taught to us by Hamaas, including punctual Islamic prayer, fasting, keeping the home and our own persons clean. Our first year of marriage was very pleasant, and the baby gave us both something to be proud of.

I still found in myself, however, the need to be alone. I had grown accustomed to my privacy. In my parent's home and in college and then on my own in Milwaukee, I had never lived with a woman or anyone who could either put demands on me or even have her own different routine. Never a great compromiser, I was not the easiest man to live with. If you've got three brothers and one afternoon you all hate each other, you've still got to sleep together that night, and the next day they'll still be there; you learn to deal with each other and develop a tolerance and a way of accepting apologies and admitting mistakes. An only child can retreat to his room and brood and never have to abandon his hatred. I'd been a loner, and when it came time to be married, I wasn't used to dealing with someone in what had been my own territory who was going to leave the cap off the toothpaste or keep the shower stall door closed when I wanted it open. More than that, I found that even though as a solo I had often been bored and lonely, there was also a comfort I derived from solitude that I couldn't find in any other way. There was nothing I could do about it— there was nothing I wanted to do about it—at some point I just felt like being by myself.

That summer I studied Arabic at Harvard University in Cambridge, Massachusetts. Habiba stayed home with the baby, but we stayed in close contact by telephone and the occasional weekend plane ride. I was consumed with my religion, wanted to learn everything I could about its history and origins and the kind of subtleties Hamaas had incorporated into his entire self. I was being powered by the energy of the D.C. community; Hamaas was a dynamic and persuasive speaker, and down there we would all be moved and turned on by the spiritual atmosphere he created like a mist.

At Harvard, however, I was confronted by some very disturbing contradictions. I was studying the Arabic language, reading the source material of the faith itself, the Qur'an and the Hadith, and I began to realize that many of the strictures that Hamaas had been teaching me weren't written anywhere. Little things started to accumulate in my mind like water around cement until the foundation of my beliefs was threatened. As trivial a disagreement as over the proper wording of the Muslim greeting began the process. (Where else would it begin but at the greeting?) *A Salaamu Alaikum,* it turned out, was sufficient; more—which Hamaas had instructed us was required— was not improper but unnecessary. Also, Hamaas would have us scrub up for prayer as if we were on *General Hospital*, but in most cases all that was required was a simple ablution.

The whole summer was devoted to learning the basics of Arabic. In *The Life of the Prophet* I read the story of Bilaal, a slave whose owner took him out in the sun and placed a large stone on his chest and told him to renounce his faith in Allah. Bilaal refused, and though he was not killed, he was persecuted mercilessly. In order not to suffer the torture of Bilaal, to escape death or violent repression, I was taught, Muslims are permitted to be secretive concerning their faith. Here was a basis in Islamic tradition for compromise and accommodation. My readings at Harvard, and Muslims whom I knew in New York, also told me quite definitively that what I had been taught as doctrine was in fact the outer edge of extreme orthodoxy. These Muslims asked how I practiced Islam, and when I told them, they said that much of what Hamaas quoted as *hadith*, which are verbal traditions of the prophet put into book form, had never appeared in any collections of *hadiths* at all.

I became very uncomfortable. Hamaas had discouraged us from checking out his edicts with other Muslims because he said they were all charlatans, and many of the people whom I had checked out in the Islamic world *were* charlatans. I had become involved in Islam because I sincerely believed in its principles—they matched my own desire for commitment and purity—and the way Hamaas had taught me about the faith and its culture made a lot of sense to me, demonstrated true insight. Now I was finding that Hamaas may have been insightful but not correct. I was shaken.

Full of my new information and armed with a long list of contradictions, I challenged Hamaas. Before I could get halfway through, he grew angry. "These things aren't written for a reason," he said hotly, "they are to be handed down from person to person. I don't know who your sources are, but I'm going to practice exactly the way my teacher taught me. I'm not changing. If you don't want to follow the way I teach you, you can go and do whatever it is you want to do."

The confrontation made me dizzy. I was full of legitimate concern, looking for a discussion of doctrines and law and intellect. Hamaas was into his moral strong-arm tactics, and for a moment I was taken off guard.

"But—" I started.

Hamaas didn't want to hear any buts. "You know," he said darkly, "maybe you should split."

The last time somebody suggested I leave, it was Hamaas who had stepped in and told me to stay.

"If you don't think we're correct," he went on slowly, "we're leaving the house."

I didn't know what to do. I had asked sincere questions and had been threatened with abandonment, but I had been given no answers. How could I accept anyone on faith except Allah? This couldn't go on.

I agonized over the decision for days. My association with them was over, then it wasn't. I flipped back and forth for hours, first alone, then still with a community of friends. My wife believed in Hamaas even more strongly than I did, would she be forfeited too? Hamaas had named me, defined me, and I had accepted his definition. If I denied him, was I unraveling my self?

Hamaas stayed in a silent rage, but I spoke privately with other members of the community. They had not been exposed to the contradictions I had learned that summer, and when I tried to give details, it became clear that there was no way these people could completely reject what they had been taught in order to make me feel comfortable. Within the community I was totally alone.

Hamaas was making no deals; the practice was going to continue the way it had, or he would move elsewhere. He would not be questioned. Finally I conceded. I had been taught so generously, and so much good had come from my experiences, that I could not continue to create disharmony. I was twenty-five years old and did not have the certainty to face down Hamaas' moral challenge. I was more exhausted than I had been all season. I was a boy, and I just gave up.

I decided then to give over the house. The membership was growing, more people were approaching to be educated and converted, and I thought we had the makings of a devout Muslim community that could take root and spread its influence throughout the country. The house hadn't cost that much, I told myself, and I had bought it with the intention of its providing a true foundation; here was a tangible commitment I could make to replace a spiritual one that I could already feel beginning to wane. My faith in Allah remained strong, but my belief in Hamaas had weakened and that caused me pain. I couldn't abandon my questions, I could only stop asking them in public.

I was in Milwaukee, had just come home from practice, on January 18, 1973, when I heard about the massacre. A secretary in the Bucks front office called and told me her phone lines were all lit up, that something horrible had happened in Washington, and everybody in the world was trying to reach me. I hung up immediately and dialed the mosque in D.C., but the line was busy. I dialed the number four times but could not get through. I flicked on the radio, and the news was already on the wires, unconfirmed reports of religious wars and Muslim murder with my name attached. I paced and dialed and paced, and when the phone finally rang I grabbed it.

"Kareem?" It was Lateef, one of the community brothers. His voice was muffled, and he was doing his best not to cry.

"Lateef, what happened?"

"Daud is dead. Abdu Nur is dead. They shot Bibi and Amina."

"*What?!*" I shouted. "Who did it? What?!"

Lateef was still in the house, and he was trying not to talk too loud, as if any sound would bring more suffering to the dead. I strained to hear him; he was stunned but coping. The police were there, he said, and they had to use the phone; he'd just wanted to get me the news firsthand; it was horrible, call me back later.

I was a thousand miles from the frenzy of a murder scene, and the frozen solitude of Wisconsin made my home's silence even more unbearable. I needed more information and the warmth of contact, but almost everyone I could call for help lived in that house. My parents called, and I told them I was all right. I listened to the news, and when Lateef finally phoned again I began to piece together what had gone on.

Hamaas had been sending letters to several Black Muslim temples around the country. Using religious philosophy and his own eloquence plus specific and extensive references to the Qur'an, he had explained to these people that Elijah Poole, who was calling himself The Honorable Elijah Muhammad, had taken some Islamic trappings and combined them with Poole's own perverted theology to arrive at the "religion" that exalted him and that the Black Muslims now practiced. In essence, Hamaas was telling them that everything they knew was wrong.

Some members of the Black Muslims had seen Hamaas as a threat to their organization and eight or nine men had been sent to kill him. The gang had stormed the house that afternoon, but when they found that Hamaas, his wife, and one of his daughters had gone out shopping, they had tied everybody up and waited for him. When Hamaas hadn't returned they'd grown impatient. They'd ransacked the rooms and then, one by one, attacked everybody there. They killed Hamaas' three sons: Daud, who was my age, Abdullah, and Rahman U Din, his ten-year-old. They put bullets in the head of his daughter Amina and his second wife, Bibi. They drowned three infants in the bathtub and the sink.

The assassins were rushing out of the back door when Hamaas had arrived home. He'd jumped the sidewalk and tried to run them down with his car, but they'd ditched their weapons and scattered, and he couldn't catch them. When he saw what they had done he could not be consoled. He went inside the house into seclusion.

The next morning the police knocked on my door. The townhouse had belonged to me—my name was on radio newsflashes every fifteen minutes all night long—and there was some speculation that because I was a highly visible member of Hamaas' community I might also be a target for his enemies. I was to be provided 'round-the-clock protection. At another time I might have laughed, but that night I thanked them and accepted gratefully. I had viewed the country as dangerous, hung around and near some dangerous people, but I'd never felt mortally threatened before, and I knew exactly how easy a target I was. Press table slights lost all meaning next to real danger. Even my objections to J. Edgar Hoover were put aside for the time being.

I left Habiba and the baby safely at home and went to D.C. to be a pallbearer at the funerals. (It was the All-Star Game break, but I couldn't have played; I was too upset, plus I wasn't pleased with the possibility of my getting shot on the court on national TV.) I visited Hamaas, and he was in bad shape. He had lost one daughter, two grandchildren, and three sons. There was no sign of the murderers, and he was still very much in danger every moment of the day. He had no trained defense, only the people in the community, but the house was like an armed camp. Hamaas had always thought of himself as a religious warrior; now he was in a battle and under siege. I tried to talk with him, but he alternated between grief, rage, and crystal clarity. My main source of support had gone out of control, and there was nothing I could do to help or be helped. We buried our dead; he returned to his house, and I went back to Wisconsin.

The next few months are still a blur to me. Everywhere I went where there were a number of Black Muslims, I had my police escort. Hamaas trusted no one. He went into the house and didn't set foot outside it for more than a year. He posted an armed guard outside the house at all times, cut down the trees to remove potential sniper's cover, stayed away from the windows.

Living in fear has a strange effect on you. The minor impulses of a normal life are disrupted by the constant potential for harm. The desire to see what's in the mail, the late-night urge to drive to the deli for a yogurt—they could cost you your life. Once you incorporate that fear into your daily routine, as you must if you really want to protect yourself, you find both your days and your character a lot less pleasant. Under different circumstances this is exactly the kind of penetrating dilemma I would have leaned on Hamaas to help me cope with, but he wasn't there this time, and I didn't find the strength to do anything but retreat into numbness.

I went to work every day, became very fatalistic, and by the time the season ended I had effectively kept paranoia from taking control. The Bucks had played erratically all year, but we won our final fourteen games and finished tied with the Lakers for the lead in the Western Conference. We were all thinking unexpectedly of the championship, and then we got beaten by Golden State in the first round of the playoffs. Having concentrated my energy so fully the last three weeks, finally getting the murder and terror to subside, I was very disappointed. I wanted to keep playing; it was better than living at home.

I had to get away. My summer semester at Harvard had whetted my appetite for the Middle East, and I decided to continue my studies, and get myself out of America, by going around the world. I left Habiba and the baby in Milwaukee and visited Libya, Saudi Arabia, Iran, Afghanistan, Thailand, and Malaysia. I lived in a thoroughly Islamic environment, speaking as much Arabic as I could make comprehensible, eating only Eastern food, praying and observing Muslim traditions in a society in which Islam was the ruling culture and not some suspected splinter group. I still felt extremely American—

there's nothing like immersion in a foreign culture to make you aware of how deeply embedded you are in your own—but there was exhilaration in knowing that, for once, I was in the majority.

In speaking with these Eastern Muslims I found that they, too, had never heard of many of the *hadiths* that Hamaas taught as orthodoxy. As a broad culture, Islam encompassed everyone from casual believers to the wholly devout, it seemed willing to accommodate many rather than accept only a few. My faith in Allah was bolstered by the numbers of brother believers I saw, and as the summer wore on, I looked forward to returning to the United States with this fortification. I was in Singapore, headed for Hong Kong to see my old friend when I heard that Bruce Lee had died. There was no escaping tragedy. I flew home.

In August seven men were indicted for the murders in D.C. They had been sent by the Philadelphia Black Muslim temple, as was suspected. They were captured and tried. Despite bullets in the skull, Bibi and Amina had survived the attack, and it was their eyewitness testimony that convicted the murderers, but Hamaas was not satisfied with the verdicts. They had killed his family, and he wanted their heads. Their capture didn't decrease his fear of more violence, it may even have strengthened it; vengeance is a strong theme in the history of religion. The happiness and sense of expansion had been taken out of Hamaas' life: He could not pursue his calling to proselytize in the name of Allah because he felt any step outside his house could be his last; he could not bring in and teach new converts, as he had when he had formed the community, because any one of them might be his killer. For a man whose major joy and purpose in this life was to live by and spread the word of Allah, this was maddening.

The community bent under his stress. His position, which he had handled with strength and power, had from the beginning been difficult to maintain. Even in the best of times the constant strain of trying to be the perfect guide for a group of people who are expected to follow your instruction totally and completely must have been terrific. He had never accepted criticism and so had no feedback; no one ever contradicted him.

The deaths must have eaten away inside Hamaas. Once, in the middle of a business conversation, he had begun shouting, *"They killed my children! They murdered my children!"* No one had mentioned the outburst to him; it wasn't like you'd sit Hamaas down and question him about it.

With Hamaas at less than his best, the moral center of the community was shaken; there was no focus. What happened was that, ultimately, people started to leave. To Hamaas this was close to blasphemy, and those who left had to do so very quietly and not come back. Anyone who abandoned the community was considered to be lost.

I had relied on Hamaas for much of my handle on the world, and when his universe became his building I was very much alone. Habiba and I had rarely sustained each other; my world was my faith and my profession, hers had been the community. When the family in D.C. began to break down, ours in Milwaukee started to do the same.

It's not easy being a Muslim woman—her hair and arms and legs must be covered in public; she can't wear clothes that are in any way tight or revealing; she can't be too aggressive; she must take care of the children—and I made a lot of demands on Habiba without offering her much in the way of emotional support. Like anyone, she needed love and companionship, and when she didn't get it from me she had turned to the women in the D.C. community. They became her confidantes, and the more they supported her the more she supported them. When I was pulling away from them she was drawing near.

Our life in Milwaukee was entirely predictable. We rarely went out, rarely had people over, spent most of our time listening to music or reading the Qur'an. The interests that had brought us together dwindled. Soon it was clear to me that the main reason we were married was that we were Muslims. Hamaas had been the man who formed this marriage, now I was out of step with him and out of love with her.

In December 1973, as winter was hitting and I was faced with months on end of silent living, Habiba and I agreed that we should separate. It was not a difficult decision; I was erasing a mistake. She took our daughter and moved to Washington, D.C. I would visit her once in a while, sometimes for as long as a week or two, but we never lived together again.

I had no home, but I didn't notice. Life in Milwaukee had been so routine that I had looked to the road to do some living. Milwaukee became just another road town, and I began to have some fun. I spent more time with my Bucks teammates, made some new friends, noticed one or two new ladies. I'd walk into a club, and the guys would look up, startled to see me, and say, "What are *you* doing here?" "Nothing," I'd say, and the night would move forward. There was a release even to having nobody but myself at home. I was familiar with this being alone business; it was comfortable, and I did it well.

I continued to call Hamaas. He would tell me, "Guard your faith; take care of your body; don't make an idiot out of yourself," and I'd still take his words to heart, but because his strength was not at its fullest, he had less to give to me. My calls began to come less frequently.

Most of what I did was play basketball. We had an excellent team that year. Oscar was still playing, and we had Jon McGlocklin off the ball, Bob Dandridge and Curtis Perry at forwards. Early in the season we picked up Cornell Warner from Cleveland, and he would come off the bench and be decisive at power forward. With Lucius spelling Oscar, and Mickey Davis behind Dandridge, we were deep. We beat everyone in the Eastern Conference consistently and had the best record in the league.

A few days before the end of the season we suffered a true setback. We were playing in Detroit with the division title wrapped up and only a couple of games to go when we lost Lucius Allen. It was during the game, one of the ballboys had left someone's warm-up jacket too close to the court, and when Lucius ran by he stepped on it. Basketball courts are slippery to begin with, so when Lucius' heel caught the cloth he slid as if doing a split and seriously damaged his knee. That was it for his season; the next day he had his knee in a cast.

Without Lucius we beat the Lakers and Bulls, and faced the Boston Celtics in the 1974 NBA finals. It was a combative playoff, and the officiating was generally poor. Richie Powers was the referee, and he allowed the Celtics' center Dave Cowens to dive on my back for rebounds and defense; he thought that was okay. Every game he refereed, we lost.

I get especially intense for the playoffs. During the regular season I play every game to win—that is the point of professional basketball, and I resent anyone believing I would ever put out less than my best—but when the championship is directly on the line I get real focused. I am good at dismissing disturbances, giving little time to things I find minor or trivial, and during the playoffs I am even harder to distract. I use the power of concentration that Bruce Lee taught me; I lock into my *chi* and kick my game up a step.

The home-court advantage didn't turn out to mean a whole lot. We lost the first game at home, won the second there, beat the Celtics in Boston in the third game, and lost there in the fourth. Got beaten in the fifth in Milwaukee and came back to Boston needing a road win to stay alive.

The sixth game was tight all the way. Neither team could establish dominance, and the lead went back and forth. The game was tied at the end of regulation time, tied at the end of overtime. With thirty seconds left in the second overtime period, we had gone down and made a tough basket, but the Celtics had come right back. John Havlicek was having an excellent series, and as the Celtics raced downcourt, Cowens set a pick for him in the corner. I switched out and jumped in the air with my arms fully extended, blocking the normal trajectory of his ball to the hoop. Havlicek was alert and smart, however, the definitive mark of a clutch ballplayer. He altered his shot, threw it almost straight up in the air like he was gunning for the top of a silo. The ball flew over me in a tremendous arc and fell straight into the bucket. They were up by one with seven seconds remaining.

We called time out, getting the ball past midcourt, and set up our final play. If this one doesn't go in, we all go home. We figured they would key on me, so Coach Costello called for Jon McGlocklin to take the jump shot from the corner with me as the outlet in case he couldn't get the ball, and we moved back onto the court.

A team is allowed only five seconds in which to get the ball inbounds, otherwise they lose possession. I posted low and set a pick to try and free Jon for the shot, but his man stayed with him, and Jon could not get open. With time escaping I ran to the free throw line at the right side of the lane and took the inbounds pass. I looked around, but the Celtics had gone man-to-man, and everyone was covered.

There were only seconds left in the season, but I had my *chi* focused and had no worry. I felt as if everything was moving in slow motion and all power was mine. There was no sound, not even a real sense of bodies. My head was clear. I don't think I've ever felt quite so totally, comfortably alone. Henry Finkel was guarding me (Cowens had fouled out), and I just dribbled to the baseline, turned, and put up the hook. It went right in.

Things went back to real time, double time, in a hurry. The Celtics' main strategy was as soon as you scored on them, they tried to inbounds quick and come back at you. The Bucks ran downcourt ready to beat them. The Celtics called time out. There were three seconds left to play. In our huddle we were intent on our functions, and when we walked back out on the court we had them zoned so well they couldn't put the ball in play and had to call another time out. When they finally did get JoJo White free, he could only take a fallaway twenty-five-foot jumper with no chance. We won the game by one point.

I often have insomnia after games, sometimes even see the dawn. That night all I could do was lie in bed and replay those last seconds. Total adrenaline OD. I got on the plane to return to Milwaukee the next day, and I had not slept.

We lost the seventh game two days later. We could have beaten them, and with Lucius available to us I'm sure we would have. The Celtics were well-coached, however, and, to their credit, they took good advantage of our weakness. Throughout the series they pressured Oscar, guarded him closely as he brought the ball up the floor and set up our plays. Lucius was an excellent ball handler, and during the season we had counted on him to take a lot of that responsibility. Without him Oscar was forced to bear all that weight as they tried to wear him down, tire him out. With no Lucius we were forced to bring Ron Williams off the bench. Ron was a good shooter, but his ball handling wasn't championship caliber. We also had Dicky Garrett who could handle the ball, but Larry Costello hadn't played him in months and he didn't have his game together for the playoffs. We ended up being undermanned in the backcourt, and it told on us.

The 1974–75 season didn't turn out so well. Oscar retired, Lucius got traded ten games into the season, and I broke my own hand like an idiot. We were playing the Celtics early in the year, and on a scramble for a rebound, Don Nelson gouged my eye with his finger. The pain was tremendous; I felt like I was blind, and I was furious. They let Cowens and all these guys climb all over me, never even gave me the most minimal protection of the

269

rules, and now because of their stupidity, I might be severely injured. Don Nelson is no wimp; he's a big strong man, and he had hurt me. I was in a rage, and when the pain in my head subsided enough for me even to be capable of retaliation, I wanted to kill him. I restrained myself because I knew Don hadn't stuck me on purpose, but I had to hit something, so I smashed my fist into the metal standard that supported the backboard and broke two bones in my hand. What a jerk. The pain was overwhelming, but once I calmed down I felt like a real idiot. All these people taking shots at me, and I personally put myself out of action. That was the stupidest I've felt in my entire life.

The eye healed in a matter of days; the hand took six weeks, and by that time the team was out of contention. I had to sit around Milwaukee, which was no treat, and hear about what a fool I was. Hey, nobody knew that better than I did. I needed to move, to put some of this behind me, to find some friends and a fun place to live. The team finished last in our division. I had never played on a loser before, and I didn't like it. My contract with Milwaukee ended after the next season, but I had had enough. Although they offered to buy me a townhouse in New York City and even suggested that I could commute to the games if I would re-sign with the Bucks, it was time to think of a change of venue. I asked to be traded and the Bucks obliged.

It was strange, though. By the time I was about to leave Milwaukee I had finally developed an appreciation of its people. The team owners treated me with respect and paid me well, and the fans turned out to be great. They are the salt of the earth; they show up when you're winning, they show up when you're losing. They come early, stay late, and let you know what's happening while they're there. When I first arrived the fans weren't very knowledgeable about basketball itself, but as the Bucks played it for them they developed rapidly, and by the time I left they were on top of the game. They were a different kind of people than any I'd met before, but I came to know them as generous and good. In New York the fans boo anybody on the opposing team; in Milwaukee they cheer anyone they appreciate. I ended up, much to my surprise, liking Milwaukee. It's too cold for me, but it's too cold for the people who live there too.

I would have played in New York with great pleasure. In fact, I tried to be traded to the Knickerbockers. My friends, my roots, even my family (though I wasn't having much to do with them at the time) were all in the city. Walt Frazier, Earl Monroe, and Bill Bradley were still playing for the Knicks, and it would have been a perfect situation for me.

Unfortunately, the Knicks screwed things up. Rather than trade for me; in which case they would have had to compensate the Bucks with a number of quality players or draft choices, the Knicks chose to try and finesse George McGinnis. George was a high-quality ballplayer working in the ABA who was for the first time becoming available to the NBA. The Knicks did not own the rights to sign him, but they signed him anyway. It was a blatant and obvious power play on the part of the Knicks' management, and the rest of the league squashed them flat, invalidating the deal and penalizing them a first-round draft choice. Meanwhile, they were diverted from signing me. I was very disappointed, but I had to look elsewhere. I could have gone to the Washington Bullets and been near Hamaas and Habiba, but I decided against that. Jack Kent Cooke, the owner of the Los Angeles Lakers, had the money for me and the players to exchange with the Bucks, and when that deal was presented I accepted.

Summer in Southern California was a dream compared to the sub-zero Milwaukee winters. I still had ties in Los Angeles, though it had been six years since I had graduated from UCLA. The big shock when I arrived was to see what it was like living there as an adult rather than as a boy in the closed-in world of the university. It's a town built on celebrity, and I had to learn how that worked.

Lucius had been traded to the Lakers the year before, and I stayed with him and his wife until I bored them stiff; then I visited Hawaii (another revelation), then settled into LA. I found a house in Bel Air whose size was accommodating and began to think about living in a world I always assumed would reject me. I started doing things I never thought I could do. Because I was a Muslim and this was a Christian society, I didn't believe I would be hired to do television commercials (living in Milwaukee, very few came my way; in LA, it seemed like everybody was in the business), but here was Johnson & Johnson paying me to do a Shower-to-Shower Powder ad. It all seemed so simple. I was single, separated from my wife, and once in a while the loneliness would descend on me, but I made the occasional romantic attachment and slowly started to enjoy my celebrity.

I was still supporting Habiba and my daughter and visited the house I'd bought them in D.C. regularly so people would not think I was shirking my responsibilities, but I had no intense contact with Hamaas or the community. My faith in Allah was still strong, but I allowed myself more room to breathe. I prayed less often and without the rigorous preparation Hamaas demanded; I curtailed my traveling all over the Islamic globe. I developed a less formal, more personal relationship with my religion. I started learning how to live in the real world.

The Lakers didn't look to be too good that year— they had traded three excellent prospects and their center to get me—but I was happy to be with them. We trained at a college facility in LA, and though nobody likes training camp, I'd always come out smiling. "What are you so happy about in this funky little gym?" a teammate asked as we were leaving a particularly tough practice.

"Just think if this funky little gym was in Wisconsin and there was snow in tomorrow's forecast," I told him.

The Lakers had Lucius and Gail Goodrich and

Cazzie Russell, but power forward was a problem, and the bench provided minimal support. I took a lot of heat in the papers, supposed to score, rebound, and bring a championship to LA all by myself. I did try. I felt, returning to the city and, it seemed, the public eye, that I had something to prove. I led the league in rebounds and blocked shots and was second in scoring, but the team was the NBA's second to worst in defense, and we finished fourth in our division. I won the MVP for the fourth time, but it was not enough. I've said often that an individual's play cannot carry one team or consistently beat another, and the 1975–76 campaign bears me out; I had the best statistical season of my career, and we missed the playoffs by two games.

Habiba and I made several stabs at reconciliation. I would visit her and little Habiba in Washington, D.C., and for a few days there would be a calm that would raise our hopes. It wasn't so much that I wanted to live with Habiba as that I didn't want to admit to a failed marriage. I kept returning to the concept of our marriage, conveniently putting out of my mind the distance we had grown apart. Neither of us could make it work happily, but neither wanted to let it go. On one of my returns Habiba became pregnant, and that summer, in Washington, D.C., my first son was born. Hamaas named him Kareem. My son was beautiful, and he has grown in the years since into a little boy of truly sterling character, but I still could not live with Habiba.

The Lakers were prepared that next fall. Working with a private coach named Pete Newell, forward Kermit Washington had spent the summer learning how to provide muscle under the boards. This rejuvenated Kermit was just what we needed. If I'm going to intimidate inside, switch off and help my teammates with my mobility, we're going to need someone with the strength and tenacity to grab the rebounds from all those missed shots. Kermit was every bit that man. On offense, if the other team tried to double-team me with the power forward, they left Kermit alone for more rebounds, which was suicide. He had developed into a disciplined player, and his solidity freed me to move around even more, safe in the knowledge that he was taking care of business underneath.

Lucius and Cazzie were back, and we had added Don Chaney in place of Gail Goodrich, so our defense was greatly improved. We moved from seventeenth in NBA team defense to fourth, and our offense remained potent. The season was going along fine; we had the best record in the league, until injury struck. Kermit went down with a knee in February 1977, and in March, Lucius got hurt again. Two of our starting five had to sit on the sidelines for the entire playoffs.

The playoffs are a time when strengths are solidified and weaknesses exploited. Without Kermit to crash for rebounds, we were vulnerable off the boards, and without Lucius, our offense suffered. We managed to beat Golden State in the opening round, but it took us seven games, and then we came up against the Portland Trail Blazers.

At full strength, Portland and the Lakers matched up excellently. We had beaten them three out of four during the regular season. Their backcourt of Lionel Hollins and Dave Twardzik was quick and smart, as were Lucius and Chaney. Forward Bob Gross had a nice shot and an uncanny court sense, almost like eyes in the back of his head; Cazzie was going fine for us. At power forward Maurice Lucas was having an All-Star year, both scoring and getting his tough rebounds. Kermit matched him, and they battled when they met.

Portland's center was Bill Walton. Bill had come out of the same UCLA program that I had, had been taught and disciplined by John Wooden, and had learned his lessons well. Playing at his best, Bill played a lot of defense. He used his size and bulk to control the crucial rebounding area, going after every ball and also getting a lot of blocked shots. He was extremely quick and mobile, which made him difficult both to guard and box out. He had good moves to the offensive boards, but that was not really his strength. His prime asset was the ability to draw the double-team and then find his open teammates with crisp and accurate passes for the easy shot. He was a great passing center, selfless, excellent with the outlet pass to start the fast break, and he was fortunate enough to have a coach who recognized and encouraged his talents and teammates who complemented them and could execute. On top of that Bill played with true playground enthusiasm, he would have played basketball even if there was no prestige or pay involved; he just liked it, and that added a dimension to his game; he was out there having fun for a living.

He was also an interesting guy. Five years younger than I was, he had graduated from high school in 1970, and the whole '60s flower power ethic was still strong in him. He wore his hair long in a pony tail and his beard kind of shaggy. He not only held firm left-wing political views, but he was not bashful about speaking them. He was a Great White Hope that was legit, a white man with the chance to show the niggers how to play basketball, but he wouldn't accept that role in life or the conditional tons of advertising money that the business establishment was prepared to give him in return.

That season and in the two previous years Bill had been in the league we had played some good games against each other. He was developing into one of the NBA's all-time great centers. He would bump me when I'd try to shoot the hook, and I had to do a lot of boardwork because he was an excellent rebounder. Fortunately, he wasn't that offensive-minded, which meant I could overplay him while he was looking to pass, then after he dished off, box him out and get the defensive rebound.

What I found offensive was the way our relative talents were treated. I knew that white players got better press—that was obvious everywhere—but I was angry when, in order to exalt Bill Walton, the media started knocking me. If he played well against me, I was over the hill; if I excelled against him, it was no big deal. I could understand people debating whether he was better than I was or I was better than he; it's the sports fan's endless speculation, part of the enjoyment of sports. But I resented people using him to knock me. When he started playing well the television commentators and newspaper columnists were tripping all over themselves saying, "Forget Kareem, it's Bill." They could promote Bill all they wanted; he deserved it. But I had been Most Valuable Player four of the last six years—one trophy would be the highlight of most players' careers—and I wanted the respect I had earned.

With Lucius and Kermit out of our playoff lineup, Portland beat us four straight. The games were close, the last three decided by under six points each, but all I read about in the papers and magazines was "Portland Shocks LA, Walton Outduels Jabbar." I averaged thirty-five points a game; I was doing everything I could do, but I was playing against tough competition and not getting great help. Maurice Lucas outrebounded Don Ford something like fifty to twelve in four games, but the press stories read . . . "Walton made Kareem look terrible," "Walton's the greatest center ever to play the game." There was something personal in the glee with which those opinions were reported; I felt as if another piece of me was being chipped away. I've had to deal with that ugly blend of racism and envy my entire career, and what it's done is sharpen my killer instinct, made me super-intense. If I've become aloof and almost impervious to criticism, it's because I've come to expect it. Still, it never feels good. You can bet if Bill and I had both been black, you wouldn't have heard such crowing.

14

Hamaas had gone haywire. He and eleven gunmen had taken over three buildings in Washington, D.C.'s Embassy Row and were holding hostages and issuing demands. This time no one from the community had called; I'd heard it on the news and seen it on TV.

The immediate cause of his attack was the planned opening of a film called *Mohammad, Messenger of God.* Muslims are extremely protective of the story of the prophet's life: There may be no tampering with the facts, context, or teachings regarding Muhammad; also, it is forbidden to create any likeness of him. This is to protect against innovations in the faith by those who had no actual contact with the prophet himself. The Qur'an is the word of Allah as revealed directly and only to Muhammad by Allah. The *hadith* was written and corroborated by eyewitnesses to the prophet's actions; it is a pure and factual account of the prophet's life. To presume to alter

277

his teachings or the facts of his life is to tamper with Allah's revelations, and that will not be tolerated. This movie depicted Muhammad and took artistic license with his story, and Hamaas found it blasphemous. There would have been riots and death if anyone had attempted to show that film in a Muslim state. Egypt would have burned from one end to the other; people are very sincere about this issue. Islam was the most serious commitment in Hamaas' life, and he was not going to permit a Muslim equivalent of *The Ten Commandments* or *The Robe* to trivialize the name and faith of Allah. He viewed this as an attempt to degrade and undermine Islamic teachings and figured it was time to go to war about it.

Hamaas and his community members took over the District Building (Washington, D.C.'s City Hall), the Islamic Center, and the headquarters of the B'nai B'rith—speaking to Christians, Muslims and Jews—and, while holding their occupants hostage, issued a list of three demands: That the showing of *Mohammad, Messenger of God* be suspended; that a seven-hundred-and-fifty-dollar contempt of court fine Hamaas was issued for an outburst at the trial of his childrens' murderers be returned to him; and that the five men convicted of those killings, plus the three convicted of killing Malcolm X, be turned over to him.

Hamaas was not a violent man, but violence was not beyond him. He did not as a rule try to use force to intimidate people—he was such a fine logician that he could usually sway people with the strength of his arguments—but on occasion he would go for the jugular. I was present during one heated argument over Islamic teachings between Hamaas and an older Muslim. Hamaas stated his position, the old man said he felt the more traditional belief was proper, and Hamaas argued that his own interpretation was correct. When the old man would not agree Hamaas took a machete off the wall, held the sharp blade to the old man's throat and threatened to kill him if he didn't concede. Hamaas won that argument and effectively prevented any others from arising in the future. I knew when I heard about the takeover that he was serious.

More even than the particular complaint that had started the action, I think Hamaas had been eaten up inside by an unvented hatred for the people who destroyed his family and the system that did not sufficiently punish them. He had been forcibly isolated, and the passion that he had willingly and constructively used to spread the word of Allah was trapped in grief and suspicion and rage until it began to fester and infect what had been a strong and righteous man. In that state, when he was confronted with this latest offense concerning a belief that was extremely deeply felt to begin with, Hamaas simply exploded.

The Washington, D.C., police tried to storm the District Building and during the shootout a twenty-four-year-old local reporter was struck by a stray bullet. He had opened an elevator door, walked into a crossfire and was killed. The ante had been raised for the police; now it was up to manslaughter. For Hamaas the death was an unintended and unfortunate side effect that happened literally in the heat of battle. I don't believe he would have killed anyone intentionally. If he was going to do something crazy from his own personal sense of outrage, he would have done it immediately after his children were killed. This was not some murderous fanatic; this was a complex man going wrong for complex reasons. His "holy war," which is what he called it, was both sincere and disturbed.

After Hamaas' men repelled the police—there were nineteen injuries inflicted—another angle was taken. Ambassadors from three Islamic nations—Egypt, Iran, and Pakistan—were summoned, and Hamaas agreed to meet with them, in the building, face to face. The three men entered. With Hamaas they read the Qur'an, the three ambassadors stressing the Islamic theme of compassion, Hamaas quoting, "There is no justice without the sword." After three hours he surrendered peacefully.

Hamaas had been my mentor, and I still felt responsible to him. I could not support what he had done, but I could not entirely abandon him. I arranged to pay for his legal fees. I spoke with him, and he explained to me why he had taken his actions. He wasn't apologizing. He said it was a blasphemous movie and it demanded firm action, that he was living in this country and would have to deal with the consequences. He felt he had nothing left to lose. He would rather be in Paradise, and he was ready to go there.

Hamaas was fifty-five years old and was sentenced to a minimum of forty-one years in prison.

With Hamaas in jail the community in D.C. began to founder. I paid for Hamaas' defense, gave him a lump sum, and didn't ask who else was being defended by it, but all of a sudden I was the only one with any money, and they wanted to hit me up for most of it. They borrowed some but were never able to pay it back, and when they wanted more I was still there. Finally, I had to start backing off. I paid off the note on the house and ended up forgiving almost all the debts, but my contact with the people there grew smaller and smaller. I stopped sending them money. I had no community.

The last time I saw Hamaas was in prison. He was in a glass cage scratched by a lifetime of visitors, and we spoke by phone. I was very sad. When I'd first met Hamaas he had been a brilliant, compassionate man. At the street academies kids had loved him because he was real; he'd cared about them; he'd spoken to them in realistic terms about what they could achieve. He hadn't come on with some bullshit about, "You're all going to be senators or play in the NBA." He'd helped them deal with reality and given them hope and direction.

I gave a large portion of my life over to Hamaas, and he taught me most of the ideas I now hold most strongly. He is responsible for ridding me of racism and helping me view life through the Faith, for which I am eternally grateful. He gave me insights into myself and the environment in which I live that no one else has ever been able to approach. He could have taken advantage of me, but he didn't. He was a concerned friend and adviser, but I found he wasn't perfect, and by the time he walked in and took over those buildings, he wasn't the same person I had known. I can't agree with or accept everything that Hamaas did; if I could, life would be real easy, but I can't. I've had to realize that and step back, allow Hamaas to live according to what he believes is right, and insist that he and everybody else allow me to make my own decisions and live by my own lights. I knew Hamaas as a man devoted to decency and Allah; his intentions from the beginning were positive. The events of his life have been very difficult, and the fact that he has ended up so changed is very sad. It's futile for me or anyone else to judge him, though; he is not the type of person who will be judged by anyone but Allah.

I turned thirty in Los Angeles that spring and found that for the first time in my life I was totally alone. Hamaas was in jail; my wife was in Washington, D.C., my parents had been shut out to the point where my occasional visit to them was abrupt and uncomfortable. I might have felt solitary, but there was a strong relief in my solitude, as if my breath had been short for years and only now could I relax and breathe deeply. I began to recognize the kind of continual stress I had assumed would always be a part of my life, and I began to hope I'd been wrong. I was meeting people in Los Angeles, starting to consider my opportunities with the ladies, beginning to think like a free man.

That all ended when I kicked the shit out of Kent Benson.

I have a temper. I play the game hard and physically; I want to win every time I get on the court, and when something or someone gets in my path I am not unwilling to go right over it. I play within the rules, however, and I know them well enough to be aware when they're being broken. Because I am large and powerful and a significant force to be reckoned with, I am constantly the target of my large, strong opponents who will try almost anything to neutralize or undermine my effectiveness. I get banged around a lot.

It is the nature of the position of center in the game of basketball as it has developed that one has to almost literally fight for space under the boards or on the court. You know you're going to run into somebody's elbow, trip over an opponent and fall hard on your hip bone, jump in the air and land on somebody's shoulder with your kidney. You can deal with that; it's part of the game. What I've had to contend with for as long as I've played the sport is my opponents' constant attempt to physically punish me and the referees' equally consistent refusal to permit the rules to protect me. Players either want to prevent me from playing successfully or prove themselves against me. Most can't do it within the rules. I take more abuse than anyone in the NBA. After a while I started to dish it back.

At first it was annoying, being distracted from playing the game by jabs to the ribs and shots to the head. Then it became painful. Then I began to expect it, got angry even before the game began at the crap I knew I was going to have to take. Finally, it developed into a matter of principle: If the rules will not defend me, I will defend myself; I will not be a punching bag.

There aren't many really hurtful players in the NBA. A lot of guys play hard—guys like Maurice Lucas, Elvin Hayes, Zelmo Beatty, Artis Gilmore, Paul Silas—but they're just doing their best. The only truly dirty player I've run into, a man who took real pleasure in his viciousness, was Dennis Awtrey. Awtrey caught me with a blindside punch, very much on purpose, knocked me down, and was fined fifty dollars. He was great with the blindsider, never saw him go face to face. He was a mediocre player, and that one shot kept him in the league for several extra years.

I'd had enough of getting pounded, and for a while there I started to give it back regularly, but sometimes I retaliated too strongly. One fight I do regret was with Tom Berleson when he was playing for Seattle. We were both playing hard in my offensive end; I was trying to make my moves and he kept trying to body me, and as I made my way to the basket, we both fell in a heap to the polished court. When two guys over two hundred thirty pounds fall to the floor, it sounds like an industrial accident. It's never fun. I hit my elbow sharply, and he landed on top of me. I was in real pain, scared that I'd been injured by a hostile player and angry at the foul. I scrambled to my feet. When he got up I decked him; then I was ready to fight the whole Seattle team. I would've taken them all on. I know now—in fact, I knew when I calmed down in the locker room—that Tom hadn't meant to hurt me. He is a big, awkward man, and he was just trying to play the game intensely. I'd simply been hammered once too often, and he bore the brunt of my anger. I never apologized to him, so I'd like to do it now.

The same kind of thing happened with Coby Dietrick of San Antonio. He tried to strip the ball from me and grabbed me by the arm. When the ref called a foul, Dietrick took the ball, flipped it back, and hit me in the head. I punched him in the mouth. Got kicked out of the game. To this day I don't know whether he meant to get me or not.

All this sounds very cavalier, but getting battered intentionally by two-hundred-twenty-pound athletes eighty-two games per season (not counting the playoffs, when everyone's blood is up and the whole deal escalates fifty percent) is no day at the beach. I've had both eyes gouged—I wear protective goggles every game because that's where I am most vulnerable—I've been punched, pulled, pinched, pummeled. The concept is I'm so big that that's the only way you can beat me, but it's dangerous and it hurts. Out on the court I am my only defender.

I decked Kent Benson because I wasn't going to be abused. Benson was another white hope fresh out of college and looking to make a name for himself. The Lakers were playing in Milwaukee. It was two minutes into the first game of the season; Milwaukee had scored, and I was jogging downcourt about to establish position to the left of the lane. There is a standardized amount of jockeying that goes on as the offensive player tries to claim and hold a space on the floor that he can use to his best advantage and the defensive man, using whatever means he can, attempts to deny him that privilege. Benson had no experience in the professional world, did not know the parameters, all he knew was that the book on me was, you muscle Kareem. He was going to show me that he didn't back down a step, that he was a man. I had gotten behind him and was ready for the ball when he glanced around, saw no one was looking, and threw a vicious elbow that caught me flush in the solar plexus. He knocked the wind right out of me. Immediately, I was back in the streets: With no breath I expected him to keep attacking me, because in New York that's exactly what would have happened. I was doubled over, on the playground, dealing with another beating. I hated it; I hated him. I kept saying to myself, If I can just get my breath back we *will* have a final confrontation.

I started to breathe again, in gasps like I was crying, and as soon as I could move, I ran out there and fired on him. I wanted to kill him. If I'd hit him a good shot in the temple, I believe I would have killed him. Fortunately, for all my training in the martial arts when it came down to delivering a blow in anger I went with the roundhouse right and hit him in the orbit of the eye. His skull absorbed some of the impact. He went down as if he'd been shot, but I was yelling at him, wanted some more. This was life and death for me, and I was fully prepared to carry it through to its conclusion. Benson was a big man, six eleven, two hundred forty-five pounds; he could have damaged me. I had organs inside that didn't need to be getting hit by him. It was early in the season, and I wasn't going to let this be established as a precedent. I wasn't going to stand for it.

Benson was not getting up. I really could have killed him. My temper was fierce, but justified or not, there was no way a man should die over a basketball game. I was angry and confused. I had been attacked, had responded in my own defense, and once again had become the villain. My temper had gone out of control and taken my new-found relaxation with it. I knew I could count on even more public hostility now.

I certainly got it. Boos from the crowds, columnists calling me a coward and saying I should have challenged Benson to a fight like two outsized gunslingers—the rookie sheriff vs. Black Bart. At that point I didn't care; I was sick to death of the whole scene. I thought seriously of retiring. Why put myself through all this hatred? Is all this money worth being despised by millions?

Around the league the players were not so much surprised as wary. The tension that builds during a season is considerable, and more than a few guys have wanted to go to blows once in a while. Most of the time cooler heads prevail. I wasn't very pleased with myself for having lost control—I had been ready to kill a man!—and I resolved to hold my temper better in the future. I haven't had a serious fight since, partly because of my new discipline and partly because some of the guys I had to play against maybe started to think I was a little crazy— "Kareem, man, he's a little . . . off . . . you know?"—and they might not have wanted to mess with me.

I had broken my hand against Benson's face and was sidelined again. The league couldn't suspend me because my hand was already in a cast, but they fined me five thousand dollars. Benson, who had caused the initial injury, was neither fined nor reprimanded. (The official explanation was that since the referees had not seen Benson foul me, the league could not discipline him.) Typical NBA justice: Discipline the nigger. Later that season in a similar incident, Ricky Sobers, who is black, punched somebody out while the refs weren't looking but got fined anyway because they caught him on video. The tape of the Milwaukee game very clearly shows Benson giving me the elbow that hurt me, yet he didn't get fined. Where's the logic? Where's the consistency? All I see is white players being excused when attacking blacks, and black players who hit whites getting leaned on hard.

The classic in this system of selective justice was the case of Kermit Washington.

Kermit was a triumph of the work ethic. He came out of college as a first-round draft pick with a great body and fine determination but short on technique and basket-ball skills. During three undistinguished years with the Lakers, he enrolled in a summer training program with former San Francisco University coach Pete Newell and, through pure hard work and determination, developed himself into one of the league's premier power forwards. He was strong and tough without being brutal. He was also a sensitive man who was always working to make his team win.

Kermit now has the reputation of a killer. It's not that way. I saw the whole scene unfold right in front of me.

We were playing the Houston Rockets, in Houston, two months after I had punched out Benson. The Rock-ets were a moderately talented team with a thin bench, and they relied on outside shooting and rebounding for their chance at success. When they went with their big front line of Rudy Tomjanovich, Moses Malone, and Kevin Kunnert they could be tough underneath. We had set up our offense and missed the shot, the ball rebounding out and the Rockets taking off on a fast break the other way. I had been caught moving in for the offensive rebound, so I was near the backboard, trailing the play. Kunnert and Kermit had been boxing each other out, hustling for the ball, and when it had bounced away from them Kermit had grabbed Kunnert's waistband to keep him from getting upcourt. Kunnert, who is white, had gotten mad and thrown first a left elbow that hit Kermit in the shoulder and then followed it with a right cross that caught him on the side of his head. You don't do that to Kermit. Kunnert started to run downcourt, but Kermit chased him, grabbed him by the shorts, turned him around and started to hit him. Kevin can't fight very well, at least he didn't show much against Kermit who does know how to handle himself. Kermit was in a rage; he would not be blindsided, would allow no one to cheap-shot him, and was going to impress that point on Kunnert in terms he would remember.

I ran to midcourt and grabbed Kunnert. When breaking up a fight between someone you do know and someone you don't, I've always found it most effective to lock onto the stranger; first, it prevents your friend from getting hurt, and second, you can reason with your friend, talk to him while shielding him off his opponent with your body. No way you're going to talk down an angry man you don't know; at least, with your body between them, you stand a chance of cooling a friend into lucidity.

I grabbed Kunnert in a bear hug and swung him around to protect him. At that moment Rudy Tomjanovich came running up from Kermit's blind side to do exactly what I'd done, hold Kermit and calm things down. Unfortunately, Kermit sensed Rudy behind him, thought of it instantaneously as another attack, turned and threw an absolutely crushing right hand. Rudy ran full speed into Kermit's fist. My back was turned momentarily, but I've seen videotapes of the blow and it's terrifying. I did hear it, however. From three feet away it sounded like a watermelon had been dropped onto a concrete floor. I spun to look, and even as Rudy was going down, there was blood pouring out of his face, all this blood on the floor. Kermit had stove his whole face in.

Kermit is not a vicious man, he hadn't meant to

injure Rudy. He had reacted with force to what he'd felt was a serious threat. That much was obvious immediately. The league saw it differently. For the second time in two months a white player had been knocked cold by a black, and they were not going to stand for it. There were tapes of the entire incident, and they were shown over and over again on local news broadcasts around the country, made it onto the networks, this nigger almost killing the white boy. The beginning of the play, the first punch thrown by Kunnert and the cause of the whole chain of events, was also available on tape, but that was given no play. This was Violence in Sports, no retaliation or self-defense; this was niggers on the rampage, and it had to be stopped.

Kunnert was never disciplined. Kermit was suspended without pay for twenty-six games and fined $10,000. What that said to me, and to all the black players in the league, was that if somebody white punches you out, you play defense and hope that the refs will try and stop it at some point. If not, just realize that the NBA needs white players to keep the white fans interested and the arenas filled and the networks on the line. Count on no support from the people who run this business.

Before he could play another game, Kermit was traded. He and Don Chaney and a number-one draft choice were sent to the Boston Celtics for Charlie Scott. It was a terrible trade for the Lakers. We lost a solid chunk of our defense and some future for another guard. Our alternate rebounding fell to a white forward, Don Ford, and died; I got double-teamed by power forwards again; we had to go another year and a half undermanned off the boards.

More important than the Lakers' fortunes on the court was something I only came to find out four years later. A highly visible and influential man in basketball management told Kermit that the league owners forced Lakers owner Jack Kent Cooke to make that trade because they would not tolerate having me and Kermit on the same team. Here were two extremely powerful black men who had both severely beaten white players, and the owners wanted us separated because they would not have us intimidating the rest of the league. That's hard to prove and easy to deny, but I fully believe it.

Professional basketball is essentially a black sport being run as a white business. All the team owners are white, as are most of the general managers and coaches. (To the NBA's credit, however, it has accepted more blacks in significant management positions than any other major sport; baseball and football are still as white as a blank ledger.) A great majority of the players are black, which more than anything else creates a marketing problem; the disposable income that pro sports needs in order to thrive is largely in the hands of white people. Blacks play the game in school and in the street, have refined its style and made it a cultural staple, but they haven't got the dollars to fill the arenas or support the television advertisers. Pro basketball is a black game being sold to white people, and the owners, who have serious dollars sunk into the league, are all out to protect their investment. White players give white fans some faith; Larry Bird can be a white fan's fantasy alter ego a whole lot easier than Micheal Ray Richardson can. If they can compete with the black players, whites represent hope that America's athletic pride has not been totally usurped by strangers. If they can outdo them, there is cause for joy. I've seen it.

Black players view fans with a reasonable amount of cynicism. Several years ago the entire eleven-man squad of the Knicks was black, and you'd hear people grumbling about the "New York Niggerbockers." That will put you off your game.

You can feel the racial makeup of the places we play. Visiting the Memorial Coliseum in Phoenix was like being in one of those movies back in the '50s where black people didn't exist. Everyone has a great tan; they're wearing white patent leather shoes and polyester sports

289

jackets with ridiculous red-and-blue patterns. If a Phoenix player executed a particularly good play, one man might rise from his seat and salute a friend several rows down with his cup of beer. Cobo Arena in Detroit, for instance, had an entirely different ambiance. At Cobo there'd be this fabulous organ player who had to be out of some great black church. He'd set the tone by playing rhythm and blues with some heat, not the grim Muzak that passes for pregame sounds in most places we play. I've always paid attention to music whenever I've heard it, and this guy put the whole night in the right key. People would come dressed to kill, men with the big hats, women in their best coats with the big fur collars, real fine. The whole atmosphere was like a black social event every time I came to town.

And they knew their basketball. The personal interplay between guys on the court got picked up on by the Cobo crowd, and if there were challenges issued, people there were aware of them; they talked to the players like they were ministers: "Whip it on him, Oscar!" "Talk to him, Mr. Bing!" Somehow in Detroit you'd see a lot of spectacular individual plays, and any time a player really lit one up, regardless of who it was, the crowd would go crazy. People would run out of the stands and give each other fives along the baseline. One guy fifteen rows up would run down the aisle, meet a friend halfway, shake it up, pop him five, and run back again. There was a lot of inner-city rhythm in the crowd, and it inspired what was happening on the court—guys love to hear a hip crowd go nuts—which would gas the fans even more. Sometimes we'd really set Cobo to rocking.

In Phoenix I'd hear, "Hey, tar baby." "Hey, you niggers." For a couple of years we had some real winners right behind our bench. It wasn't just Phoenix.

The only time I've felt sorry for a referee was during a game in New Orleans. Tommy Nunez might have made a poor call, but some customer with a baseline seat yelled out, "You stupid-ass spic!" I wanted to go over and knock the guy out. I felt for Tommy; you've got to deal with professional criticism, but there's no place for that. It's one of the few times I was ready to fight for the rights of an official.

Cobo was located in Detroit's black ghetto. Every night was a party. Then the team moved its games to the Pontiac Silverdome, replaced the organ player, and took most of the fun out of it. More "convenient," better parking, fewer "problems," and a whole lot less soul.

The other major public relations problem for the NBA is drugs. Drugs are an open secret on all strata of American society: Stockbrokers are smoking pot after hours; lawyers are snorting cocaine and wearing gold razor blades around their neck; at least one major car manufacturer has been caught holding several kilos of powder; doctors are shooting heroin and hospital morphine. There are plenty of street junkies, and people on welfare are buying nickel bags. None of this is any big surprise. When an athlete gets caught doing drugs, however, all hell breaks loose.

Athletes are supposed to be America's heroes. Without ever having volunteered, we are all called upon to personify and uphold the country's honor. Kids look up to us; we are role models for future grandeur. This is nonsense. Athletes should be called upon to be equally as moral as every single individual in society, no more and no less. We are more visible, but not more valuable, than doctors, teachers, cabdrivers and businessmen. If the society has decided to dump the burden of perfection on us alone, or us in higher percentage than other segments, then it is in trouble, because we are no more able or willing to accept that burden than any random group of steelworkers or politicians. Morality is an individual concern. Celebrities should be celebrated for what they do best, not for some mythical persona that has been created for them. Because a guy can bury a twenty-foot jumper or glide to the hoop like an angel doesn't make

291

him the one to tell you how to live. Each man and woman, from the most known to the least, should have the confidence and the strength to create and live by his or her own beliefs and not be led blindly by others who may not be qualified for the job. *Listen* to celebrities; they may be morons.

The uproar over drugs in the NBA is less about morality than it is about commerce. The media makes tremendous money publicizing, analyzing, and criticizing professional sports, and if the product is tarnished, so are the profits. Scandal is good to a degree—it sells newspapers—but there is the constant pressure to maintain the image of cleanliness and not upset the dollar figures. There is also the element of gambling—no doubt about it, millions of dollars are bet annually on pro sports—and an athlete on drugs is more difficult to gauge and make a successful cash determination on than a straight one.

I don't really care who's doing drugs in the NBA as long as the scene isn't adversely affecting my team and teammates. I've known enough drug users—going as far back as grade school and the streets of New York—not to view them as pariahs or lost souls. I've certainly smoked more than my quota of weed. For a while there at UCLA I didn't want to hang out with anyone who didn't smoke reefer, but that was as parochial a view of the world as any uptight antidoper's, and I got over it pretty quickly.

Hard drugs are another story. I've seen friends have their lives destroyed, some die of OD's. Got to stay away from things that will kill you. Once in college I snorted some heroin. I threw up all out the window, and the next day I was sick. That was the end of that.

The drug scene in the NBA has changed greatly since I entered the league in 1969. The drug scene in the whole country has changed, too. The NBA was still predominantly white when I arrived, and the drug of choice was alcohol. Most of the players had never had the opportunity to try drugs unless they came from a big city like New York, Detroit, or Philadelphia. The Summer of Love had happened, and guys in college were learning all about the possibilities, but the older players were more tradition-bound and some were pretty resistant to change. They still believed the myths, so whatever drugs got used were done, as was true in the rest of society, secretively.

As things progressed and more black people came into the league bringing their lifestyle and the social drugs that they used, the drug uses changed. More white guys used it, too. Professional basketball players almost all come out of college, and the campus at the time was the new cultural breeding ground, so almost everyone who was coming into the NBA had at least been exposed to the idea of recreational drugs.

Things started to change when excess set in. Serious drug use, whether it's pot, cocaine, amphetamines or heroin, will wrestle with your conditioning. Pro basketball demands a physical discipline that is a lot greater than the casual "being in shape." The game itself is grueling, full-tilt exertion for two hours or more, back-and-forth non-stop action. Five minutes up and down the floor at a professional pace is enough to put away most weekend athletes. Then the travel schedule, constant time-zone changes, cramped airplane rides, interrupted sleep, and insistent social temptations all work against your getting any rest. Physical conditioning is an absolute necessity, and if that goes, your game will go with it. Habitual drug users have a hard time in the NBA. Most burn out in a year or two.

What happens is that a boy coming out of school, likely as not having been less than affluent most of his life, all of a sudden has all this new money to play with and a lifetime of backlogged temptation to spend it on. Marijuana is something college kids can afford; cocaine is much more expensive and harder to find. Now it's all available, the financial wherewithal and the easy connection, and it's hard to resist. The guys who have trouble are the ones who say, "I can handle it." Before, they were spending twenty bucks on some grass, now they're blowing thousands on coke. It's a seductive scene—and they are able to go as far as they want—and before they know it they're way past their ability to exercise some discipline.

Most of the NBA drug-taking is recreational. Players are under pressure to perform by management, the fans, their peers, themselves. Relaxation is a necessity, and drugs help that right along. Some guys drink; that's just as dangerous, but it's legal. Others get high. Most guys can take it, having developed the ability to withstand and even channel the pressure to their benefit, the same way they developed their inside moves. A truly complete ballplayer learns to play the NBA as well as to play the ballgame. An extended career free of injury or setbacks is one long contest. You don't want to foul out.

You do learn to be careful. Before going to play against the Knicks one night, one player asked another to hold a gram of coke. When they got to the airport after the game and the guy wanted his gram back, his teammate realized he had left it in his locker in Madison Square Garden. They stood there trying to figure out how to get back and score those drugs without getting arrested.

Nobody wants to get caught with it. I saw one joint clear out an entire locker room. This big, tightly-packed cigarette fell out of someone's pocket after a game one night and rolled to the center of the floor. Seemed like everybody saw it at once because all of a sudden guys were grabbing their clothes, pulling at their overnight bags, bundling everything they had to have, and hightailing it out of there as if the room were on fire. Some of the guys were half-naked! In fifteen seconds the place was empty! Sooner or later somebody must have picked it up, but it wasn't a pro ballplayer.

One player I know bought a pound of weed in one city and was bringing it home on the plane when he ran into a hijacking check at the airport. The security woman opened his bag and saw the brick—she saw it; he knew she saw it. She didn't say anything and let him get on the flight. In the air the guy got the serious paranoia—he didn't like something he'd seen in her eyes—so he flushed sixteen ounces of reefer down the toilet. Sure enough, when they got off the plane the sky marshalls were waiting for him. He was clean.

Drugs were a problem long before the NBA did anything about it. The league office used to send around some doctor from Johns Hopkins to warn us about possible effects, but they didn't really want to know about it. As long as no scandal hit the news everybody was happy. Meanwhile there was one player totally strung out, shooting heroin, drinking a bottle of Caro syrup a day, stealing jewelry from guys on his team to buy drugs. He's at this meeting, nodding, and the doctor is droning, "If any of you have some problems, I'm at University Hospital . . ." The whole thing was a joke.

There have been cases made public involving NBA players and their problems with drugs. Bernard King and Eddie Johnson had the courage to deal with it out in the open, which I admire. I've seen out-of-control drug use firsthand involving my teammates, and it's never easy. One guy retired and then took the fall. He got so deeply involved with drugs that it took all his money. He stopped making house payments; all his savings were gone. His wife took his Porsche because that was paid for, but they repossessed his Mercedes. His wife had to get a job to support the children. She tried to tell him his troubles were really her fault and get him to a marriage counselor just to get him some special help, but he wouldn't admit he had a problem. It ended up with her moving out after he put a gun to her head.

Another teammate almost decimated our team. He was doing freebase (cocaine cooked with ether to refine it to its most potent elements, and then smoked), and he went down the squad from one man to another trying to get a bunch of them to join him. Some were tempted, but other people pulled their coattails, and ultimately he was left alone. He started going through severe, crazy personality changes: wildness, paranoia. Kept talking about how nobody liked him, how the coach was a liar. Everybody knew something was up but nobody felt it was their place to say anything to him. He was freebasing all the time, and his conditioning went all to hell. Ultimately he became an undeniable detriment to the team, and although he had once been an excellent player, they had to let him go. He was hurt and angry and outraged the way dopers are when they can't deal with reality, but something must have registered. It took him several years, but he finally did straighten out.

At least one entire team was undermined by drugs. I'd heard rumors about common-knowledge out-in-the-open freebasing involving five guys on a team out of our division, and then I started to notice in the sports pages they'd mention that this one All-Star was sick and couldn't come to the game. Or he'd have one great game, then four crummy ones, then he'd get hurt. That's a sure sign, because when your conditioning goes you lose some of your strength, and then it's easy to get hurt.

It turned out the rumors were true. That summer I visited one of the guys I knew, and there were four players over there doing freebase. I was a little surprised. Then the star of the team dropped by. He saw me and tried to come over and talk, I heard something about "ether," how they were using ether, but he couldn't handle the simplest conversation and had to go slump in a corner so he could be supported by both walls and wouldn't fall. He was babbling like a man who had been in a prison camp, an Andersonville survivor. He was completely incoherent and a little scary.

They had been a good team with a lot of offense and a decent shot at the playoffs, but they'd died. What could you expect?

I got involved with cocaine between college and the pros, but not for long. What turned me off was a minor brush with death. A friend and I were out driving, about to get on the Major Deegan Expressway in the

Bronx. We had been snorting some stuff, and I was behind the wheel, whipping in and out of traffic playing Mario Andretti, shouting at drivers, looking for blood challenge on the road. I had hooked up in a nice little drag race to the entrance ramp when my steering column froze. Doing forty miles an hour, the car hopped the curb, just missed a lamp pillar, spun totally around twice in the grass, and came to a halt. Nobody was hurt; the worst thing that happened was the tires got muddy, but I knew that would never have happened if I hadn't been high, and I didn't want to blow my pro career, not to mention my life, on a drug that would get me so crazy—no matter how good it felt at the time.

I was approached about freebasing the year I got back to LA in the pros. There was a whole ritual involved— you not only got high, you got a floor show. A special guy would invite a select and extremely hip blend of celebrities, power brokers, and entourage to his house for their initiation. The cooking process was a secret—they'd whip that up in the kitchen—but first you'd give them money for a gram of cocaine. They'd disappear, then reemerge with your smoke. There was something very wrong here, from the hushed hipness of the whole deal to the fact that they could be keeping half of your coke and you'd never know about it. I knew right away that this was not the way I wanted to be spending my time. There was a deferential silence—this stuff has never failed; here's another fish on the line. They were waiting for me to go for my wallet and put all this money on the table, but I grabbed my keys and left. And stayed gone. And have been very glad I did.

Freebasing is a whole culture. Richard Pryor can tell you about it. It will keep you inside for days. Big guys, seven-foot NBA centers, fall over in a heap after a couple of hours and you need to call the AAA and a tow truck to cart them away. One guy's wife had to pound on a friend's door and make her husband come home because he'd been gone for forty-eight hours.

Freebasing is developing its own terminology. One of my teammates was "Count Basie." Mostly it's called "baseball." Lots of jokes. One guy in the league is nicknamed Chico Esquela, because "baseball been very, very good to him." They call one particularly heavy user Bowie Kuhn, because he was the "Commissioner" of baseball.

It's a coed sport. I was on the road, and I saw this woman after the game. She was tall, gorgeous, with the right curves in the right places. We made some eye contact, exchanged a few words, nothing serious. She called me later at the hotel.

"What you playing tonight?" she asked me.

"I'm not playing."

"Want to go a few innings?"

"A few innings of what?" I said.

She purred, "I know you play basketball, but I hear you like . . . baseball."

Sorry, baby. I'm not ready to play baseball.

She wouldn't believe me. "What's the matter, honey, afraid of a few errors? Afraid you're going to strike out?" Made it seem that I wasn't man enough to do some base with her. I let her slide. People who play "baseball" are losers. I play to win.

15

That couldn't be Sophia Loren running up the escalator in Century City. I haven't been that good in this or any other life that I should be so blessed.

Whoever she was, she didn't want any part of me. Maybe five feet four, dressed in pants and a loose but ample cotton checked shirt, she had all the requisites and a light in her eyes, but when I spoke to her, she pretended I wasn't there. I was going down as she was climbing; she was waving a sheet of paper shouting, "Happy! Happy!"

"Here I am," I said, and reached over the railing to snatch the letter. She looked at me like I was crazy. That didn't happen very often. Who was this woman?

She seemed to be heading toward Happy Hairston. Hairston, a former Laker player whose business office was in the same building as mine, was standing one step in front of me looking bored. Must have been an off day for Hap. He pocketed the letter when she handed it to him and, as she disappeared around a corner, rode the escalator down.

I wasn't one of Hairston's intimate friends—we'd played against each other, one time come to blows, without striking up any significant conversations—but this was important, and I wasn't going to let a little thing like a blood feud stand in the way of my getting next to this beauty.

Happy wasn't real loose with the details. "That's my secretary," he told me when I asked. Her name was Cheryl Pistono. Hairston had never hit on her, but he treated her like his little sister whom he wasn't going to let anyone touch. Not that she couldn't take care of herself. When he got back to his office he told her, "Do you know who that was? He wants to meet you." She said, "Forget it."

I'd never had the good social cools, and my years of marriage had divorced me from the scene even further. It was the summer of 1977; I was four years separated from my wife, a recent immigrant to LA, and not at all on sure ground. I asked Phyllis, one of the secretaries who worked in my office, to call and leave her a message. Cheryl was on another line, said she would call back. She didn't, forgot about it. The next day Phyllis called her twice and finally made contact. "Listen, Cheryl, Kareem is really nice," she said.

"Phyllis, do me a favor," the woman answered, "tell him that I'm not interested in a fling with a superstar, and that's all I've got to say."

Phyllis spared me that, just said Cheryl didn't want to get involved. I hadn't met a whole lot of women who were that actively not interested, which intrigued me, but there was something I had sensed just looking at the way she carried herself that made me pursue her. I make a lot of snap judgments, most of them negative; when I find someone I respond to positively and instinctively, I've got to chase them down.

300

"Just ask her if she'll talk with me on the phone," I told Phyllis.

Cheryl had thought she was through with me, but my persistence must have intrigued her and she said, "I'll talk to anybody, Phyllis. I'll talk to him, sure. Fine."

I don't know why I didn't just call up in the first place. I certainly knew how to deal with women who wanted me—I could be as charming as I had to be to get the job done—it was getting through to someone who might not find me appealing that made me hesitate. I made the call, but no one picked up. It rang ten times, twenty—Phyllis had just spoken to her; I knew someone was there—and then Cheryl answered.

I really concentrated on this woman. As voices over the phone, there was none of the physical intrusion there would have been if we'd been sitting and talking. On the line I was no disorienting giant, and size was no topic of conversation; she could talk to me, not some behemoth. For her, this was one time when she didn't have to deal with some guy's furtive staring at her body or taking the bedroom inventory. I found it easy to ask her where she came from, what she liked to do. I paid attention to her, and she must have liked it, and though she still came on pretty tough, I began to get the feeling I was getting through. I asked her out for dinner. "I can't," she said, "I'm busy this week."

"What about this weekend?" I asked.

"I'm going away."

"What about next week?"

She weakened. "Maybe we can have lunch or something," she said. "Call me."

Office intrigue comes to a boil very fast. The next day Hairston was putting me down. "If I wanted to see you," he told Cheryl, "I'd come to you myself. I wouldn't go through friends and secretaries. What is this? The guy doesn't have any guts."

It wasn't one minute later that I walked in the door of that office with a rose in my hand. I had picked it from my own garden, and I handed it to Cheryl and introduced myself.

People took the long way to their desks. Quick errands to the front room all of a sudden had to be made; the Xerox machine started working overtime. I've never felt very comfortable as the center of attention, always preferred to be the silent observer, and I was ill-at-ease making the romantic gesture to begin with. Cheryl felt my discomfort and got us out of there. "Let's go for a walk," she said and, without waiting for me to hold it, swung the door open and walked on down the hall.

I taped an appearance on Merv Griffin that night. There is a talk-show convention when a guest isn't going to move down on the couch and listen to the rest of the parade—"I know you have a pressing engagement, and you have to leave us." My pressing engagement was dinner with Cheryl. I brought my business manager along as a buffer, in case I'd made some terrible mistake.

But I hadn't. Cheryl had a fierce combination of arrogance and compassion that drew me to her. She insisted that I pick her up at her girlfriend's house, gave me her friend's phone number; if she wanted to ditch me, I would have a hard time tracking her down. This was a woman who was leery. Tell me about it. The friend's name wasn't even on the mailbox, so I had to call, and then wait twenty minutes for her to get off the line so I could get through.

For all that arrogance, in spite of every sign that told me she was wrapped up tight, there was a soul attraction that pushed me toward her. Cheryl was smart; that was clear in our first conversation. She read; she had strong opinions on topics from religion to sports, and she could explain them and defend herself with no help from me or anyone. She was sharply critical, just like I was, but she saw life positively, and I really warmed when she both lashed out at easy hypocrisies and hoped for a better future.

302

Cheryl had been a Catholic and had "fallen" like I had. Now she was a Buddhist. She had left her home in LaSalle, Illinois, at sixteen and lived with relatives in LA, attended Beverly Hills High School. Men had a definite way of looking at her, and for a time she hung out at Hugh Hefner's, spent weekends in Vegas, lived the high life. Though she was nine years younger than I was, she knew how to handle herself in traffic—among men, in public, with her emotions—a whole lot better than I did. She had been dealing with a world I had opted out of, and the most important sign I got from her that first evening—intuitively, it was just something I could feel— was that she knew how little I knew, and she liked me for it.

I was never a great one for hustling to make the good impression. If casual women wanted to be around, that was fine with me; if not, see you later. Cheryl had been hit on by the best and didn't have time for a man who wasn't interested, and I liked talking to this confident, brassy girl who was so very unimpressed. I don't know why, but I took her hand and began blurting out feelings I didn't know I'd had, wasn't sure, in fact, that I truly believed, but which sounded so good coming out of me I didn't try and stop them.

Cheryl had heard all those lines before. Guys had been trying to get into her pants for years, and she assumed this eruption of romance was part of my seduction arsenal. She had gotten a glimmer of my innocence but took it for cynicism, couldn't believe I was so naive, and chalked me off as a confused if somewhat disarming LA Romeo. She made me take her back to her girlfriend's house, gave me a peck on the cheek, and said goodnight.

She was every bit as emotionally impenetrable as I was, but while I would normally have let such an unforthcoming date go her own way—I had told her stuff I hadn't known, and she'd said "Thanks" and split—there was something about Cheryl I could not allow to leave. I had felt happy in pursuit, and whether she had caused it or I was simply ready to display some affection didn't matter to me. I was pleased to know I wanted Cheryl; I hadn't felt that happy inclination in years.

The next morning I walked into the office where she worked and said, "We're flying to Mazatlan. Come upstairs and see my office. We're going. I already asked your boss if you could have the days off, he said yes." She was shocked. Why did she look a little annoyed? I took her upstairs. Called her that afternoon, took her to lunch the next day. I really liked Cheryl, and I loved the feeling of liking her.

Finally she told me, "Kareem, I can't go with you." Damn it. I knew she was going to say it; I'd been too open, too happy. The other shoe hadn't fallen. "I'm not at that point with you where I can go somewhere."

At least she hadn't booted me out of her life. I was thirty years old, but I hadn't dated in a decade and had never gotten good at the personal negotiations, the meaningful pieces of each other that potential intimates exchange like lovers' currency. I had to learn what she valued; I knew I valued her.

"Hey," I started, "you don't have to come with me. As long as you'll talk to me, I'll be here."

Cheryl thought that was bullshit. She'd heard it from enough men who had said they were going to be in touch but when she hadn't come across were never heard from again. But though she was skeptical, I continued to call. I surprised her and astonished myself. I was really starting to feel again.

Over the next few months we grew close together. Because she carried with her an ejection-seat view of relationships she was free of the fear of losing me and found it very easy to say what she saw. She is a very perceptive woman, and the more I began opening myself to her the more she began telling me things about myself that I had never considered. On my part, I began to love her.

Cheryl had an aggressor's optimism about life. She'll

fight until she gets what she wants. By the time I met her I had been beaten into thinking that nothing's ever finished till it fails. My parents, my mentor, my wife, all had fallen from me, and I assumed more of the same was all that would follow. I had learned the hard way to stay away from public displays of any kind so I wouldn't be criticized on any level except my work, at which I excelled and was still taken for granted. I viewed everything with extreme wariness.

Cheryl tried to coax me out of my cynicism. On our first date I had told her, "Yeah, well, I dribble a ball up and down a court—if you could consider that a job." She was in the process of trying to make me enjoy my life when I punched out Kent Benson.

I was steaming with stupid futility that night. I hadn't seen anybody, but I knew that as soon as the press showed up I was going to want to kill all over again. Not only would I be blamed for defending myself, mocked if I complained, and left just as unprotected as I'd always been, now my hand was broken, and I couldn't even do the one thing that made all this bullshit worthwhile: play basketball. Life was terrible, and I was doing a lousy job of it.

The team had traveled to Indiana, and I went straight to the hospital, where I found out that yes, the hand was broken, and they put it in a cast. I went back to the hotel to pick up my bags and return home to LA when this package arrived. I fumbled it open and found a single rose. There was a card endorsed. It read: "In every situation in life there is a beauty that you must discover. Love, Cheryl."

She was wonderful. The whole flight home I thought about her and how she could possibly see anything positive in this awful time, and the more I thought the calmer I became. When the plane landed I stuck the rose in my cast and there was Cheryl to meet me.

We did a lot of talking that night and all while I healed. She wrote me a letter, one of those late-night evocations that appears on the page through a force of its own. She wrote that I was fortunate, living in a style and doing a job for which millions of men would trade years off their life. She was both sympathetic (she was beginning to understand the roots of my isolation) and at the same time angry at me for missing all the satisfying things that were open to me. "All the knowledge and intelligence about basketball just stay within your body. You play and never say a word," she told me. "You have money, you have fame. People want to meet you, they stand and stare at you, and when they say something they try and somehow compliment you on your life. These people *like* you. You have to find something within you, some kind of appreciation, because all you have inside is ugliness: 'I'm stuck here, this is ugly, that is bad.' Your life is not a jail sentence."

I realized, with my hand broken and reputation damaged, that my temper could ruin my career and that I'd have to control it, but Cheryl went deeper and told me that I was missing out on not only my career but my whole peace of mind. I had stopped caring to the point that though I could not feel pain, I could also not be pleased, wasn't there to hurt or to love. Now all of a sudden I'd been hit by both and didn't know how to deal with it.

Cheryl and I spent a lot of time talking, although what I was hearing from her, and realizing myself, took years to take hold. She forced me to think about myself in relation to the fans, for instance. I never used to give a lot of autographs, could never really understand the appeal of my signature on a scrap of paper. (Once when I was in grade school I had waited on an autumn Sunday outside the Yankee Stadium locker room door and gotten a whole sheet full of football Giant autographs. I took them to St. Jude's the next day. By the end of the week they were lost, and I found them that summer stuck down inside the couch.) Often people are incredibly inconsiderate, interrupting meals and conversations to plunk down paper and make rude demands. A lifetime of this kind of interruption—constantly, at every public meal every day, year in, year out—will make the most even-tempered person abrupt. Plus I felt signing autographs somehow demeaned the people who received them, made them acknowledge a lack of their own significance. Cheryl told me that no matter how commonplace the experience was for me, these people were showing gratitude and admiration, and it was insulting to ignore them when they were honoring me. I'd never thought of it that way; I'd thought of it as an inconvenience imposed by pests. From then on I tried to be easier about it.

(It's strange but when I sign "Kareem" people get upset. "Kareem Abdul-Jabbar" is so long it cuts down on the number of autographs I can give by half, so now I sign "Abdul-Jabbar" and everyone seems to be happy.)

When I began playing ball again Cheryl and I had become a definite couple, and little by little, I began to trust her. It was a very new and difficult feeling, flying in the face of the whole course of my life. We were not always great partners; we fought, abandoned each other, returned to fight some more. Somehow we stuck it out. All of what she told me registered, but it was years before much of it showed up in my actions. She kept bothering me; she was aggressive in her own defense as well as mine. Part of her strength was her ability, her *willingness*, to tell me when she thought I was full of shit. Not too many people are willing to risk the consequences, but she knew I paid real attention to her, and she could get away with it.

We had our separations and our shouting fights. It became clear to me that the idealized Cinderella image that I had endowed Cheryl with was one more in a lifetime of fantasies concerning women. She wasn't the flawless gem I'd always been searching for, but finally I could not deny that I loved her. In spite of the birth of my beautiful second daughter, Sultana, I received a Muslim divorce from Habiba, and two years after I'd met her, Cheryl moved in with me.

Slowly, by no means overnight, my outlook brightened. Cheryl, who is an extremely outgoing person, mentioned one day, "I remember when I first started going out with you, you'd never smile. You always seemed like such a serious person." She caught me in a contemplative mood, and I had to admit that she was absolutely correct. That started me wondering about what other people might be thinking when they met me. It seems foolish that it took me thirty years to consider it, but I had been pretty self-absorbed in my little niche. The people I worked for catered to me, and because I did a good job they made me comfortable. I've never been particularly interested in meeting strangers; I think I dwell too much on a person's negative attributes; once I see those, I'm not interested in whatever else he or she might want to show me. Winds up the only people I could really hang out with would be renaissance men and women, and there aren't many of them around anymore.

Cheryl's comment made me recall a newspaper article about me written by a Boston writer named George Kimball. Crazy George was fun, and at the end of the interview I smiled at him. He wrote: "The smile was bigger than life, just like Kareem." It disturbed me that someone would be taken aback by the fact that I smiled. What had I turned into? It made me realize that, gee, I don't smile that much. I had always smiled as a little kid, flashing around the supermarket talking to everybody. Somewhere all of that had gotten squashed. I began to think about it. Cheryl helped me come to that.

My recuperation after decking Benson had given me time for reevaluation. Largely because of the fight, I was left off the All-Star team for the only time in my career, and I thought about quitting the game altogether, but I pulled through that one. I began to resurrect my enjoyment in basketball. When playoff time came round I was ready. Unfortunately, with Kermit Washington traded we were undermanned off the boards. Jamaal Wilkes, newly arrived from Golden State, had to play Jack Sikma. He was giving away five inches and forty pounds, and he was supposed to keep Sikma off the backboards. It was disappointing, but we lost the 1977–78 playoffs in the opening round.

I spent the next year trying to absorb the changes I was going through. I had a standoff with the press; they were too intimidated to ask me the questions I wanted to answer, while I was still too wary to invite them to take a closer look. Something must have registered within the Laker organization, however, because I was named team captain. I was pleased and honored, though I never quite went and said so. I'd always been one to lead by example, and that's the way I chose to express myself. Rousing speeches get old early, consistent full effort is there every day for everyone to see.

The Lakers of 1978–79 had the same strategic weakness as the year before, however: no power forward. When I play defense and block or intimidate shots, there must be someone on the scene who can grab them. Much as I try, I can't be expected to jump out, cause the miss, and then turn around and have the rebound fall my way every time. I need to be complemented by a strong rebounder. The 1978–79 Lakers went with two small forwards, Jamaal Wilkes and Adrian Dantley, and a thin bench. We placed third in our division and met the Denver Nuggets in the opening round of the playoffs.

Denver had beaten us three games out of four during the regular season with their run-and-gun offense. We split the first two playoff games, losing on their court by five and winning at home by twelve, and had to play the deciding game in Denver. The press really kicked us around. The day of the game the *Los Angeles Times* went out on a limb. They said Jerry West was not a capable coach, Abdul-Jabbar was not a leader, the Lakers had no leadership, and they would lose that final game to the Nuggets. I knew we didn't have the squad strength to win the championship, but I was not about to be degraded. We went out and beat the Nuggets 112–111 on their home court and surprised the shit out of everybody.

Then all kinds of things started going on. Ted Dawson, a TV sportscaster whom I suspected might not like me either, told his viewers, "Hey, you guys should send Kareem and the Lakers a telegram or mailgram, let them know how much you appreciate them," because what we'd been reading in the papers, he said, wasn't what was happening. The team had flown straight from Denver to Seattle for the start of the second round, and the next morning I was presented with stacks of mail. I was amazed. You mean, these people really do appreciate me?! I kept the whole load; I still have them. I called Cheryl to tell her the astounding news, and she said, "I told you so." I felt great. I started looking at faces in the crowd and realizing that there could be a lot of friends up there, that the people who stopped me for autographs might really be interested in getting them. If someone wanted to shake my hand, hey, I'd do it.

Of course, all that well-wishing didn't mean we still weren't a couple of guys short. Seattle pounded us off the boards again, beat us in five games, and went on and took the NBA title. But that last Western Union barrage really made my year.

I was trying real hard the next season to be more outgoing. Not that I was going to tap dance for the media, but I began to feel at least receptive to people who in previous years I might not have bothered with. Cheryl also made a point of reestablishing contact with my parents. (Her father had a hard time handling the fact that his little girl was openly living with an affluent athlete. A big basketball fan, he refused to come home the first time we visited them. He's lightened up a lot since.) She invited my mother and father to Los Angeles, something I had never done, and paid more attention to them in two months than I had in a decade. I've never been good at airing my grievances—I'm still not—but at least Cheryl made me willing to reintroduce them into my life. Usually, once I've kissed someone off they're gone for good.

My public image pivoted on a friendly gesture I made for my mother. Cora likes "Hot Rod" Hundley, a lively former ballplayer who does pro basketball color commentary on TV. She's never met him, but she likes his personality, and I thought she would like him to say hello to her . . . on the air. I'd never seen it done on any of the NBA broadcasts, always thought it was taboo, but I figured I could come out of my shell one time and try it. I told Rod, "My mother's a big fan of yours; she watches you; you should say hi to her." Rod's a happy-go-lucky guy, he'll try almost anything; he was probably pleased to get an easy phrase out of me, so on national television he said hello to Mrs. Alcindor.

My mother missed it. She was away from the set. All her friends, however, called and told her, and she was a big hit in her social circle that week. She was a little upset at herself, though, for not having been there to hear it, so the next time we were on a national broadcast I did it again. "Hot Rod, say hello to Moms for me." But Rod was slick, he came right back with, "Why don't you do it?" Yeah, I'm gonna do it. I looked at the camera and said, "Hi to Moms and Pops in New York!"

My folks loved it, this transcontinental notice and affection from their silent son, and I got a kick out of it—I went back to the huddle feeling like I'd just pulled a fast one—so I did it at pregame shows, half-time, post-game interviews, every time I got a chance.

I hadn't given it even a second's thought, but it turns out that lots of people liked the touch. They hadn't expected me to be so warm to anyone, and when I did it seemed to cheer them a little. Even the big fellow says hi to his folks. Fine with me, no need to be nasty. Journalists saw it, or got wind of a new attitude on my part, and the whole deal began to feed on itself. Images work that way; one friendly story begets another; one civilized interview attracts more civilized questions. I may have been a bit more patient with the same old lines of inquiry, and therefore a better interview, but I was still the same guy with the same beliefs. I was simply being perceived as more approachable and therefore being approached more often. Also, my career had continued so long I may have outlasted a generation of sportswriters. The older, more traditional beat reporters who were inundated and insulted by the old anti-Olympic, pro-black power media images were being replaced by younger, hipper, more sociologically appreciative journalists who had had to deal with Vietnam and had accepted racial awareness as part of growing up. To them I wasn't an intruder; I was an institution.

There was also an easy journalistic hook to hang my "transformation" on: Earvin "Magic" Johnson. Earvin came out of college after his sophomore year as a twenty-year-old kid with tremendous exuberance and outstanding basketball skills. In games, at practice, at pickup scrimmages, wherever he happened to be, Magic was very thrilled to be playing basketball. He was a boy living a dream, and his enthusiasm was infectious. He was also a showman who was totally capable of playing the kind of intense winning basketball that I responded to and at the same time making the crowd feel like they were participating. And in some sense they were, because the more a place roared the more he would make it roar. He would bring smiles to people's faces, mine included.

Earvin likes to make eye contact. He's got an expressive face, and he enjoys the good challenge, so whenever possible he'll look right at a defender to let him know that not only is a basket and two points on the line but so is this guy's pride. He'll lock his opponent in a personal duel. When Earvin is going strong there is a real person out there for the fans to latch onto. He loves the attention and really basks in that public warmth.

Earvin broke into the league as a humorous fellow with basketball as his life. Even his style of play was humorous. He likes to have a laugh on the court, and it's always at the opponent's expense. He keys everybody up: his teammates because he's such an extraordinary passer that he's liable to get you the ball at any moment, and the other team because they don't like being the foil to some of his sleight of hand. He loves to fool someone, dash by, get the lay-up, not even look as the ball is going down, but beam downcourt and make some gesture that brings the crowd to its feet laughing and applauding while his defender seethes. Guys don't like having that done to them, so it raises the level of the game for all of us—we've got to deal with the other team's coming back in our face—and puts a buzz on everyone who's watching.

Most important in what makes Earvin an outstanding ballplayer, however, is his expertise. He's one of the great passers, and at six feet nine, he's a guard who can crash the boards hard and often. He does his job well and consistently. That, more than anything, makes him a pleasure to work with.

So I was enjoying the 1979–80 season, and people began to notice. The press figured it was my "liberation" by "Magic," but it was a combination of factors. First, Cheryl was constantly telling me I had significant things to say and encouraging me to share them, with my teammates and the public. Second, Dr. Jerry Buss, who had recently bought the team, stepped in and renegotiated my contract, which I took as a statement that he valued my contributions very highly. Third, during the off-season the Lakers had obtained two strong rebounding forwards, Spencer Haywood and Jim Chones, who I knew would make a tremendous difference in the capacity of the team to go all the way to the championship. With Jamaal Wilkes at small forward, Norman Nixon having developed into a truly excellent guard, Earvin, Spencer, and myself in the starting lineup, and for the first time a strong bench, we were looking very good. As the season started I was a happy man.

The first game of the season was on national TV. We were playing in San Diego against Bill Walton and the

Clippers, and the game came down to the wire. With only a few seconds left and the Lakers down by a point, we called time out and set up a play. I was concentrating, but my life wasn't on the line. We had eighty-one games to go, and then the playoffs. I was just going to work. The ball came in to me, I turned and, as the buzzer sounded, put up the hook. The ball went in, we won by a point. Good. Nice way to start off a season. I turned to jog back to the locker room and get on with the rest of the day when I felt someone running at me, pinning my arms to my side. I was shocked. It was Earvin, both arms around me, his cheek to my chest, hugging me as if we'd just won the seventh game of the championships. The last game he'd played had been for the NCAA title (which his team had won), and he'd gotten so excited that this single Sunday afternoon NBA contest had taken on almost cosmic proportions for him.

I was a little embarrassed—such a public display, so little cools—but he was so happy that it dawned on me, I'd had a lot of fun making that last shot! If Earvin had any effect on me, it was because he helped the team win and reminded me just how good that made me feel.

The Lakers played well all season long, finished first in our division, beat defending champion Seattle in the Western Conference Finals, and came up against the very strong Philadelphia '76ers in the 1980 World Championship Series.

I hadn't been in a final in six years, and I wanted to win this one something fierce. I looked at our squad, looked at theirs with Julius Erving, Darryl Dawkins, Maurice Cheeks, and Caldwell Jones, and knew we could get it done. After three straight NCAA championships at UCLA and another in the NBA only two years later at Milwaukee, I had gotten used to winning, almost taken it for granted and lost the thrill of victory. Now, nine years after my team's last title, I had become all too familiar with the agony of defeat. There had been reasons for each loss, and I had tried to blunt the disappointment by being extremely rational about exactly why we'd been beaten, but what I hated most was becoming resigned to losing. For this championship series I kicked that feeling in the ass and went out there and raised my game even more.

We split the first two games in Los Angeles, went out and split two in Philadelphia. We were back on home court, and it was time to make our move. I had been scoring about thirty points a game, but I wanted more. If we won this, we only had to split a home-and-home series to be the champs. If we lost, we'd have to sweep.

There was tension, but it didn't bother me; I'd been playing under pressure since I was twelve years old. People expect me to win; other people's expectations are a constant in my life, but the true pressure is in the preparation, which I impose on myself. I have my personal standards to maintain that are higher and more exacting than any outsider could know. I've been asked about tournament pressure, but that's like, "What does your blood pressure feel like?" It's part of my system.

I was, however, very pumped up for that fifth game. Philly wanted this championship just as much as we did; they'd been coming close for years. The game was tight when, late in the third quarter, I made a lay-up, came down on the side of my foot and felt a tremendous pain jump through my left ankle and run up my leg. I knew just from the way it was hurting that it was serious. I work on my ankles; they are very strong, and most of the time I don't sprain them even when I turn them over, but this time it went all the way. Dr. Kerlan, the team physician, thought it was fractured, and the medical team wanted to know if I wanted to go to the hospital right away or wait and watch the game.

"Can I hurt it any more?" I asked.

"If we tape it up, you won't be able to injure it further," Dr. Kerlan told me, "but it's going to hurt a lot."

"I'll try it," I said. "I want to play."

They taped it tightly, and when I stood up and tried to move it, I found they were right; it hurt like a motherfucker. But I was deep into my *chi*, using all of what Bruce Lee had taught me about focusing my energy and harnessing my power, and after asking Allah for some special strength, I moved out of the locker room as if in my own concentrated cloud.

I stepped onto the court and, no doubt about it, there was pain. I had to adjust for the fact that I couldn't jump off my left foot, and I had to fight off Darryl Dawkins at the same time. The first few times up and down the court it intruded like an electrical storm, let me know I was in a struggle. But there was a more pressing battle going on, and I shut out all pain and focused tightly on the job at hand. I was no longer mobile, I had to be concise. My foot would let me know when I screwed up.

I scored forty points that night, and we won by five. After the game I headed straight for the hospital and then to bed. I couldn't even travel with the team to Philly for the sixth game. My ankle had swollen up the size of a grapefruit, and if there had to be a deciding seventh game, there was no way I was sitting it out, so I spent that day at home on the mend.

What a frustrating feeling, watching my team play for the World Championship two thousand miles away while I was laid up in bed. I hobbled to the television, shouted at the referees and rooted loudly for the Lakers. Earvin played center for that game and scored 42 points. Jamaal went wild with his jumper and popped in 37. We won!

The vacuum in my bedroom, knowing what a sweaty, steamy madhouse the locker room was like, left me kind of numb. You win a championship in a single moment; you share the victory with the guys by spritzing champagne and yelling and jumping and popping apocalyptic fives. Then a team goes its separate ways. No tickertape parade the next day is worth the one hour immediately following the final victory—and I missed it. I met the airplane when the team came home, held the trophy, congratulated the guys, but I felt the fates had denied me that one solid burst you play all year to win.

They gave the playoff MVP award to Magic. I had averaged more than thirty-three points over five games, played the good defense, grabbed the rebounds, but Magic had worked his show in the spotlight, had his one brilliant performance, had been the better story. He was right there on the scene to receive the trophy, get his picture taken, be the shining star; I was in Los Angeles, on crutches, no guarantee of being a properly receptive recipient. I understood why they passed on me, but I wasn't happy about it.

Cheryl talked me down. Where only a few years before I might have been bitter, blamed and hated an antagonistic media, now I could see why the machine worked that way and accept it as the real world. Magic, in accepting the championship trophy, said they'd won it for "the big fellow," which was gracious and thoughtful of him.

I felt a whole lot better when, several weeks later, I was voted the league's MVP. It was my sixth time; no one had won it more often.

The best thing that happened to me in 1980 was Cheryl's giving birth on November 18th to our son, Amir. In the Middle East an *amir* is a man with authority, not a prince but an emissary with the right to rule. Amir is all of that. He was the first of my children with whom I've had the opportunity to function as the father I should be and want to be. He's a real little dynamo, and I love helping him grow.

My parents have had a great time with Amir, too. He is the first grandchild they've had the chance to develop a strong relationship with, and they are definitely thrilled. Amir has made all of us think more about each other and has brought us closer together. If there have ever been the classic doting grandparents, it's Cora and Al. They visited us in Los Angeles when Amir was only four months old, and they never left him alone. Cora would carry him around and read to him, take him on long walks in the stroller. "This is a tree," she'd tell him, "and that is a bird, this is a house. . . ." Although Amir couldn't talk or really understand, my Mom was introducing him to the world. It's up to me and Cheryl to tell him what it's all about.

My father can't take his hands off him. As quiet as he was, all Al wants to do now is take Amir to the park, play baseball with him, throw him in the air, chase him around, spend a lot of time with him. It looks like everyone in the family has begun to mellow.

We didn't repeat in 1981 as NBA Champs because Earvin got injured, and when he came back he had forgotten what had made him and us so successful. Mammoth public success is hard to handle at any age; at twenty-one it's got to be real difficult. He had been an unselfish and joyful passer who could hit his outside shot if he had to. After the championship the team got put in the back seat and, for public relations purposes, Magic was moved out front. It took losing to Houston in the miniseries for it to become clear to everyone that the Lakers were a team—one of the best—and we needed to blend all of our individual talents to survive.

In 1981–82 we worked perfectly: Earvin worked the ball, ran the break, and made sure everybody was happily in the flow of the game; Norman Nixon finally got the respect he deserved as an All-Star; Jamaal Wilkes maintained his smooth game in trying times; Kurt Rambis arrived and shocked the media and the rest of us with his banging; Michael Cooper became indispensable; and Bob McAdoo showed his critics he could still play. We beat Philadelphia again, and this time I was there to share in that victory flashfire. I got used to winning again. Want to do it all the time.

The 1982–83 season started where our championship had left off, only we looked to be even better. Our confidence was high and we had deepened our squad by adding the number one draft pick, James Worthy, a slick and impressive forward out of North Carolina. We were looking to be the first NBA team since 1969 to repeat as champions.

At midseason, however, I was faced with a problem that put basketball in a much diminished perspective. My home, containing almost all of the most valuable possessions I had gathered during my life, burned to the ground in January.

I was on the road when it happened. An electrical fire started in one of the walls, and in the middle of the night Cheryl woke up with the house totally in flames. Fortunately, she and Amir and several of our friends got out safely, but my collection of oriental rugs burned up, disappeared as if they'd never been there. I had four priceless and completely irreplaceable Qur'ans from the middle ages and they simply do not exist anymore. My three thousand jazz albums melted. The beautiful pieces of glass and art that I had bought and gathered over the years were gone, as were my basketball trophies, my childhood pictures, all my clothes.

I was shocked, and for a while somewhat disoriented; I would think about reading a book, or listening to an album, or putting on a favorite shirt, and they'd be gone. It surprised me, at first, how much I leaned on these things.

Islam had taught me how to face the world, and once again I turned to it for strength.

"In the name of Allah the Compassionate, the Merciful. ALM," the Qur'an says.

"Do men imagine that they will be left at ease because they say 'We believe' and will not be tested with affliction? Truly! we tested those who were before you. Thus Allah knoweth those who are sincere and those who feign." (Chapter 29, verses 1–3)

"In the name of Allah the Compassionate, the Merciful. And surely we shall try you with something of fear and

hunger and loss of wealth and lives and crops; but give
glad tidings to the steadfast who say when the misfortune
striketh them: Truly! we are Allah's and truly! unto Him
we are returning." (Chapter 2, verses 155–156)

My faith soothed me.

But Cheryl and Amir had gotten out alive, and when placed next to life itself my possessions began to seem rather small. With so little left, I found I hadn't really needed much of what I'd collected and owned. Material possessons, which had been a mark of both success and contentment to me, lost some power once they were gone. Plus, people kept giving me things. A radio station sent over fifteen hundred jazz records—backed up a truck! From all over the country I began to receive gifts and notes of sympathy. Once again I found people cared about me, and once again I was surprised and pleased.

With my charred house a constantly painful memory, I channeled my energy into my work. The Lakers won the Western Division title easily. Unfortunately, late in the season Bob McAdoo went down with a foot injury. And when James Worthy broke his leg in a freak accident going for a rebound, we found ourselves at a distant disadvantage going into the playoffs. We beat Portland, took San Antonio in six, and then faced the Philadelphia '76ers.

They were tough. Strong, well-balanced, and deep, the '76ers would have been a battle even if we had been at full strength. But when Norman Nixon went down with a separated shoulder in the first game, things got even more difficult. They played excellent basketball and beat us in four straight.

The 1983–84 season had several true and lasting highlights and one serious lowlight. I started the season with a good shot at Wilt Chamberlain's all-time NBA career scoring record and by mid-March it was within reach. It developed into a real media event, the kind that only a few years ago would have made me very cynical and suspicious. The Lakers would come to play in a city during the weeks that the points were piling up and the press would gather around and ask: "How does it feel to be breaking Wilt's record?" "What does it mean to you?" "Do you think you are better that Wilt?" And then we'd move on to the next town and the reporters would say, "I know you've been asked this before, but . . ." and I'd get the same barrage. As the day approached the questions flew faster, the crush got thicker. I had some answers: I like breaking Wilt's record, it's an achievement of quality and durability. I leave the question of whether I'm better than Wilt to the students of the game; that kind of speculation is a fan's birthright. What does it mean? Even now I'm not sure. I still haven't sat back and savored the satisfaction of being the all-time leading scorer. At the time I was keying on the playoffs, which is what playing in the NBA is all about.

There was a lot of pressure, but there was also a lot of warmth. Because of the historical aspect of the record—this thing spanned fifteen years and a lot of people's adolescence and adulthood—all sorts of people wanted to witness and somehow share in the event. With all the media coverage it started to snowball, and when that started happening people who had never paid much attention or shown much respect started to get behind it. "Ah, he's going to do it. What's it about?" I watched at first warily and then with a growing pleasure as basketball fans around the country made me a part of their lives in a way that I really hadn't been before. I truly did feel like I was a part of people's lives. It was a strange and very pleasant experience for me. I'd be driving down the thruway in Los Angeles and some guy in the next lane would recognize me, roll down his window and start weaving down the road yelling, "Pass Wilt, Kareem! Go ahead and do it!" White people, black people, I was finding out who my friends were.

I finally got the record against the Utah Jazz. We were playing in Las Vegas and I had had a hot first half.

It was definitely going to be that night. But the Jazz weren't going to roll over; they didn't trick up the whole game to stop me but they weren't going to make it easy, either. They collapsed their defense on me to begin the second half and, just on the brink of the record, I missed several shots in a row. The buckets weren't coming because the Jazz were conscious of it.

Earvin Johnson's whole career has been based around his being a playmaker and helping everyone on his team do their best. He'd said before the game that he wanted the honor of getting the assist on my record-breaking basket, a fine and genuine gesture. But I just kept missing. Finally I set up to the right of the basket and the Jazz started to throw up a double team, almost a triple team. Magic got me the ball and when I saw them coming I stopped. They froze for a split second to see if I was going to pass the ball out for the open jumper, and when they did I went on ahead and put up the hook and—at last—it went in.

The fans went wild, the officials stopped the game and gave me the ball. My mother and father came on the court. It was a wonderful moment.

The next night, at the Forum in Los Angeles, I saw Wilt. The Lakers organized a tribute and during the ceremonies he and I got a chance to speak. Wilt has never gotten the proper respect, people didn't appreciate what Wilt did when he did it; they tossed it off as somebody with superior physical ability doing something that didn't count for much. But I took it seriously, and so did the guys in the NBA, and so does Wilt. Out there on the floor, while other introductions were being made, he leaned over to me privately and said, "I'm glad to see you do it. I'm glad it was you." Wilt would rather his record had stood forever, but he'd been my mentor, had taken an interest in my career before I'd ever had a professional career. It was a very gracious thing to say.

I told the fans in LA that I was happy they could share the moment with me. That was something of a transformation for me, and I think *Giant Steps* had a lot to do with it. While writing and promoting the book, I talked to many more people than I'd ever been comfortable speaking with before. I tried to let people see through my eyes and the results were surprising. Reviewers and readers were startled by my openness and I was pleased by their warm response. They could see that the problems I've dealt with are the same ones they've had to face and that in many ways we are similar, regardless of our physical or cultural differences. I could feel people identifying with me. They approached more easily, and for my part I was more easily approachable. I don't see strangers as attackers any longer, don't feel they're out to tear down what I've accomplished. I can't be everybody's favorite, but at least now people can respect and appreciate what I've done.

Unfortunately, the NBA season ended in a dud. The Lakers lost in the playoffs to the Boston Celtics. Now I know what my man Popeye Doyle in *The French Connection* felt like. He went through a whole lot of tough hard work, busted up a big heroin ring, confiscated dope by the pound, and in the end the bad guy got away. I don't even want to talk about it.

The 1984—85 season will be my last. It will have been sixteen years and I deserve a vacation. I don't want to hang on just to be hanging on. The money definitely tempts me; it would tempt anybody. But at age 38 I'd have to work harder for it and if my production declined then in everybody's eyes it would be seen as a "shame," a "tragedy." It wouldn't be. I'd still be competing with the best in my profession, but if I competed less successfully it would mess with everybody's head, including mine. I have to accept that age has its effect, but I don't want to hear anyone saying, "He's over the hill." I'd rather go out on top.

I like knowing I'm at the top of my profession; it's taken me a short lifetime to appreciate it, but now I am aware of my position. I'd be surprised if I can attain the kind of dominance I've had over basketball in another field, but I'm definitely going to try. I'm considering going to law school, there's enough competition in that field to keep me interested. I want to resume my Islamic studies. I also want to lie on the beach in Hawaii for years on end. My children demand and deserve my attention.

I have played organized basketball since I was eight years old and have accumulated a certain amount of knowledge. Basketball demands both ability and thought; there are a lot of hugely talented players at work in the NBA who will never achieve all that they're capable of because they're either too disinterested, smug, or stupid to learn the angles. I don't have the patience to be a coach, but I've got this information, and as I am approaching the end of my playing career, I've begun to feel both an impulse and a willingness to pass it along.

It's taken me some searching to come up with this. Teammates come and go according to the whims and desires of both management and themselves; you don't want to lay out the whole NBA for somebody and then have them traded and tear up the league or beat you in the playoffs. I also have never been one to push myself on anyone, don't want any innocent chalk talk to be interpreted as arrogance. Ballplayers are very sensitive about being told what to do by their peers; everyone in the league has excellent skills, and most hardly listen to the coaches, let alone a teammate. I've always preferred to lead by example, give advice only when it's requested. Unfortunately, either because they thought it was uncool or figured I wouldn't give them my time, few guys ever asked.

Recently, however, the opportunity arose and I took it. The Lakers chose James Worthy as the number one selection in the 1982 NBA draft. When he arrived at training camp it was immediately obvious that he was a player. He had size, speed, strength, quickness, agility, a good shot, and the clear willingness to learn what he didn't already know. He also seemed like a nice guy, and after a while we hit it off. I risked volunteering, and he risked asking.

There were definitely gaps. He was sixteen years younger than I was, for starters. I'd begun to get used to that sort of thing, the longevity of my career putting more and more distance between me and the players. Worthy was drafted after his junior year in college, though, and was almost the youngest guy in the league. No way I could talk to him about Sandy Amoros' great catch against the Yankees in the '55 Series; it was five years older than he was.

We did talk basketball, though, and I found it satisfying to be able to put into words my pieces of personal information—subtle, specialized, valuable only to the very few people who could share in its benefit and understand the effort it had taken to gather and test it. When I saw Worthy respond, by absorbing what I was telling him and thanking me, and by using it to play well, I got a private pleasure totally unlike anything basketball had offered me before. James Worthy is his own ballplayer and ought to succeed on his talents, but there was a continuity started that I was beginning to enjoy.

There's always continuity in New York. Whether you're there or not, New York is where it's always going on. I made my way back uptown one summer not too long ago, and if things had changed, there was still a pounding in the streets that my years in Bel Air hadn't muffled in me. I was back in town when I got a call from my man Tyrone. Fifteen, twenty years before we had baby-sat for Monk's drummer's kid, played some ball, made the jazz club circuit together. Tyrone was my age, and he had a game, and he was excited.

"Hey, man, we're playing for the championship!" He wanted me to come and see him play. "Don't go to the Rucker," he told me; "you'll go crazy down there." And I would have—a whole lot of people, big local attraction, I would've gotten mobbed.

"What championship?" I asked him.

"The Over-the-Hill Game!" he said.

They were playing at the Battlegrounds. This wasn't some Revolutionary War memorial; this was a playground near Riverside Church at Amsterdam and 151st Street where all the time I was growing up they were waging some serious on-court warfare. I had honed my game there from grade school on, but hadn't been back since college, and when I got there and looked around, some things had changed and others survived.

There were ballet dancers in the police station. "No, man," Tyrone explained, "the precinct is down into the block now; the city gave the building over as a community center." Diagonally across the street was a single-family wooden-frame house, the kind you just don't see inside of New York City anymore, had to have been built around 1910. That was still standing, and in good shape too.

I arrived at the court, and all the guys I used to play with from eighth grade through high school were there! Liggins, Bobby Lloyd, Sonny Johnson, Tony Greer. Other guys whose names I'd forgotten but whom I knew by face. They were all there! These were the guys I had tagged along with, hung out at Roy's and eyed the ladies, watched for signs of cool and developed my own style in league with. Standing around shooting were guys who had come up after me and some who seemed like they'd always been exactly where they were. Nobody was more than four, five years older than I was, and some were much younger. It was like coming home.

My friend Ray came by and was talking to everybody in his normal hurry. I was sitting by the mesh fence. "Man, Ray," I said evenly, "you're not going to speak to me?" He looked at me like I couldn't *be* there. Kareem wasn't sitting here, in this park, that was yesteryear.

We all just about ignited. Roy's, with its thirty-five-cent hamburgers, had been closed for years, but we went off and got some beer and just sat around and talked, reminisced. Like, Sonny, we all laughed; Sonny was a good ballplayer; he ran all day. But Sonny was a real belligerent kind of guy and made a lot of enemies, so when we'd go to party there'd always be somebody there who didn't like Sonny and was laying to kick his ass, and we'd always had to deal with that.

We laughed all afternoon. They wanted to know about everything. I gave them the scoop about Kent Benson, and why Kermit Washington had punched out Rudy T.; they updated me on the old crowd.

This wino came running across the street at us. We started to tense up. Damn neighborhood. But it was one of the dudes! He saw us and just for a couple of seconds something must have registered and he growled, "*Hey!*" and maybe ran some old game through what was left of his mind. He looked terrible. His face and hands were all swollen up, teeth missing. But just for a moment he looked real young again before he staggered off.

The Over-the-Hill Game got played. I sat it out. Didn't want to disrupt the good feeling by having to get in someone's face or having someone insist on getting in mine. Some of the guys were in top shape; they'd stayed with it and could still take on each new wave of playground kid. Most had kids of their own. Some had put on the good poundage, lost more than the first step to the hoop, but they were still out there playing for the crown. It was the best time I'd had in years.

Hey, check out the moves, watch the shot. No way these guys are over the hill.

ABOUT PETER KNOBLER

Peter Knobler and Kareem Abdul-Jabbar have been friends since high school. Mr. Knobler, the former editor-in-chief of **Crawdaddy** magazine, has also written for such publications as **The New York Times, The International Herald Tribune** and **Sports Illustrated.**

Congratulations— But...

What about all those questions and problems that arrive with a new addition to the family? Here are several invaluable books for any new or expectant mother. They are filled with helpful hints for raising healthy children in a happy home. Best of luck and may all your problems be little ones!

☐	24642	**HAVING A BABY AFTER 30** by Bing & Colman	$3.95
☐	24020	**NO NONSENSE NUTRITION FOR YOUR BABY'S FIRST YEAR** by Heslin/Natow/Rave	$3.95
☐	23821	**BH&G NEW BABY BOOK**	$3.95
☐	01398	**THE BABY CHECKUP BOOK: A Parent Guide to Well Baby Care** by Sheila Hillman (A Large Format Book)	$7.95
☐	01409	**INFANT MASSAGE: A Handbook for Loving Parents** by Vimala Schneider	$4.95
☐	24412	**CARING FOR YOUR UNBORN CHILD** by Gots, M.D.'s	$3.95
☐	24022	**UNDERSTANDING PREGNANCY AND CHILDBIRTH** by Sheldon H. Cherry, M.D.	$3.50
☐	23122	**NINE MONTHS READING** by Robert E. Hall, M.D.	$3.95
☐	22721	**FEED ME! I'M YOURS** by Vicki Lansky	$2.95
☐	24973	**SIX PRACTICAL LESSONS FOR AN EASIER CHILDBIRTH** by Elisabeth Bing	$3.50
☐	23407	**NAME YOUR BABY** by Lareina Rule	$2.95
☐	24496	**THE EARLY CHILDHOOD YEARS: THE 2 TO 6 YEAR OLD** by Theresa & Frank Caplan	$3.95
☐	24233	**THE FIRST TWELVE MONTHS OF LIFE** by Frank Caplan, ed.	$4.95
☐	23249	**SECOND TWELVE MONTHS OF LIFE** by Frank Caplan	$4.95
☐	23419	**COMPLETE BOOK OF BREASTFEEDING** by M. Eiger, M.D. & S. Olds	$3.50
☐	24405	**MAKING YOUR OWN BABY FOOD** by James Turner	$2.75
☐	20347	**MOVING THROUGH PREGNANCY** by Elisabeth Bing	$2.95
☐	14523	**MAKING LOVE DURING PREGNANCY** by Bing & Colman	$2.95

Prices and availability subject to change without notice.

Buy them at your local bookstore or use this handy coupon for ordering:

Bantam Books, Inc., Dept. BB, 414 East Golf Road, Des Plaines, Ill. 60016

Please send me the books I have checked above. I am enclosing $_____
(please add $1.25 to cover postage and handling). Send check or money order
—no cash or C.O.D.'s please.

Mr/Mrs/Miss_____

Address_____

City_____State/Zip_____

BB—1/85

Please allow four to six weeks for delivery. This offer expires 7/85.

SPECIAL
MONEY SAVING
OFFER

Now you can have an up-to-date listing of Bantam's hundreds of titles plus take advantage of our unique and exciting bonus book offer. A special offer which gives you the opportunity to purchase a Bantam book for only 50¢. Here's how!

By ordering any five books at the regular price per order, you can also choose any other single book listed (up to a $4.95 value) for just 50¢. Some restrictions do apply, but for further details why not send for Bantam's listing of titles today!

Just send us your name and address plus 50¢ to defray the postage and handling costs.